FIRE!

On the evening of June 9, 1980, at eight p.m., Northridge's most celebrated resident came screaming from behind his Rolls-Royce convertible. Rushing quickly down the tree-lined driveway, his course erratic, his cries punctuated by shouts for help, he threw himself against the gate. The door gave and he stumbled into the street, his head bowed and his body bent forward.

A neighbor saw the man pass, smoke curling from his body. She scooped up the phone and anxiously advised the operator, "A man is running down the street and he's on fire." An ambulance was dispatched to the address she provided.

"I think you should stop," suggested Officer Zielinski. "We've got to get you to a hospital." He took Pryor lightly about the wrist, but the comedian wrenched free.

"I'm *goin'* to the hospital," Pryor said, his voice even, his words coherent. "Just show me where the hospital is, I'll get there."

The officer shook his head. "You can't walk there. Why don't you just stop and wait for—"

"I *can't* stop," Pryor shot back. "If I stop I'll die."

RICHARD PRYOR:
Black and Blue

Jeff Rovin

BANTAM BOOKS
TORONTO · NEW YORK · LONDON · SYDNEY

RICHARD PRYOR: BLACK AND BLUE
A Bantam Book/January 1984

ISBN 0-553-23809-4

Published simultaneously in the United States and Canada

Bantam Books are published by Bantam Books, Inc. Its trade-
mark, consisting of the words ''Bantam Books'' and the por-
trayal of a rooster, is Registered in U.S. Patent and Trademark
Office and in other countries. Marca Registrada. Bantam
Books, Inc., 666 Fifth Avenue, New York, New York 10103.

PRINTED IN THE UNITED STATES OF AMERICA

O   0 9 8 7 6 5 4 3 2 1

RICHARD PRYOR:
Black and Blue

Prologue

The Spanish ranch house is set back from the road more than one hundred yards, hidden behind a rusted, ivy-covered chain-link fence and thick fruit trees. Gone is the sign that hung on the door of the occupant's previous home: "Uninvited guests are not welcome at any time whatsoever. To avoid rejection, please do not take the liberty of 'dropping by.' " It would have been unnecessary, since the grounds are virtually impregnable. The only way in is through the driveway, past an eight-foot-high, electronically operated iron gate. In case of a fire, the only way for anyone to enter would be by ladder.

The fifty-five-year-old estate, once owned by the Wrigley family, covers one-third of a huge block in Northridge, a wealthy community nestled in the San Fernando Valley, across the Santa Monica Mountains from Hollywood. The home cost half a million dollars and has all the dignity of a Beverly Hills mansion, with none of the chill. Tens of thousands of dollars' worth of changes have been made in the original design. There are many new windows glaring from the stucco walls beneath the brownish roof tiles, since the owner dislikes air-conditioning, preferring the natural breeze that sweeps across the valley. Other additions include quarters for the live-in Mexican housekeepers, the costly basement screening room, and the gymnasium and boxing ring behind the main house.

The eight-and-one-half-acre estate is covered with citrus and nut trees and includes a guest cottage, a tennis court, a

1

hedged-in rectangular pool, and a basketball court. There are also large kennels for the owner's pair of Alaskan malamutes and waist-high Falabella miniature horse. However, the estate's most exotic feature is the aviary-atrium in the main house, between the master bedroom and the dining room. Filled with colorful birds and flowers, the tranquillity of the courtyard is heightened by the gentle splashing of huge Japanese goldfish in a small central pool.

Such exotic trappings are not what one would expect from a man who calls people "motherfuckers" for a living and has made headlines by shooting cars, punching actors, stabbing hotel clerks, and beating up women. But in his life, as in his art, the occupant of 17267 Parthenia is anything but conventional.

On the evening of June 9, 1980, at eight o'clock, the calm of the residential neighborhood was violated when Northridge's most celebrated resident came screaming from his house. Rushing past his Rolls-Royce convertible, he ran down the tree-lined driveway, his course erratic, his cries punctuated by shouts for help. He threw himself against the gate and stumbled onto the sidewalk, then ran west along Parthenia, his head bowed and his body bent forward.

A neighbor, alerted by the commotion, glanced out her window and saw the man pass, smoke curling from his body. She immediately called the police, and an ambulance was dispatched to the address she provided.

Outside, several cars had stopped, their occupants running to the side of the injured man. He ignored their offers of help and most of them just stood staring in his wake. Through the dissipating smoke they saw that his polyester shirt was in tatters, scraps of fabric clinging to his flesh, his khaki pants blackened around the waist. As he chugged off, a short, elderly woman rushed from the house. She ran after him, yelling for him to stop, but he paid no attention. Simultaneously, a patrol car arrived, having intercepted the ambulance call and spotted the commotion.

Officer Carl Helm squinted ahead. "Hey—isn't that Richard Pryor?" he said to his partner. Officer Richard

Zielinski stared for a moment before concurring. The officers jumped from the car.

Pryor's aunt Dee and the police officers reached him at the same moment.

"He just exploded into flames," Dee said breathlessly. "Help him!" Pryor ignored them and continued walking briskly toward the police car. His chest was covered with doughnutlike craters, his shirt not only burned but melted on in spots. There was a massive ulcer running along his left side, and his hands and lower neck were horribly singed. He held his arms arched out from his body, allowing the cool air to brush against his severely charred underarms. Pryor's face, too, was disfigured. Part of his nose was missing, most of his mustache was reduced to stubble, his left cheek and lips were badly blistered, and his earlobes and eyelids had been seared away.

While Helm rushed back to the police car to check on the whereabouts of the ambulance, Zielinski and Dee walked alongside Pryor.

"I think you really ought to stop," suggested the twenty-nine-year-old officer. "We've got to get you to a hospital." Zielinski then took Pryor lightly by the wrist, but the forty-year-old comedian wrenched free.

"I'm *goin'* to the hospital," Pryor said evenly. "Just show me where the hospital is; I'll get there."

The officer shook his head. "You can't walk there. Why don't you just stop and wait for—"

"I can't stop," Pryor shot back. "If I stop, I'm gonna die."

Zielinski didn't argue. He simply informed Pryor that he would stay right beside him.

Pryor lifted his head and whined, "God, I really screwed up, man. I fucked up. Please give me a second chance. I know I did wrong, but there's a lot of good in me. Haven't I brought happiness to anyone in this world?"

"Sure you have," said the officer, talking to keep Pryor's mind active and focused. "We all love your stuff."

"Yeah," Pryor agreed, without conviction. He was silent for a second, then said suddenly, "I just want to see an airplane before I die. I—I gotta run."

Pryor began to jog, and the policeman, though startled, kept pace. Dee dropped back, weeping.

When Helm glanced up and saw the two men running off, he radioed their course to the ambulance, then followed them in the car.

Zielinski and Pryor were now a mile from Pryor's house, in front of the San Fernando Valley Christian School at the corner of Parthenia and Hayvenhurst. Pryor stopped for a second, whimpering with pain and shaking like a runner warming up for a heat. Then he headed south along tree-lined Hayvenhurst.

Zielinski trotted in front of him, trying to block his path. "Look," he said softly, "we've got to stay where the ambulance can find us. Why don't we turn back?"

"No, I gotta go this way. If I go any other way I'll die."

"All right, we'll do it your way," Zielinski answered. "Just try and hold on."

"Yeah—yeah. Hold on. God," Pryor began again, heedless of the passersby who stopped to stare at him, "I've really done it now. They told me just *yesterday* not to smoke that shit, and this is what I get. Why didn't I listen? God's paying me back! Man, I've *really* done it this time, haven't I?"

Pryor and the officer had gone only two blocks more when the ambulance squealed to a stop beside them. The police car pulled up behind it, and Helm and Dee jumped out.

"We had the wrong address," one of the paramedics snapped to Helm as they pulled out a large sheet soaked in antibiotics.

Zielinski again stepped in front of Pryor. "They're here," he soothed. "Just cooperate and you'll be all right." He held up his hands, gesturing for the comedian to stop.

Showing surprising agility, Pryor jumped around him and ran on, faster than before. "I'm not stoppin'," he called over his shoulder. "Don't wanna die *sittin' down*. Got a weak heart and I wanna bust it. If I run fast enough, my heart's gonna *die*."

As Zielinski and Helm exchanged words, the two men from the ambulance joined them. Together, the four approached Pryor. "Hey, man, we're trying to help you," said one of the medics as the other men managed to wrap the medically treated sheet around him. "Be careful, he's in shock," the medic cautioned. Dee watched anxiously as her nephew yelled and began to struggle, but the attendants were able to secure the wrap and tie his hands.

Pryor snickered humorlessly as his eyes roamed from man to man. "Okay, ya got me. Lord, ya got me now. Just give me a second chance!" The men were not sure whether Pryor was talking to them or to God.

Dee stood beside her nephew as the paramedics brought out a stretcher, quickly laid Pryor on it, and strapped him down. "Aunt Dee," he looked up with wide, bloodshot eyes, "I done wrong. God help me, I done wrong."

Dee held back her tears as Pryor began crying hysterically. When she looked at her nephew now, all she could see was the nightmare of him engulfed in flame, screaming as he threw off the blanket with which she had smothered the fire, gasping as he raced from the bedroom, looking desperately for someplace without walls, someplace where he wouldn't have to stop moving.

With his aunt and Officer Helm at his side, Pryor was rushed to the burn center of the Sherman Oaks Community Hospital. During the brief ride, Pryor heard the siren shriek over his own involuntary wailing. He calmed slightly as the treated wrap began to ease the torment of the third-degree burns over sixty percent of his body. Thinking more lucidly now, Pryor refused to believe that he had come so far only to perish in such a useless manner. Muttering under his breath that he had beaten the odds before, he swore he would beat them again.

Chapter One

More than once Richard Pryor has said of his career, "I never would have imagined *this* fame and recognition," yet the odds were against him having made *anything* of his life.

Pryor is a native of Peoria, Illinois, an area that reeks of Americana. Values are traditional, politics a shade to the right.

Named for the Indian tribe that once inhabited the area, Peoria is the state's third-largest city. Its present urban population is eighty percent white. In the nineteenth century, Peoria was one of the great theatrical centers of the nation. Since 1925, the city's principal claim to fame has been its Caterpillars—not the insect, but the line of farming and construction tractors. In every respect, Peoria has always been a pleasant, prosperous city.

Richard Pryor has another explanation for why Peoria is considered a model city: "It means that the Negroes are all under control."

That's not exactly the case, but, like so many of the comedian's comments, it is laced with truth.

Oppression in the Midwest was never as severe as in the South, nor were Midwestern blacks as discontent as blacks in the crowded, rundown cities of the Northeast. Until the civil rights movement of the 1960s, white society and black society in Peoria simply lived as two separate planets, each with its own orbit, rarely intersecting. When cities from Watts to Detroit were exploding with violence, Peoria was relatively calm.

7

Late in the nineteenth century, centered in a four-block stretch of Washington Street, in the heart of Peoria's ghetto, was a business that rose along with Caterpillar as a potent force in the local economy. The business was prostitution.

Despite the illicit nature of its industry, Washington Street, the core of Peoria's red-light district, was paradoxically "respectable." It was relatively clean in the 1930s and '40s, and could almost be described as quaint, with its brownstones and century-old wooden mansions converted into apartments. There were clean, one-story taverns, pool halls, and an abundance of liquor stores. Pryor would one day malign his old neighborhood by describing it as "(a) 'bring your hat' neighborhood. You go down there with your hat on and then later they hand it to you with your head in it." But the ghetto had a little of everything, from the stately to the derelict—though, he says, "there were very few banks."

Crime was not a serious problem in the Peoria ghetto in the 1940s; the environment was one of community. Adults looked out for children no matter whose they were. As a teacher who taught in this area puts it, "The grownups knew who all the children were and where they lived, and they'd watch them." They would immediately discipline children who were misbehaving, or would haul them back to their parents. Even the police, most of them blacks partnered with whites—what Pryor would later dub "*I Spy* Cops"—preferred to bring children home rather than detain them. "You might have to boot them in the ass to get them to go," Peoria police Captain "Torsey" Helm recalls, "but you could count on the fact that if a kid embarrassed his family they'd beat the hell out of him."

Though Washington Street was the hub of prostitution, there were no streetwalkers. At the more aggressive parlors, the women would stand in windows, waving or blowing kisses at passersby and sometimes rapping on the pane. In the more "sophisticated" houses, the women would simply sit and wait for their pimps to bring in customers.

At the northern end of Washington Street, the pimps and their prostitutes were predominantly black. The sole exception was Joe Eagle, an Italian who ran the spur's only brothel staffed with white women. Eagle's relationship with the black pimps was strained, though not because they competed for local business. While the blacks took pride in their operations, Eagle's one-story brick building was a wreck, despite the fact that he charged up to fifty dollars per visit. The blacks felt that his slipshod operation would give prostitution a bad name.

Black pimps had no problem meeting Eagle's competitive challenge. They drummed up business not by pitching lower prices—almost every john who came to North Washington Street was a wealthy or middle-class white—but by touting the common mythology that black women were better sexually than white women. (As Pryor expressively puts it, "Black women *fuuuuuuck!*") It was a value judgment most customers were too drunk or too excited to make.

No matter who ran or staffed the brothels, all sought exclusively white customers. Black men did not patronize these establishments but went to their own places a block away, where the women were older, the buildings not so attractive, the prices only a dollar or two. The reason was not solely financial. The madams were afraid that the presence of black customers would drive the lucrative white trade to Eagle or to higher-priced call girls.

The brothels were tasteful by contemporary standards. Most had maids who cleaned the sink and set out fresh towels in each room after a trick. Some of the classier establishments employed caterers and jazz musicians. Of course, with such a colorful cast of characters, these places were anything but clandestine. However, until 1954, when a new administration came in and "cleaned house," arrests were uncommon. Kickback money is said to have bought the silence of key police officers, and raids were authorized only, as one officer says, "to keep the public satisfied," or on those rare occasions when a customer was rolled or became violent.

As a rule, the madams were very good to their girls. Though they took twenty-five to fifty percent of the fees, the madams earned every penny. They provided rooms and meals and shelter from the police, and regularly sent the girls to clinics to cure the inevitable cases of "bad blood."

To the credit of both the madams and the pimps, young girls were not encouraged to join the trade. The only pressure came from white men who were passing through the neighborhood or attending conventions at the nearby Mayer Hotel. These men would boldly approach any attractive black woman who caught their eye. Though their style was more in the vein of lewd remarks than actual solicitation, such encounters contributed to the awareness among young blacks that they must look out for one another in the white-dominated society. Richard Pryor would learn this lesson very early in life.

During the 1940s, the most powerful madam on Washington Street was China Bee. A former policewoman who knew Bee well says, "I wouldn't say she was exactly *respectable;* I know I wouldn't have wanted her in my house. But she was very nice, a beautiful person; we even went to the same beauty shop." China Bee controlled more girls than anyone else in town, housing them in a former mansion best described as tackily plush. Hers was the most popular brothel on the street.

Next door to China Bee, benefiting from spillover and boasting its own faithful clientele, was the house run by another successful madam, Marie Bryant.

Born Marie Carter in 1899, she was a black Creole from New Orleans. Marie had been part of a great wave of migration from the South to the Midwest early in this century. The bulk of the exodus consisted of jazz musicians who found work on the excursion boats sailing the Mississippi River. Discovering that they could enjoy comparatively more freedom than they had known in the South, many of these blacks jumped ship in cities along the route. Illinois eventually became home to many of them.

A second migration, solely from New Orleans, helped pave the way for Marie's future occupation. Until 1917, New Orleans law permitted prostitution in the district known as Storyville. However, with so many sailors coming ashore during World War I, the secretary of war asked the city to help keep the seamen healthy by outlawing prostitution. Thus, many of the girls, pimps, and madams relocated in the Midwest. Their presence caused a sudden proliferation of brothels in cities like Memphis, St. Louis, and Peoria, where officials found it was easier to control prostitution than to stamp it out.

Marie and her family moved to Decatur, Illinois, when she was a child. She went to school there and later married Roy Pryor, the brother of her best friend, Amanda. Marie and Roy had four children: "Dickey," Maxine, Leroy "Buck," and Billy.

Marie's marriage was an unhappy one, and eventually she divorced Roy and moved to Peoria with the children. The country was in the grip of the Depression and employment opportunities were scarce. It was not long before Marie turned to prostitution.

Possessing a good business sense, Marie established her own brothel in a two-story brick building that at one time had been a dance hall. There was a modest yard bordered by a picket fence in the back; at one side was a short stairwell that led to the basement. Possibly as a "front," Marie turned the kitchen into a soda fountain for the neighborhood kids. Upstairs, the ambiance was slightly different. There was a huge central room in which the girls waited for customers, and off of it were smaller chambers where the men could relax while waiting for the girl of their choice. On the floor above that were the rooms in which the prostitutes both lived and worked.

Big-boned and described by one of her neighbors as "very masculine," Marie was not a sweet-talking hustler like so many of her peers. She was pleasant, businesslike, and very protective of her girls. Marie was not one of those madams who would send a prostitute to the hospital for a "checkup" and have her sterilized. Her compassion transcended her desire to become a local power; as a result, prostitution did not drag her to its ranker level. The work was done as efficiently and tastefully as possible.

Marie's very professional attitude and diligence are typical of the ethnic and immigrant poor of that era, for whom the only way out of the ghetto was hard work. Work did not have to be qualified. If no one was hurt, if one was making a living and not seeking a fix, then anything went, from

prostitution to gambling to black-marketeering. For this reason, Marie did not find her profession in conflict with her
very Catholic upbringing. One was to provide for the body,
the other for the spirit. Richard Pryor would have this ethic
drummed into him, although he would often lose sight of it.

Once her business was established, Marie opened two
other houses, controlling numbers 313, 317, and 324, all
located on the same block. She also married a man named
Tommy Bryant. A good-natured soul, Bryant operated Pop's
Poolroom at 618 Sixth Street, where, as one frequent visitor
put it, "he really didn't do much of anything." After he
married Marie, he didn't have to: he moved into the living
quarters of the first brothel, where Marie supported the entire
Pryor-Bryant clan.

Although Marie was not ashamed of her work, she never
coaxed the children to follow in her footsteps. They all lived
at the brothel, but she made their home life as normal as
possible. They went to church regularly, and the family
frequently went fishing.

Marie's efforts were successful where Dickey was concerned. He married an attractive young woman named DeWitt—
"Dee" to her friends—and took over Tommy's pool hall,
which was considered respectable. This suited Tommy just
fine, since it meant he had even less to do. Maxine also
married, and Billy died young; only Leroy lacked direction.
He tried his hand at various kinds of work, from truck driving
to construction work, but ultimately decided that pimping was
more to his liking. Marie reluctantly took him into the family
business.

Leroy, a handsome man, was six-foot-one and weighed
230 pounds. It is said that his sexual appetite matched his
size. He would often sneak away with one of the girls. His
favorite was a sweet, gentle five-foot-two-inch woman named
Gertrude Thomas, who went by the professional name of
Hildegarde. She adored Leroy, who was very protective of
her, and in March 1940 she allowed herself to become
pregnant by him.

Leroy wasn't fazed at first. He probably assumed she
would get rid of the child, like most prostitutes did. He didn't

want to be a parent, and he didn't want Gertrude to have to stop working. But Gertrude, who would not stand up to the volatile Leroy in most matters, wanted to keep the baby. When Marie came out in Gertrude's corner, Leroy had no choice but to go along with them—although it would be fully three years before he married Gertrude to give their only child his legal name.

Gertrude's baby was born in St. Francis Hospital on December 1. He was christened Richard Franklin Lenox Thomas Pryor III, after his uncle Dickey. His family and friends called him simply Richie.

Richard's hospital delivery was unusual, for most of his contemporaries were born at home, in the kitchen. But Richard's family was not as poor as most. There was no need to discard him in a trashbin or in a shoebox, where Richard himself once discovered a dead baby.

Like his father, young Richard spent most of his childhood days at the brothel. It's no coincidence that for forty years Pryor treated women alternately with gentleness and with violence: during the first eighteen years of his life, he rarely saw a woman who was not being caressed or abused in some manner.

Actually, Pryor had little direct contact with the customers. His style was more covert. Pulling a chair to the door, he would spy through the transom on his mother and the other women as they entertained their customers. ("You couldn't peek through the keyhole," he says, " 'cause your head kept hittin' the door.")

Marie made repeated efforts to shield Richard from these goings-on. She would grab him by the ear and send him outside to play; there, during the summer months, he would entertain cousins from out-of-town, or when he was alone he would carry on conversations with an imaginary friend named Charlie Eggy. But curiosity and a sense of danger were what made Richie Pryor tick, and he would slip back in through a window or back door.

Though he admits that he "watched things when I didn't exactly know what they were," Richard didn't ask his mother or grandmother to explain them. He knew that they would probably have yelled at him for watching and shooed him away. But more important than understanding was Richard's perception of the brothel. He describes it as having been "fantasylike" and was happy just letting his imagination fly. "It was an adventure, it was two worlds," he says, referring to the thrill of being where he shouldn't have been and the chance to glimpse the secret, incomprehensible world of adults.

Richard's family didn't worry about him when he was young and his escapades were restricted to the house. But his curiosity didn't stop at the gate of his grandmother's picket fence, and the rules changed when Richard was old enough to venture out on his own. Whatever qualities of "neighborhood" Washington Street possessed, it was still a place where children could fall in with gangs or minor-league hoods, or experience peer pressure to smoke, drink, or steal.

Not surprisingly, it was Richard's grandmother who took responsibility for his behavior. The boy's mother loved him dearly, but she wasn't equipped to handle him. Gertrude would speak openly and from the heart about the values she felt her son should have: honesty and a sense of dignity— qualities that had been hardened by Marie's conviction that while prostitution was her livelihood, it was not her life. Richard's mother also tried to share with him the comfort she took in religion, though the nuances of faith were lost on him. The fire-and-brimstone preachers who spoke from the pulpit and at tent revivals frightened him, and later they became recurring targets for his most scathing humor. It would be years before Richard understood his mother's quiet devotion.

Gentle Gertrude could not bring herself to discipline Richard the way Marie did. For all practical purposes, Marie was his mother, the only one with the time and patience to deal with his indiscretions. And there were indiscretions aplenty. Because of Richard's plucky and inquisitive nature, Marie ended up having to discipline him daily. Sometimes this took the form of a severe warning or a quick, cleansing trip to church; more often it involved physical punishment.

Typical was the time Richard and some friends went rafting on the Illinois River. It was a stunt they would try only once. It was bad enough that none of the boys could swim and had to be rescued by the Coast Guard, but, compounding their sin, they'd used Marie's fence to build their raft.

Marie Bryant was from the old school in what Pryor has described as the art of "whipping behind." She had ample opportunity to display her prowess. Whether Marie came to the scene of the crime or watched for her grandson from the bay window—the same one in which her girls beckoned to potential johns—the welcome was invariably the same. Richard would arrive, sometimes in then-rookie Torsey Helm's police car, and Marie would be enraged. Doubling over in fury, she would cry, "How could you *do* such a thing, why oh why oh *why*?" Calming, she would glower down at Richard and, wagging a finger, say, "Now, boy, go and get me something to beat your ass with."

Richard knew better than to plead. Groveling only made Marie angrier, sometimes earning him a warmup beating with whatever was handy, be it a wooden spoon or a douche bag. So, he would obediently turn and, eyes downcast, search out a switch.

Richard always walked slowly on these assignments. Whimpering, he would pray for it to snow before he could find a suitable tree. These quests made a greater impact on Pryor than did the beatings themselves; he vividly recalls finding a switch that was just the right size, stripping it of leaves, and crying on the return trip as he impulsively slashed at the air and listened to the whoosh of the stick. There was no sense in returning with a branch that was too small. On the infrequent occasions when he tried that tack, Marie, depending on her mood, either went out and selected a branch that was barely smaller than the tree itself, or simply thrashed him with whatever was handy.

Years later, in his film *Live in Concert*, Pryor informed his audience, "I see them trees today, I will *kill* one of them motherfuckers." He pretends to wrench a sapling from the

15

ground as he says, "You ain't never gonna grow up. You won't be beatin' nobody's ass."

Richard may not have learned to stay out of trouble, but one strategy he did pick up was never to talk when Marie was applying the switch. If he uttered even an involuntary exclamation like, "I won't do it no more!" Marie would extend the punishment one stroke per word as she answered, "Oh—I—*know*—you—ain't—gonna—do—it—no—more—'cause—you—shouldn'ta—done—it—the—first—time—when—I—told—you—not—to—do—it."

Inevitably, when Marie ran out of steam, she would sit Richard on her lap and minister to his sore seat while muttering softly, "See? You shouldn't *do* that, goddammit." She always concluded with the gentle reminder, "And the next time you *do*, I'm goin' to tear your ass up again."

Richard always had a great time adventuring, but, as he would one day realize, he caused his grandmother so much grief that "she died worrying about us, her kids, her people." As many times as the boys were told not to, they still participated in stunts which might include the likes of letting loose "bad dogs" and trying to get away from them, or waiting for a bus to stop at a light, then slipping cinderblocks under its tires. It wasn't that Richard took his grandmother lightly; he simply believed that she would never find him out. Sometimes she didn't, but the police did; and whenever they did, so did his father. When that happened, Leroy would, as Richard puts it, "kick ass all the way up Washington."

Leroy Pryor was not a man to mess with. He was brash, blunt, and impatient with both his wife and his son, and Richard describes him as "so scary... I piss on myself sometimes when he call me." Whether he was taking his son hunting or presiding over the dinner table, Leroy was a man of little sentiment. He addressed Richard not as "son" or "boy" as Gertrude and Marie did, but with strident, demeaning exclamations. "Shit, nigger!" was one of the milder oaths he used. It wasn't until years later that Richard understood the insurmountable barrier between him and his father—the fact that Leroy "had a child but he didn't need a child."

As much as Richard feared his grandmother's stinging

justice, it was a treat compared to his father's unpredictability. Richard jokes that Leroy's idea of discipline was for Richard to stand in front of a moving car. Perhaps Leroy really wouldn't have gone quite that far, but Captain Helm remembers him as "the reason Richard could never have gotten into *real* trouble. At the first sign of it, I'd just march him up to his father and he'd kill him."

Gertrude, too, suffered from Leroy's volcanic temper. At night Richard would lie in bed and listen as his mother turned over the money she'd earned during the day, angry words often erupting over some small matter. Frequently, these fights expanded to include Richard and whatever trouble he'd gotten into that day. Pryor remembers, "It would scare me when my mother and father were fighting. They'd hit each other, go after each other. My father beat me up one time because I jumped in when he was beatin' up my mother. He slapped me, knocked me down and said, 'This is *my* wife!'"

The abuse Gertrude took from her husband and her customers gave Richard a keen sense of her unhappiness. He would later say that she and his father "shouldn't have had to do what they did to live," but he seems to have developed a guilt complex where Gertrude is concerned. While he would one day joke a great deal about most of the people in his life, his mother would rarely be included. In one of the few bits in which she was mentioned, Gertrude was not portrayed like the caricatured figures he made of his grandmother, father, or Uncle Dickey, but as an almost pathetic figure moaning plaintively, "You don't know the pain I went through when you were born, you have no idea," to which he weepingly responded, "I'm sorry. I'll go back."

Richard's long-time friend, actor and ex-football star Jim Brown, believes that Richard's early penchant for comedy was inspired by his need to escape from the tension of his home. "If you grow up where you don't have . . . unqualified love around you," Brown says, "then you must fortify yourself; if you don't, then you're not gonna survive."

Brown overstates the lack of "unqualified love" in the Pryor household, for, like most children, Richard seems to have taken at face value the fact that his parents were doing what was best for him. However, Brown is correct about Richard's need to fortify himself. And while Richard freely credits his mother and grandmother with having shaped his values, his real strength—his humor—came from his father.

Leroy Pryor was not much different from other men in the ghetto, men who had not shaken the stigma of the "emasculating matriarch." Having had doors slammed in their faces for years, most black men were without career opportunities. But black women could train for work as teachers, nurses, or social workers—professions that didn't carry the taint of white supremacy, as did the traditionally "male-oriented" professions. Or they could find satisfaction at home, raising a family. Black men did not have those options and were even further dehumanized by the popular impression that they had to be either Uncle Toms (honorable, hardworking, forebearing, faithful to whites) or Coons (well-meaning but incompetent).

Hardened by poverty, black men asserted themselves at home, taking out their anger and frustration on their women and establishing far from exemplary role models for their children. How much of Leroy's personality was influenced by his professional lot is difficult to say. But the example he set for Richard was one of never suppressing what he felt. He refused to put up false fronts, expressing himself freely regardless of how cutting or inappropriate his remarks might be. He was also free in his use of street language, although Marie did not appreciate hearing it around the house. Richard didn't pick up swearing from other kids in the neighborhood; he taught *them*.

A more extreme example of Leroy's candor was his reaction to his wife's death. As Richard tells it, "We went to the funeral and it was about fourteen below zero. My dad was sitting in the car and he was crying, and as he was crying he says, 'If it gets any colder they'll have to bury the bitch by herself.' "

What appears to be selfish or insensitive behavior was obviously Leroy's way of surviving the ghetto, of living with the demeaning nature of his own profession and that of his wife, and of having to watch his sister open a brothel in nearby Bloomington in order to survive. Looking back on his youth, Richard didn't condemn his father but perceptively referred to Leroy's surliness as "heart."

Richard would one day expand that "heart" into violence. However, as a five-year-old he took from his father only those superficial mannerisms that were within his reach—Leroy's brusque delivery and assertiveness. Unfortunately, adults and teachers found these cheeky qualities off-putting, but Richard's big mouth *did* come in handy on the street. And that, for a time, was all that mattered to him.

Richard Pryor was a moderately "with it" child. He saw a lot of the world by hanging out at Pop's Poolroom and living in the brothel, and was quick to pick up on everything the people around him said or did. He became sexually "active" early in life—early even by ghetto standards. He was five years old when an older girl gave him the hands-on lowdown about sex, although it was some time before the information was of any use to him. Discovering masturbation several years later made much more of an impression. Pryor relates that he was in the bathtub when he touched himself and thought, " 'Hey . . . I'm onto something here!' " He adds, "I came; I thought something was wrong with me. Hour later I was back, jack: 'Can you do it *again*?' "

Being brash and aware gave Richard a needed advantage, since he mixed with kids who were beefier, taller, and merciless. One of Richard's mentors, Juliette Whittaker, of the Carver Community Center, describes him as "so skinny and little that he looked nine when he was thirteen."

No matter how conciliatory Richard was, the toughs always found a reason to beat him up, whether it was to take his pocket money or comic books, or because he had looked at them the wrong way. He wasn't strong enough to fight back, and for a while experimented with drugs to help him over the psychological hump of "accepting the fact that I was no street-fighter." He soon found less dangerous ways of coping. Belligerent humor was one of the two weapons guaranteed to save Richard's hide, and he was usually successful at smart-alecking his way out of trouble. He would run away only if he couldn't think of something clever to say. And even that was calculated.

"I developed a cool run," he boasted to Johnny Carson during a "Tonight Show" appearance in 1968. He demonstrated how he would cock his arms back, downturned index fingers jabbing the air like pistons as his determined, upturned face rocked from side to side. "Girls would see me and say, 'Look, Richard's running!' " Pryor considered himself fortunate, however, for at least one of the girls would always sigh, " 'Yeah, but at least he's cool!' "

According to Ms. Whittaker, Richard's humor allowed him not only to survive in the streets but to hobnob with the Clarks, a family of twenty and the most powerful kids in the neighborhood. She recalls that Richard became something of a gang jester because "he made the Clark boys laugh so hard they wouldn't touch him, nor would they let anybody *else* touch him."

Potential victims of the Clarks also liked having Richard around. After watching a kid get beaten silly, Pryor was likely to amble to his side and admonish, "Hey—put your teeth in your mouth and get up." Richard would then go on for a minute or two about the fight, causing so much laughter among the gang that their quaking victim would have a chance to slink off.

As a result of his quick wit, Pryor remembers, "I wasn't afraid like the other kids were." More than that, he enjoyed the attention he got. Once in a while a tough kid would become jealous of this attention, and if he didn't slap Pryor around, he'd tell his own jokes—always badly, yet earning more laughs than Pryor ever heard. But such conflicts were rare. The kids enjoyed Pryor's characterizations, in particular "Rummage Sale Ranger," a sort of godfather of the Salvation Army. The impact these vignettes had on Pryor was even more profound. "Niggers don't have theater groups," he would later explain. "Niggers train on the corner."

Pryor's problem wasn't getting the laughs; it was knowing when to stop. Smart-mouthing the kids was one thing; sassing his teachers was quite another.

Richard's troubles at school stemmed from the fact that

20

teachers were constantly telling him things he didn't want to hear. One of his earliest and most traumatic experiences involved the nickname "Sun," which he had given to himself as a child. Richard chose it because when he looked at himself he saw that he was orange, like the sun. "Then," he says, "one day in school the teacher told me I was black, and I was really upset about that. I said, 'But I'm orange.' And the teacher—a white teacher—said, 'No, you're Negro.'" Richard shot back that not only was he orange, he really didn't *want* to be a Negro. This and similar conflicts helped to make school Richard's private battleground.

Chapter Two

Richard's problems in school were heightened by his fascination with movies and movie stars. He was already hyperactive and full of nerve; motion pictures gave him the confidence to take on the world—which, for the time being, was the Peoria school system.

From the time he was six years old, Richard spent as much time as he could in movie theaters. "No movie ever opened that I didn't sneak in to see," he says—adding that he stopped this practice only when he started owning a piece of them—and would frequently play hooky to do so. Only the sternest warnings from his father could deter him, and then only for a day or two. Not coincidentally, the characters Richard idolized were figures who wouldn't have lasted long under the thumb of a first-grade teacher and whose fathers, if shown at all, were cantankerous but harmless old men.

Richard's favorite stars were Lash LaRue and John Wayne, two sides of the same heroic mold. Pryor desperately wanted to *be* LaRue, a white cowboy who dressed all in black and packed a big black whip. LaRue was splashy and self-aggrandizing, John Wayne without the stuffed shirt. Wayne was the kind of hero who would have punched out one of the Clarks and the rest would have fled; LaRue would have taken on all twenty in a grand, rock 'em, sock 'em battle.

"I didn't know he hated my guts," Pryor would later say of Wayne, who swaggered through right-wing rhetoric as easily as through the streets of Dodge City. Pryor had adored Wayne and trusted him to do what was right. It would always hurt Pryor not to be liked, but it hurt him far more to be betrayed.

However, in the late 1940s, Pryor's sole criterion for judging movie stars was whether their pictures made him feel good. He wasn't oblivious to race; it just didn't matter to him. However, that attitude was not universal. In his classic autobiography, *Nigger,* comedian-activist Dick Gregory reports that going to certain movies could actually be dangerous for blacks. Growing up in nearby St. Louis, he remembers that "[in one movie] Tarzan jumped down from a tree and grabbed about a hundred Africans. We didn't mind when Tarzan beat up five or ten, but this was just too many . . . and we took the movie house apart, ran up on the stage and kicked the screen and fought the guys who still dug Tarzan." Richard was usually so involved in the movie that he would probably have ignored a fire, let alone a mere rumble.

Richard's identification with movies and movie stars was much deeper than that of other kids his age. "I used to play with Popsicle sticks and make believe they were people," he says. "Also, my grandmother had a bunch of records upstairs, old Doris Day records. I'd listen to those and imagine that I was in a play. That I was in Hollywood." In fact, Richard's belief in movies was so overwhelming that they gave him one of his "first big traumatic experiences." He had gone to see a Red Ryder western featuring Little Beaver, the continuing character played by a young Robert Blake. "When it was over," Pryor relates, "I tried to get back behind the screen. I thought Little Beaver would be there, you know, and I wanted to talk to him." Brokenhearted, Pryor slunk from the theater, though he still didn't accept movies strictly for what they were.

While Pryor enjoyed a good screen brawl, what he really

admired were characters who used bravura to get out of trouble. They didn't have to be like Wayne or LaRue, carved from the heroic mold. Pryor was just as happy watching Abbott and Costello, Bob Hope, and Jerry Lewis, as well as less prominent comedy teams and singles. He literally took lessons from the way they "plea bargained" to avoid punishment. Then he would mime not only their routines but their delivery, turning his impressions loose on friends and, if need be, on enemies. At home, Richard would carry the fantasy one step farther. Flopping on his bed, he'd write RICHIE PRYOR on a piece of paper and paste it over photos of theater marquees in *Life* magazine and the local papers. At the age of seven, he knew what he was going to do when he didn't grow up.

As much as Pryor adored motion pictures, his fullest attention went to the animated cartoons. The wild antics of Donald Duck, Tom and Jerry, and Mighty Mouse were in tune with his own slightly frenetic personality. More importantly, these cartoons showed him how to imbue inanimate objects with life, and that lesson was of enormous help in the street. Richard started improvising outrageous anthropomorphisms, taking the part of a fist or a broken bottle hovering inches from someone's face. The kids loved it. Pryor's ability to bring dogs, deer, lions, and other animals to vivid life on the stage can be traced to this early fascination.

When television entered the Pryor household early in the 1950s, Richard was instantly smitten with its odd cast of characters. And he didn't have to skip school to enjoy them. As in the movies, he was devoted to heroes like the Lone Ranger and Superman, and he is still one of the world's biggest Superman fans. However, again, his real heroes were the comedians. He was especially taken with Jonathan Winters, a master of improvisation and characterization, and was a big fan of Red Skelton and Lucille Ball.

To say that Richard was preoccupied with these figures is an understatement. If he wasn't watching them he was pretending to be them, and if he wasn't acting out little skits he was thinking about doing so. However, it wasn't only

Richard's love of movies that kept him from attending classes or paying attention while he was there. It was his disdain for the classes themselves.

Richard's first weeks at school set the tone for the unrest that followed. When he was five years old, his mother sent him to St. Joseph's Catholic school, which has since been shut down. Richard feared the nuns, so he was well behaved and earned A's. Unfortunately, when the school board discovered what his mother did for a living, Richard was expelled. His grandmother worked feverishly to have him reinstated, allegedly going so far as to make certain that the nuns weren't using Gertrude's occupation as a cover for racial prejudice. As Richard revealed in one of his record albums, "She took me with her to get the preacher to take the devil out of me. He prayed over me, and says for the devil to come out." The effort backfired. While he was being "redeemed," all Richard kept thinking was, "If you have one, you should keep it with you. It makes you experiment."

Despite his cleansing, Richard was not accepted back into St. Joseph's. Instead, he was shuttled off to the Irving Grammar School, where his *real* demons bubbled to the surface. Richard's sharp tongue and inherent restlessness convinced his teachers that he was ineducable, so they put him in the slowest classes. In fact, they were so concerned about his limited attention span and attendant low grades that during summer vacation they sent him to the Blaine School, where he was placed in a class for the retarded.

The slow, stifling setting served only to nurture further unrest. To amuse himself, Richard stole paper and pencils and played practical jokes without regard to race, creed, or authority. He went through a cataclysmic phase of imitating Tarzan, letting loose the Ape Man's famous yell during lectures and tests. Witnesses rate his imitation of the chimpanzee Cheetah the better of the two. Pryor himself claims to have cut off a girl's hair, which is likely, but his claim of having "pasted it back on—her dress!" is doubtful.

"I didn't like it," Pryor says succinctly of school. He accuses his teachers of trying to destroy his character, adding that the best he could do under the circumstances was to "hold on to it and try to have your principles about you."

The one teacher who managed to earn his respect and cooperation in six years of elementary school was Miss Leeks, who found the ideal way to make the seven-year-old behave. If he paid attention, she allowed him to put on little shows for the class. "She used to let me do about five minutes on Fridays . . . get in front of the class and do stuff I'd heard on the radio." She realized that Pryor enjoyed doing the shows and getting attention. "It was the only place I'd be accepted and felt secure," he says fondly. "I could hide by exposing." Of course, he didn't see things quite so lucidly back then. All he knew was that, for the most part, he'd rather have been somewhere else.

Not all of his teachers blamed him. One said that "when Richard was in school he was bored most of the time. His problem, if you can call it that, was that Richard was really a genius. The school system gives children with that kind of quality very short shrift. As a result, a child will . . . withdraw and just be incommunicado, or do something the teacher would consider disruptive. In Richard's case, it was the latter. He would make comments about what was going on, and, understandably, most of the comments were critical of what the teacher was doing. I don't think very many teachers can put up with that kind of barbed humor aimed directly at them." Not only was Richard insolent, the woman pointed out, but teachers resented the fact that usually what Richard said was true.

Public school was educational in one way, however: it introduced Pryor to racism. He had never learned about prejudice from his parents or on the streets, where black-white confrontations were merely name-calling spats, barely distinguishable from the fights blacks had with other blacks. Richard was aware that blacks were allowed to sit only in the balconies of local movie theaters, but that discrimination wasn't aimed at him personally. Then one day he innocently professed his love for a little white girl at school.

"I brought her one of those gray cardboard things you draw on," Pryor reports, "where you lift up the plastic and the picture's gone. The next day her daddy comes to school and says, 'Don't you *dare* give my little girl a present.' " Scared and confused, Richard just nodded compliantly. When Richard told his father what had happened, Leroy shook his head and said nothing. He felt that experience would explain it far more eloquently than he could, and hoped that Richard would fortify himself accordingly. Leroy must also have felt that there was no sense filling his son's head with his own anger, for Richard was still a boy with a boy's perspective of things.

Richard did not feel the full impact of discrimination because at the time he "wasn't aware of the sophisticated subtleties of racism." But if incidents such as these did not breed resentment until much later (he feels "more harshly" today), they did heighten his sense of isolation. There he was, a kid who hadn't even *wanted* to be a Negro—and he was being punished for it. Discussing the intolerance of the girl's father and similar incidents years later, Pryor says he wouldn't be so bitter today if his parents, or any parents, had gone to school to "pitch a bitch, just for their child, just scream and yell, 'There is no *nigger* in my family!' " Not for the bigot, says Pryor, but "for that child, so he will know, so he won't accept it."

Although Richard wasn't alone in this struggle, snide asides from adults, whether store clerks, parents, or teachers, made him feel uncomfortable. Too, he had one albatross none of his friends had to carry: day after day he saw his mother crawl into bed with men who were not his father, and who were white.

Richard made it through elementary school and attended Woodruff High, but he didn't always show up for classes. Now it was more than just going to the movies. He enjoyed being in the streets, "hanging out with a dude, trying to be like the other cats, cats I admired because they played basketball and chased girls." He regrets not having realized that "standing on a corner, you ain't going to learn nothing . . . because it's the same old corner." In later years he would agonize that he wasn't smart enough for some women and couldn't keep up with attorneys and accountants.

Richard couldn't stand the regimentation of public school, but he managed to hang on until he was fourteen. Then he made a remark that angered a science teacher. As the man approached Richard to escort him to the principal's office, "Lash" Pryor punched him in the face. Richard was expelled.

Richard's mother was heartbroken. As a result of her son's problems, she became the brunt of neighborhood criticism. "You don't take care of that boy," Richard remembers them telling her. When she and her son were alone, Gertrude would hold him close and make certain he knew this wasn't true, that all she wanted was for him to be more than *they* were, to be "somebody." But Richard was content to be just what he was: an ex-student working in his uncle Dickey's pool hall, where he racked up balls for pennies and handled odd jobs. He often mimicked players when they were winning (the losers had no sense of humor) and cracked jokes.

During the day, Richard's Aunt Dee was like a third mother, looking after him in an environment that was far from ideal for a youngster. Dickey worked him hard but gave him time to hang out with his friends and pursue girls. Richard also spent a lot of time alone, walking the streets, watching men who slept off drunken stupors against alley walls, and listening to the colorful figures who sat on their front stoops playing instruments or spinning yarns about the South. Richard was particularly fascinated by a Southern black man whose name he never knew but who "used to sit out in front of Johnnie Mae's Barbecue Pit. The nigger had a goatee, he was toothless, and he had a guitar and a harmonica with tape on the end." Pryor would sit with the man for hours as he played a little, talked a little, and sometimes dozed a bit. His manner and his stories inspired the popular Mudbone character that Pryor created years later.

Not surprisingly, Richard's biggest concerns at the time were romantic ones. He laments having been caught up in "the great pussy drought of the fifties," though he says that most of the time if he spent enough money, he scored afterward. ("Nigger spend thirty-four dollars, he gonna fuck *somebody,*" Pryor would one day assert in his act. If the girl still didn't put out, he would demand that she wake up her father, who, in Pryor's world of wishful-thinking, would be so thoroughly embarrassed by his daughter's ungratefulness that he'd order her not only to do what Richard asked but to "wake up your mama too.")

In truth, encountering fathers was the last thing Pryor wanted. If virginity were the fort, the fathers were the diligent scouts who threatened, as Pryor puts it, "to wear your ass out" if they learned of any young man who was dallying with their daughters. Even if Pryor had been desperate enough to brave their wrath, most of the girls were not. But Pryor's amorous endeavors were not inhibited solely by the girls' fathers.

In the mid-1950s, Peoria's teens were governed by a very strict curfew to avert gang warfare and other youth-oriented crimes. Anyone under the age of twenty-one had to be home by eleven o'clock on weekdays and by midnight on weekends. The boys were reluctant to comply, of course, since nothing started cooking in the bars, park, or parked cars—which didn't always belong to the kids—until after curfew. But there was no arguing with the police, and kids caught breaking curfew were brought to juvenile lockup. The teens' fathers would come and claim them, paying a minimum of ten dollars for their release. It's fair to say that most of the teen-agers would have paid twice that amount to be released before their fathers arrived.

Richard says only half-jokingly that whenever he was caught he would beg the police to leave him locked up. Leroy would post bail, stand glowering as the slim, terrified boy was brought over, then wallop him from one end of Peoria to the other.

That was what Richard and most of his friends got for breaking curfew, which was a comparatively minor infraction. They were treated more severely when they were caught doing something worse, like "till tapping"—trying to steal pocket change—or hiding behind trash cans and shooting BB guns at passing vehicles. What frustrated the kids almost as much as being caught was the fact that the black officers were much harder on them than the whites were. Captain Helm says that the kids were looked upon as spokespeople for blacks and, as such, "were *going* to behave."

Black or white, Pryor says he "was raised to hate cops." He admitted even then that police were necessary, " 'cause there are some niggers that'll pull the truck up to your house and say, 'Give the furniture up!' " But that didn't change the fact that he neither liked nor trusted them. Not only did they spoil his fun, but his grandmother and father had to watch their own activities very carefully where the police were concerned, and some of that rubbed off on Richard.

Though Richard hints he would have preferred imprisonment to facing his father, he found jail extremely demeaning. One trip to the joint was especially memorable. When a fight erupted between two local gangs, the Love Veedles and the Love Licks, Richard impulsively joined in. Fists, blades, and rubber hoses mixed furiously until the police arrived and carted everyone off to jail. There, Pryor reports, the officers beat him. "That bothered me a lot and I swore not to be the motherfucker who was going to get hit in the kidney again."

But with Pryor, reality of one moment gives way to the passion of the next. Though he regarded jail as the most dehumanizing and lonely experience of all, a place where "you can't learn anything . . . but self-humiliation," he often found himself in jail. This was true particularly after he left Peoria and went on the road, where the pressures were enormous. Rather than encourage reform, his run-ins with the law inspired disdain for the people and institutions that inhibited him, and vitriol that would come out in his comedy. (The only part of due process Pryor ever enjoyed was the line-up, which he regarded as akin to "being in show business . . . unless you got picked, that was yo' *ass*.")

Yet, there were fates worse than prison. In Richard's early teens, eluding the police after curfew was a meaningless victory. Arriving home, he would be greeted by his father, who would boom, "You *can* tell time, can't you, nigger?" after which there was usually a one-sided showdown. On those rare occasions when Richard was so frustrated that he stood up to his father, Leroy would step back and sneer, "So you're a *man*, are you?'' then send him straight to the floor with a fist-sized tattoo on his chest.

Marie and Gertrude eventually got Richard back into school. Using his Uncle Richard's address, they enrolled him in Peoria Central High, where Richard plodded through a single semester. He held on to his sanity by working in the pool parlor after classes.

One of Richard's more astute teachers, sensing his unhappiness, suggested that he try some extracurricular activities. One of those activities would change his life.

Across town was the Carver Community Center, whose activities were designed to keep kids off the streets. Having nothing better to do one afternoon, Richard took the short bus ride over to check it out.

The community center was not a new or particularly attractive building, but it had what Richard would have called "heart.'' And that heart came from the staff and the kids, all of whom gave everything they had for Carver projects.

By far the most popular activities were the plays staged by Juliette Whittaker. A drama graduate of the University of Iowa, Ms. Whittaker had a firm but elegant manner that commanded the kids' respect, although the care and concern she lavished on them would have earned it just the same.

On the afternoon that Richard dropped by, Ms. Whittaker and the kids were rehearsing *Rumpelstiltskin*. The teacher spotted him in the auditorium and handed him a script. She told him that the part of a servant had yet to be filled and, apologizing for the meagerness of the role, offered it to Richard. To her surprise, his face lit up and he gushed, "I'll take anything, anything.''

Ms. Whittaker had no inkling of Richard's affection for movies and ambition to be a movie star. She says fondly, "I was simply impressed by his very commendable attitude to take whatever was offered,'' though she was soon to be impressed by much, much more.

Richard had never done any structured performing. In elementary school, and before that at the age of four, when he was given a cowboy uniform by his grandfather and put on a horse opera for the family, everything was improvised. (He discounts, as acting, that cowboy skit on his front lawn, because he "kept slipping in the dog poo-poo and falling and they laughed. It was beautiful, my first *comedy* routine.") The idea of having a script, just like in the movies, was exhilarating. Ms. Whittaker continues, "Unknown to any of us, Richard went home and learned the entire script, everybody's role. And one day, when the king didn't show up for rehearsal, Richard piped up and said, 'I know that part.' So he got up there, and not only did he know the script, he had added in his own mind so much comic business that the part became hilarious. The boy who'd done the king had never done it that way; Richard had everybody rolling in the aisles."

When the other boy heard that Richard had knocked 'em dead, he let him keep the part. Ms. Whittaker suspects that he was afraid of following in Richard's footsteps. "So," she says, "Richard stayed on that throne—and he hasn't come down since."

(Pryor later fictionalized the staging of *Rumpelstiltskin* in one of his most unforgettable routines. Not only does he play the parts of the principal and the children, he acts out the children playing their characters. He's superb as Young Harvey Frumpf mumbling out the Pledge of Allegiance before the play begins, but the *pièce de résistance* is the bickering between the kid playing Rumpelstiltskin and the boy playing the Prince. The former refuses to die, as written, so the Prince snorts, "Vanish!" But Rumpelstiltskin lives on in defiance, so the Prince steps out of character and growls, "You *better* vanish—my mother's here!")

Pryor's participation in *Rumpelstiltskin* and subsequent Carver plays helped ease the friction at school. According to Ms. Whittaker, "Richard had something he could really get into; it was a positive approach to himself. He was being appreciated, and that minimized the problems he was having in class."

Richard's enthusiasm notwithstanding, it was not always easy to get him to the Carver Center. Ms. Whittaker remembers, "Because of the job at his uncle's poolroom, he was

31

often late for rehearsals. When that happened, I had no choice but to go down to the pool hall and get him. His uncle was always very cooperative. I would walk in and say, 'I'm sorry, Mr. Pryor, but I have to have Richard now. I'll send him back in an hour.' And he'd be very gracious, he'd say, 'Fine. Take him, take him,' and hurry him out. I thought that was very understanding of him, until Richard told me afterward it was *me* he wanted out of there, not Richard, because when I came in it would be like church. Everyone who was cussin' and fussin' would get quiet; people who had pool sticks raised in the air to strike somebody would suddenly freeze. Then, the minute I'd leave, they'd go back to whatever they were doing.'' Ms. Whittaker admits that she didn't like going there, but, as she says, "Richard had something worth salvaging. I'd have gone to hell itself to get that boy."

After each rehearsal, Ms. Whittaker made sure that Richard went back to work. Though she did not approve of the pool hall, it was important to her that Richard develop a sense of responsibility. If he protested and tried to hang around the center, she'd tell him, "I'd love for you to stay, but you've got to go back because your uncle expects it."

Despite his ability to perform onstage, Richard was an extremely private person at the Carver Center. Nearly thirty years later he would say, "It's so much easier for me to talk about my life in front of two thousand people than it is one-to-one. I'm a real defensive person because if you were sensitive in my neighborhood you were something to eat." He felt that the more someone knew about him, the easier it was to hurt or manipulate him. Thus, Dickey and Marie were the only other Pryors whom Ms. Whittaker ever met. She says, "I never knew his father," and in fact didn't know Richard even had a father since "I never even heard him mentioned in all the time I knew Richard."

Richard became more and more of a fixture at the community center because, as he acknowledges, Ms. Whittaker believed in him. One day he would repay his debt to her by establishing seventy scholarships to The Learning Tree, Ms.

Whittaker's school in Peoria. At the time, however, he did the work solely because it challenged him.

Challenging a child as imaginative as Richard was not easy. "They just don't write plays for fourteen-year-old geniuses," Ms. Whittaker laments. As a result, she did something she hadn't done before or since—she began writing a play for him. "He never knew about it," she says, "and still doesn't. The play was called *The Magic Violin*. Set in an Italian village, it was about a boy who had a magnificent gift that was brought out when he played a special violin: he'd play it and people would change for the better. Unfortunately, I never had a reason to complete the play, since I began writing it just about the time Richard got interested in boxing. Once that caught his fancy, I didn't see very much of him."

Richard did indeed begin spending more and more of his spare time at a local gym. There, much to his father's delight—Leroy himself had been an amateur boxer—the fifteen-year-old worked out almost every day. After a few months he was proficient enough to enter Peoria's Golden Gloves, and he even won his first bout. However, his father was convinced that he did this "by telling a joke, which made the guy double up. And then he punched him out."

Richard's new distraction upset Ms. Whittaker more than she let on. She did everything she could to get him back to the Carver Center, but the only times she could count on him to show up were for the regularly scheduled talent shows. At first, the only performing he would do was with a singing group he'd formed. Richard had loved music since his early teens, when he would sneak from the house at night to visit Peoria's Famous Door Cabaret. He would stand in the back of the club and listen to the likes of Pearl Bailey, Louis Armstrong, Count Basie, and Duke Ellington. Between sets the musicians would allow Richard to sit at the drums and jam with them, after which he'd fight off sleep until the bands had finished their final number.

Richard loved the group, but with a changing voice and, the evidence suggests, some creative dissonance among the members, he soon broke away. Afraid that she would lose him altogether and that his talent would stagnate, Ms. Whittaker offered him the job of emceeing the talent shows, figuring that it was a solo spotlight he couldn't refuse. She was right. "Originally," she says with a smile, "I let him have five minutes to introduce the show. But he developed his act and it just enlarged to where it overshadowed everything else and people were coming just to see Richard. At that point it became quite evident that he had a talent which wasn't seasonal—that it was going to be with him for all his life. He just needed to explore the possibilities."

Instead, despite her best efforts, for a time Richard Pryor explored everything *but* his talent.

Chapter Three

Richard felt that he'd taken performing as far as he could. He'd tried all kinds of routines, from impressions of popular singers and comedians to a slew of joke-book jokes. It had quickly become dreary through repetition.

High school was even less rewarding, so Richard dropped out. He pared his visits to Carver and also gave up boxing, having made a discovery that caused his jaw considerable discomfort: unlike the punching bag in the gym, boxers hit back. Although Richard would always love the sport—he's the only actor with a live-in spiritual adviser and sparring partner—he retired from the ring before his features or pride could be seriously damaged.

While he devoted himself to odd jobs, such as driving a truck, sweeping floors, shining shoes, and working in a packing house, the only area in which his energies did not let up was where women were concerned. After his aborted start in kindergarten, Richard did not do any "serious fucking" until he was nine. That, he says, is when he first had sex. "This whore gave me some pussy," he says, though he

34

suspects his father "had her give me some to see what kind of dude I was." What Leroy found out was that Richard had inherited his energetic libido. Richard's attitude toward sex was simple: "If I ain't horny, I check to see if my heart's beatin'."

Shortly before his sixteenth birthday, Richard found out that he was going to be a father. He had gotten another girl pregnant not long before, and the odds are that she wasn't the first. In Richard's world, getting girls pregnant was a matter of playing the odds. But this girl claimed that she had been a virgin, and she intended to keep the baby.

The prospect of being a father stunned Pryor. "I went home to my father when she told me she was pregnant," he revealed to Barbara Walters, "and I cried. I was standing in the dining room and I was crying. My mother said, 'What's wrong with you, boy?' Father says, 'There ain't nothing wrong with him, he got some girl pregnant.' " When Richard heard this, he wondered how his father could possibly have known. Leroy explained that he knew because the girl had told him; he'd been sleeping with her as well. Richard was more surprised than hurt, explaining to Walters, "I thought she'd never made love to nobody."

The fact that he hadn't made an "innocent" girl pregnant helped to clear up Richard's guilt. Discovering that she had lied to him cleaned up the residue. He was still going to be a father, but at least it wasn't his *fault*. The girl had known what she was getting into.

A daughter, Renee, was born in 1957. Though in later years she and her father would be very close, Richard did not see much of her at the time. He married, stayed at his job at the pork packing plant for a few months longer, then impulsively enlisted in the army.

Richard approached the military with a sense of relief spiced by expectation. He saw it as his ticket from the ghetto and as freedom from adult responsibilities. His room and board would be free, he'd have money in his pocket, and his leisure time would be worry-free; too, he would see new places and be well dressed in a uniform. These factors helped convince Richard that he would make the army his career.

Richard's first hint that his dream was about to turn into a nightmare was his immediate conflict with authority figures. Like Richard's teachers, they didn't understand him; unlike his teachers, they didn't give a damn. Officers are not known for being gentle, and while the hard work itself didn't bother Richard, he disliked the military macho, the pompous, unassailable swagger behind the commands. He was a man now, not a kid; that's what the recruiter had told him. He expected to be treated with some equality.

Not surprisingly, Pryor's disapproval of officers would eventually surface in his comedy, the most biting humor centered on the way they handled self-defense instruction. Violence had never seemed abhorrent to Pryor in its natural environment—the street. But he was unsettled to find that in the army, murder and dismemberment were taught calmly, as though they were conditions that could be undone when the curtain fell, like the destruction of Rumpelstiltskin. He would one day lampoon these classes in a routine that opens with a fictitious drill sergeant booming, "I killed some—and I *was* killed some." The officer and his men proceed to massacre one another in the name of patriotism. This casual attitude toward death took a further drubbing in Pryor's account of a submarine crew, whose commander welcomes the men with a sportive, "Men, some of you gonna get *wiped out*."

Fortunately, Richard didn't see much action, and none that was authorized by the military. During the early weeks of enlistment he had wanted to get into the paratroops. However, when his superiors saw the results of his testing, they declared, he says, " 'This nigger's too dumb. Let's send him to plumbing school,' " which is exactly what they did. The results of the written test cannot have been very accurate, for as comedian Bill Cosby has said of his associate, "Pryor's a man who, if he sat down for an IQ test, would run the chart off the paper."

Embarrassed, Richard wrote to friends and family telling them that he'd made the grade. He saw nothing wrong with lying, having always done so "just to be popular and stuff." Today, he feels lies helped his concentration when he became

36

a performer. "I'd have to remember those lies," he explains, "and that took work."

Assigned to a base in West Germany, plumber Pryor found himself grabbing pipes for more than just the execution of his duties, which brings up the second problem he had with the army—the inevitable confrontations with racists.

Richard got a much harsher dose of prejudice from fellow soldiers than he had ever experienced in Peoria. There was no longer the deterrent of numbers, nor had his fellow soldiers necessarily grown up with blacks. He suffered the usual rash of back-to-Africa taunts, but for the most part he was able to ignore these or use humor as a shield. However, when that failed, it failed dramatically.

Richard's most vivid and frightening recollection is of a bout in an armory, where he was cornered by three soldiers, each holding a tire iron. Pryor grabbed the nearest weapon, which happened to be a length of pipe. Surprising the rednecks by assuming the offensive, Pryor spun and "hit one of them in the head." The fight ended abruptly, the white youth looking blankly at Pryor and slurring, "Well, damn! You're all right with me, I'll tell you that." He staggered into the arms of his friends and the three of them left.

This was not the last such incident, nor was it the most serious. A few months later, Richard was forced to stab another soldier in self-defense. These confrontations convinced Richard that the army was not for him, and he did not reenlist when he was discharged at the age of nineteen.

Having nowhere else to go, Pryor returned to Peoria, picking up where he'd left off, working odd jobs. Despite the fact that his first marriage had been terminated, he impulsively married a young girl named Patricia. "I like to be in love," he shrugs, though he seems to have had trouble sustaining it. His self-respect had been frayed by the army, and he lacked direction; he thought Patricia would help give that to him. Instead, she gave him a son, Richard, Jr., born in 1962. Shortly thereafter, some old conflicts with women seethed to the surface.

As if his opinion of women had not been confused

enough by his years at the brothel, Pryor was beginning to realize that women weren't as easygoing as men. He couldn't "hang out" with them the same way; he felt they were too emotional and had to be manipulated rather than confronted; and, as he'd learned after getting his first wife pregnant, apparently he couldn't trust many of them. This time around it wasn't trust but a blend of frustration and suffocation that unsettled Pryor. Since his home life failed to satisfy him— indeed, it complicated matters with emotional demands—he was divorced a second time. This second failed marriage was not enough to make him swear off relationships with women, but, predictably, he resolved henceforth to "take the pussy and . . . deal with the rest of the shit later."

What Richard needed wasn't casual sex. He needed self-respect, though he wouldn't get it until years later, when a bizarre encounter in Africa changed his life. In the meantime, he governed his personal relationships with a corollary of the survival instinct, which he later enunciated as "self-love . . . the greatest love of all." It wasn't that Pryor was selfish; he was simply defensive, the legacy of the time he spent on the streets.

Pryor was much more aware of what he needed professionally. In the past few years he'd tried two extremes— bumming around and then going into a strictly disciplined situation. Neither had satisfied him. What he needed was something in the middle—a job that had purpose without being suffocating.

Being onstage was the one activity that had totally satisfied him. "Performing has never let me down," he says. "It has always given me love and respect, humanity and refinement." Deciding to cash in on his local reputation, he approached one of the local nightclubs. He wasn't thinking of it in terms of a career but as something of an exercise that would allow him "to get out there and do it and bump heads, [to] feel proud about myself for going through that and coming out the other end."

Pryor hadn't done any serious performing in years, but he had appeared in a few army shows and occasionally done impromptu, stand-up routines for his few buddies. When he offered to work cheaply, he landed a job entertaining at a Washington Street tavern called Harold's Club.

According to Captain Helm, who would stop by to watch his former adversary, "Harold's was one of the most popular spots in town. They used to have bands there, and when Richard first started there he'd come onstage during intermission, do a little singing along with imitations, jokes, and skits." Originally, Pryor's act consisted of more singing than joking. "I wanted to be Johnny Mathis," he says of his short-lived ambition. "I had everything but the voice and the looks. Short of that, there was nothing going to stop me." He remembers that one of the first times he got onstage and opened his mouth, someone in the audience yelled out, "You can freeze that singing." Even without hearing his jokes, the crowd encouraged him to stick to comedy.

Richard took their advice and limited his singing to impressions of Louis Armstrong, Dean Martin, and others. He followed his stay at Harold's Club with a lengthy, more lucrative engagement at a North Washington Street nightspot called Collins Corner. The club's owner, Bris Collins, paid Richard seventy-two dollars a week to do a fifteen-minute monologue. His act still consisted primarily of gags lifted from old movies and joke books ("I was in a plane, heard the pilot call the tower. 'My left wing's on fire, my right wing's on fire, I'm over Russian territory. What do I do?' They say, 'Repeat after me, *Our Father Who Art in Heaven . . .*'") However, his delivery was animated enough to see him through the clichés.

Richard's days were free, and rather than spend them trying to write material for his act, he decided to go for the flexible hours and big bucks of a pimp. His reasoning was sound: he knew the ropes and he certainly had the connections. Finding himself a prostitute to manage, Pryor quickly discovered that he hadn't learned everything there was to know about sex and women.

Following the example set by other pimps, he made the prostitute "his woman," sleeping with her and looking after her. As far as he was concerned, it was the Life of Riley;

there were no emotional entanglements, no romance—just sex. But there was a twist. The prostitute wanted him to beat her, which literally stopped Pryor in his tracks. "I had no idea what she was talking about," he confided to reporter Sander Vanocur. "I didn't know there was any romantic connotation to physical violence."

When Richard went to his father and explained the situation, Leroy did not react the way Richard had hoped. Annoyed by his son's incompetence, he took the woman away. "You don't understand her," he charged; "you don't *need* her." In Leroy's eyes, Richard had failed as a man. Disgusted, he threw his twenty-two-year-old son from the house. Not even Marie could overturn his edict.

On the heels of his woman's disappointment, Leroy's rejection hit Richard with the impact of a one-two punch. Packing a few articles of clothing and stuffing into his pocket all the money he had, which was twenty dollars, Richard left Peoria. He didn't know where he would go or what he would do, but he had to get away. More than the need to find happiness by succeeding at something, Richard wanted to come back to town a king, to "be accepted by the people who had told me I wasn't shit." His grandmother tried to temper his anger, telling him that whatever he did, "you can come down a lot faster than you come up." She also cautioned him to remember that, out in the world, he would be representing more than just himself. "Peoria is your home. Everybody knows you went to school around here, and I raised you. So don't forget us back here."

He knew there was only one clear course, and that was to try and make show business his career. Though he was not a very confident performer, he felt he would be able to live hand-to-mouth playing whatever clubs would have him. His ultimate ambition was to make three or four hundred dollars a week and, he later admitted, "work maybe six months a year—if I was lucky."

Armed with his mixed bag of humor and the ability to play the piano and drums, Pryor took to the road. He mapped out a route of clubs on the "comedy circuit"—those cities and stages that all aspiring comics had to play to get noticed by talent scouts, newspaper critics, and the like. He began his tour at the Faust Club in East St. Louis, Illinois, followed by engagements in Lake Geneva, Wisconsin, and Youngstown. In the mob-run Ohio club, he says, "I had to pull a blank pistol on the cat to get my money," an event dramatized in Pryor's concert film *Live on the Sunset Strip*. Not only did he manage to escape with his life, but the manager was so impressed with his bravado that he actually paid him. Pryor followed these dates with stops in Detroit, Buffalo, Toronto, and Pittsburgh, where he was jailed for a month after beating a girl he was dating. Pryor didn't contest the charge, confessing, "I really assaulted her and I really battered her."

Most of Pryor's experiences on the road were considerably less exceptional. He continued to stock his routine with old jokes, grateful that the audiences were either too drunk or too unsophisticated to care and admitting that "it took me a long time to find my own direction, to stop using other people's stuff." He added a bagful of impressions to his act, of which Bobby Darin and Sammy Davis, Jr., were his favorites; he was determined to get the singing in there somehow.

Pryor's biggest problem wasn't his stale material or his erratic delivery, but the fact that he was an unknown. Invariably sent onstage to warm up an unreceptive house for the star, more often than not he was hooted off the stage by men who'd come to see the strippers, torch singers, leggy dancers, or female impersonators—of whom, in those days, more than half actually *were* women.

Richard's best dates were those in which he was able to strike up a quick sexual liaison with the female star. His relationship with the prostitute hadn't turned him off sex, but he never allowed anyone to get close to him. He lived by the maxim that it was "'breaking and entering' if anybody touches me," and simply used these female stars to help get him a good position in the show. Pryor was good at persuading these ladies, but being allowed to work with them or after them didn't guarantee that he would be a success. Usually he was either ignored or played to an emptying house, but the worst part was when the club owners themselves put him down. Pryor remembers one man who, after hearing his Dean Martin impersonation, ambled over and growled, "You got no talent, boy, but you sure got guts."

That he did. Pryor pressed on, taking comfort in the fact that he was making enough money to survive and thinking that things could only get better. At one engagement he was actually the opener for a dancing bear, which managed to get drunk, then broke loose and smashed up the club. Another time Pryor was in the middle of his act when a brawl broke out between lumberjacks in the audience. Stopping in the middle of his joke, Pryor left the stage to sit out the battle.

Apart from being a newcomer, there was one other problem Pryor faced when it came to getting bookings—the fact that he was black. In her treatise *Black Macho,* Michele Wallace wrote of this era, "If you were the average white person, blacks still didn't exist for you. You might catch a glimpse of [one] shaking out the living-room rug or hanging out the wash, or shining shoes," but there were very few whites who would pay to see black performers. The exceptions, such as Sammy Davis, Jr., and Nat King Cole, were nonthreatening, and even their acceptance wasn't universal. Ms. Wallace adds that during this period, blacks didn't help the situation by hiding in their own culture, which didn't appeal to most whites, and their own language, which was designed to exclude whites. Ironically, it would only be after Pryor embraced his ethnic culture that he would reach whites as an audience.

In those early days of the civil rights movement, Pryor was limited to appearing in clubs that specifically allowed black entertainers. Generally it was commerce, not prejudice per se, that forced club owners to turn away black comics. All it took was for one customer to call a comedian "nigger"; the other patrons were bound to feel uncomfortable, and, long after they had forgotten why, they would link that uneasy feeling to the club and stay away.

One of the first talents any comic acquires is that of putting down hecklers. Pryor was no exception, and he had no problem dealing with the hecklers, drunks, and rowdies who tried to shout him off the stage. He had a slew of comebacks, from "Let's play horsey—I'll be the head and shoulders and you just sit there," to "I'm gettin' paid to make an ass out of myself, what's your excuse?" But the bigots got to him, no matter how hard he tried to remain aloof. Racism, he said, "can't make you feel good, no matter how strong you try to be about it." Depending on the circumstance, Pryor would either yell back, leave the stage, or try to ignore the remarks until the offender was removed. Once in a while the audience would actually come to his rescue by berating the heckler.

In contrast, Pryor's contemporary Dick Gregory always stayed cool, employing one or two comebacks that never failed. He would say, "You hear what that guy just called me? Roy Rogers's horse. He called me Trigger!" which would ease the tension. If the attack went on, he would add, "My contract reads that every time I hear the word I get fifty dollars. Will everyone in the room please stand up and yell 'nigger'?" Usually the audience's cooperation would fluster the redneck and he would leave.

Pryor was never that diplomatic. If anything, his resentment increased as time went on. Offstage as well as on, he was constantly reminded of our society's intolerance, particularly when he'd try to register at a local hotel, only to find that it was restricted; and the fact that he couldn't afford many of the hotels that weren't didn't help matters.

Pryor has said that if he could have taken audiences to these hotels, he'd have become a famous comedian a lot sooner. He met people there who were stranger than even he, with his vivid imagination, could have conceived. He vividly remembers the group of gay wrestlers with whom he spent some time at one hotel. "I couldn't believe it. I mean, you'd see them brutally murdering each other in Saturday-night wrestling matches, and then you'd see them back at the hotel, kissing and holding hands." It seems that men, too, could still surprise young Richard.

Richard's days on the road were marked by frequent bouts of deep depression. Being excluded from many clubs hurt him professionally and emotionally, leaving him to wonder, as he told one interviewer, "Why can't they like me for what I do?" But he was even more frustrated by the painstaking process of developing an act, a stage persona, an approach that would knock 'em dead.

Not long into the tour, Pryor realized that he would have to rely less on jokes. "I'm probably the worst joketeller in the world," he acknowledges, and his tired "Didja hear the one about . . ." throwaways didn't help. Pryor wasn't simply giving in to his lack of confidence. His record *Insane*, assembled from very early tapes, reveals not only his awkward delivery but the awful silence of the audience. At one point, the producers spliced in laughs from a different track to keep a routine from falling flat.

Faced with a dilemma, Pryor decided to emulate his idol Jonathan Winters, and began leaning more toward characterizations. Pryor's impressions might never have been on target, but his ability to sustain a voice was masterful, and he felt he could synthesize personalities the way Winters did. However, he wouldn't do the same kind of people as Winters did—the aunts, teachers, and corporate chairmen. Instead, he would dip into his past and parody the people he'd known.

For the first time, Pryor tried writing his own material. He'd ferret through the streets and back rooms of Peoria, think about the streetcorner philosophers and drunks, the pimps and the tough kids. "I'd *see* that man in my mind and go with him," Pryor explains. The biggest problem he faced was cleaning up the characters; ghetto language was deep blue, and audiences were still relatively white. They weren't lily white, for Sophie Tucker and Lenny Bruce had opened the doors enough to allow a fair amount of off-color material on the stage. But that was for white performers only. "They would rather use the dirtiest ofay cat in the world than to use a black cat," Pryor would complain bitterly. (Black comedian Redd Foxx, whose language made Lenny Bruce look like Mother Goose, was limited to performing at black nightspots in Harlem and elsewhere, so his breakthroughs were not of any use to Prior—yet.)

The only way to know if the material is any good is to try it before an audience. This is the harshest trial in the life of any comedian. Pryor was game, comforted by the fact that if the routine failed, he could jump right to the old jokes and later crawl back to the drawing board.

Hammering out a passable act took Pryor nearly a year. Remarkably, through all the hard times when he was broke and exhausted, there was never any question about throwing in the towel. On one level, there was the very real fear of returning to Peoria with his tail between his legs. Facing his father on those terms would have been unthinkable. However, Pryor had come to understand something important about himself. He would never be John Wayne strutting toward a showdown, never be Joe Louis pounding his way to a heavy-weight championship. If he had the talent to be a hero anywhere, it was here, in the spotlight. Over the months he had weighed his experiences and come to realize, "God gave me a magic. I believe there was a gift given to me, probably when I was a child; that God searched me out and found me and said, 'Try that one.' Somebody said, 'Uh? *That* one?' And God said, 'Try him, I'm telling you. There's something about him.' "

Pryor's determination is not typical of most aspiring performers, who enter show business wanting to be wealthy and well known, wanting the attention and the glamour. They don't *need* the stage the way Pryor did. In his autobiography, *This Life*, Sidney Poitier summarized breaking into the enter-tainment field when he wrote, "Many kids [have] the inten-tion of becoming stars within a matter of weeks. I have seen them arrive year after year with a bankroll of five hundred dollars. They share a one-room efficiency apartment; some-times three or four of them need to pool their resources in order to secure adequate housing. Generally, in less than three months their funds are gone—and so are they."

That was not a description of Richard Pryor. If nothing else, he never had the luxury of five hundred dollars in his pocket.

Chapter Four

In the early 1960s, there was one city that every comic had to play to make the big time. That city was New York, home to the national press, legendary stages, well-attended nightclubs, and, most important, the variety and talk shows. Though these programs have since moved to Los Angeles, comedians or singers who hoped to achieve the ultimate and play Las Vegas had first to make a splash on "The Ed Sullivan Show," "The Tonight Show," or on New York–based TV showcases.

Pryor only dreamed of being on TV. In 1963, when he decided to go to New York, he hoped only for the chance to appear in a few of the clubs. Success there would mean recognition and a slow climb to good money; on the flip side, a bomb dropped in New York would be heard, instantly and pitilessly, throughout the local entertainment industry. But television—that was for comics who died and went to heaven.

Pryor headed for New York with less than one hundred dollars to his name. But it was more money than he'd had when he left Peoria, so he felt he was making progress, and he even managed to send some of his earnings home from time to time. With one exception, he'd never taken money from home. That exception was when an acquaintance of Pryor's grandmother landed in the Pittsburgh jail where Pryor had been tossed for beating his girl. Unable to post bail, Pryor was resigned to cooling his heels there for quite some time. However, when the man was released he contacted Marie and she forwarded the cash for her grandson's bail.

Because of the tension surrounding his departure from Peoria, Richard had mixed feelings about contact with his family. His parents' marriage would not survive, and both his mother and father would remarry. At the time, however, while he desperately missed his mother and grandmother, he could not bear even to speak on the phone with his father. Richard was not so much angry at him as disappointed that they could not relate on any level. "Only cash related. If I didn't hurry up and say, 'I'm sending some money tomorrow,' it was *click,* they'd hang up. I couldn't call and say, 'I'm miserable,' or, 'I'm not feeling well,' or, 'I need to talk to somebody.'" The money he sent to his mother and grandmother was a token, a "kiss" from Richie; he genuinely regretted that he could do nothing like that for his father.

It's likely that Pryor thought about Peoria a great deal, nostalgia and animosity combining to form a feeling of desperation. This despair was compounded by the difficulty of building a career, and eventually he turned to alcohol for solace. Pryor hadn't been a drinker in Peoria: at the age of twenty-two he had never been drunk or smoked grass. But that changed on the road, Pryor finding comfort first in drink and then, just before reaching New York, starting his long and highly publicized relationship with cocaine.

As an embittered Pryor would one day lament to a reporter, he hadn't sought drugs out but they seduced him just the same. Because he was always so flip when discussing drugs in his act, his downbeat soliloquy is at once tragic and revealing.

"You're lonely and you feel rejected," he began, "so you get real low in your house and you take a walk or get in your car and drive around looking for someone to talk to . . . to love you. You run into some man or some lady and they say, 'Here, take this. Go ahead. Try some.' So you try it and you fantasize that you're feeling better, that you've found good friends.

"So you say to them, 'Gee, thanks, that wasn't bad. May I have a little of that to take home with me?' And later you go back and look for that same person, or you look for the person he or she represents—anybody who can make you think you're happy and not being rejected. And it builds and builds.

"You create a new you . . . a much-loved, very happy you. Then you find that you have to start competing with that

47

person you've created . . . that image you want to think you are . . . that hip motherfucker who knows everything . . . about life and people and getting high. But man, I didn't know shit about it. I didn't know a damn thing, but I went ahead and did it.''

Pryor was once again begging for acceptance. He knew it would be some time, if ever, before he would get it on the stage. New York would not be like the Carver Community Center. Drugs, alcohol, and the crowd that used them would have to do for now.

Despite his nervousness on the bus ride to New York, Pryor was reasonably confident of his material. Though second-guessing himself has always been a Pryor trait—even today, until he sees healthy box-office returns or hears audience laughter, he refuses to believe that what he's done is good— he had evolved a well-balanced program of characterizations and slightly off-color humor. While his sexual and scatalogical observations weren't terribly blue, they were outrageous enough to keep things moving; one example is his "apostrophe" about Jacqueline Kennedy farting.

Pryor's comedy was still rough by current standards, but he had evolved some of the characters that would become a part of his repertoire for the next decade. These included a self-impressed preacher, military figures, and the cantankerous street-historian wino whose list of great Americans was topped by a young man who was able to book the numbers and "didn't need paper *or* pencil!" Surprisingly, very few of the blacks who had seen Pryor's shows on the road found his portrayals of downtrodden blacks objectionable. He suspects that this was because they knew he wasn't making fun of them, only "doing what I was doing. They didn't intellectualize it . . . either liked it or they didn't.''

The first thing Pryor did upon reaching New York was buy a new suit. This was not so much for his appearance as for his pride: "When you ain't got no money, you gotta get yourself an attitude." That expense left him with thirty-three cents to his name. But, spruced up and as ready as he'd ever be, he gathered up his hopes and desires and bolted from the starting gate.

Being both black and a relative newcomer, Pryor knew that the clubs in which he stood the best chance of landing a gig were the more progressive, experimental houses in Greenwich Village. He visited them all, auditioning well at most and landing a tryout at the Café Wha? Although he was nervous, the audience reacted well to his enthusiasm, his energy, and his humor, in that order. He didn't care *what* it was they liked; all that mattered was he got to stay. The pay was five dollars per night, ten dollars on the weekends.

Like the other clubs in the Village, the Café Wha? was a small, dark, informal place. Most had been coffeeshops in the thirties and forties, then in the postwar years became places where painters, dancers, actors, singers, and composers could find kindred souls; where poets were able to read their latest works and comedians could literally stand up and perform—whence the term "stand-up comic." The clubs that emerged in the fifties were merely a formalized version of what had existed for years.

Two of the earliest and most celebrated alumni of these cafés were Lenny Bruce and Lord Buckley, though only Bruce found an audience outside the Village. Locally, Buckley was the more highly regarded of the two, especially by up-and-coming comedians. He was what one critic described as a master of "verbal jazz that dealt with political, social, and religious subjects." But his appeal was limited because he was too abstract for the masses; he was not an iconoclast of popular culture, as Bruce was.

Bruce's liberal use of language would help make it possible for Pryor to come into his own later in the decade. At the time, however, Pryor knew nothing of the comic or his work. There was only one comedian of whom he was acutely aware, and that awareness swung from reverence to envy.

Progressive though the downtown clubs were, in 1963 there was only one black comedian who was enjoying widespread success there. George Kirby had managed to win a small crossover audience in the early 1950s, doing impressions of everyone from Marlon Brando to Pearl Bailey; Redd Foxx, Nipsey Russell, Moms Mabley, and Godfrey Cambridge were popular among the blacks and more liberal white crowds; and Dick Gregory had built a reputation as a brutally incisive but increasingly angry comic, consumed by what Steve Allen once referred to as "serious political paranoia." But these comedians enjoyed their biggest triumphs uptown in the Harlem clubs, not in the Village, and certainly not on a national scale to compare with their white counterparts from the Smothers Brothers to Woody Allen. As Dick Gregory observed, "A white man will come to the Negro club, so nervous and afraid of the neighborhood and the people that anything the comic says to relieve his tension will absolutely knock him out, but in the white man's house he's comfortable and secure and won't laugh at racial material that he really didn't want to hear."

Among the black comedians, only twenty-six-year-old Bill Cosby cut across all audiences, young and old, black and white. Cosby's humor was eclectic, his subjects ranging from a young man's first shave to the story of Noah to the misadventures of his semifictional childhood cronies Fat Albert, Dumb Donald, Weird Harold, and others. It's important to note that Cosby didn't *become* other people the way Pryor did; rather, he was a narrator who occasionally spoke his dialogue in character.

Cosby's material was folksy and was told with ease and charm, which made it impossible not to like him or at least not to be entertained by him. But Nipsey Russell was likable too. The difference was that Cosby's material was nonthreatening. In the beginning of his career, Cosby experimented with mild racial humor, such as the vignette of a black man who goes to a segregated barbershop and is hustled to the dog groomer down the street. Though far more tame than what Redd Foxx or Dick Gregory were doing, bits like this conflicted with Cosby's boyish manner and left people cold. He eliminated it from his act and thereafter stuck to material that didn't embarrass his predominantly white audiences.

As Cosby himself jokes, why bother being militant when he wasn't even black? "One morning I woke and looked in the mirror. There was this freckle and it just got bigger and bigger...." He was certainly a dramatic contrast to Dick Gregory, who would mock his audience by saying, "Wouldn't it be a hell of a thing if all this was burnt cork and you people were being tolerant for nothing?''

Like Pryor, the Philadelphia-born Cosby had a difficult youth, but Cosby wasn't at odds with society. Despite being left as the sole support of his family, he was schooled as a gifted child and became a star athlete in college, both of which gave him enormous confidence. His show-business apprenticeship was equally auspicious. He went to Greenwich Village with an eye on performing and used his job as a bartender to polish his talents. His easygoing chatter made customers laugh, which wasn't lost on his employer. One night the manager told Cosby to leave the bar and go onstage in an adjoining room. A folk singer had just finished and people were filing out when Cosby strolled into the room. ''But there's no one there,'' he complained. The manager nodded. ''It's going to be a while before the next show, and you're going to keep the customers happy until then.'' Cosby saw nothing to lose and went on. He was a hit, and within a year had made the big time—television. A record contract, TV series, and Las Vegas appearances then propelled him into superstardom.

It would be several months before Pryor said jealously, ''Goddammit. This nigger's doin' what I'm fixin' to do,'' and started slipping Cosby-like bits into his act. He had gotten a toehold at the Café Wha? by doing Richard Pryor, and he was going to keep that up—but he was still not exactly sure who Richard Pryor was, comedically.

Pryor's problem was not so much his routines as his often self-conscious delivery, particularly when he was out of character. He would stand there, lanky, goateed, constantly shifting; depending on his mood and the crowd—college kids in the winter, tourists in the summer—he'd wear a suit or huddle in a leather jacket like a hotrodding JD. Continually smoking cigarettes, he would snicker anxiously as his eyes darted across the audience, searching for acceptance. His delivery was rapid, anxious, even squealing at times, like a cornered fox. If the audience was receptive to him, Pryor's juices would flow and he kept the act rolling, improvising with great success. Conversely, if a routine fell flat, he would grow quiet, nervous, or belligerent, depending on his mood. He would become particularly incensed if anyone left the room during his performance. This happened much more frequently in New York than it had on the road, due primarily to the hurried urban lifestyle. Stopping in mid-sentence, Pryor would snap, as he did on one occasion, "I hope y'all get raped by black folks with clap!" or, if anger didn't overwhelm him, he would stay in character to damn the early departers. Once, playing a dull Midwesterner giving directions to a motorist, he said, "I tell ya what ya do. Ya go up here about six miles to Junction Flats and y'see a big sign—and run over those people as yer goin'."

Pryor's skittishness often made audiences uneasy, especially when he felt that he was stagnating. At such times he would literally stop whatever he was doing and apologize. Nor did it take much to unnerve him—a few lead-balloon quips, an ad lib that made no sense, a full and demanding house, or an empty one. During the first few minutes of a faltering set he was likely to half-joke, "I'd like to make you laugh for about ten minutes—though I'm gonna be on for an hour," or, "I'm very nervous—yeah, *really* nervous—because I ain't had no cocaine all day," then seconds later come back, "I hope I'm funny, because it's dangerous just to be a nigger standing up here and just be sayin' *nothin'*." Or else he would step back from the microphone, survey the audience, and sigh, "This ain't as funny as we thought it was gonna be," a line that ironically got Pryor his biggest laugh, due to its helpless honesty.

Inevitably, after the dead silence that followed, Pryor would slip into a character. Whether he was using it to escape discomfort or simply doing what he did best, he could always depend on winning audiences over with his impersonations. What was most uncanny was that he could do so even with skits that contained no humor. An example of this art at its finest is his playlette *2001: A Space Odyssey,* which he first performed in 1968. Pryor would recreate the sequence of the film in which an astronaut lobotomizes the deadly computer HAL, doing the scene word for word without a single joke or ad lib. When he finished, there would always be a moment of quiet as the audience reacclimated themselves, remembering that they were in a nightclub and not a movie theater. Vigorous applause always followed.

But back in 1963, Pryor couldn't build a reputation solely on dramatic, slice-of-life renditions. Since he had not yet evolved a stage personality uniquely his own, he borrowed from other "hot" comedians. He was able to assimilate their styles quite successfully, and, as one club insider said, seeing Pryor when he first hit New York was equivalent to having a smorgasbord of what was current in the Village.

"I did everybody else's act for a while," Pryor admits, layering their style and sometimes their jokes atop his own. He doesn't apologize for this, claiming, "It takes at least fifteen years to find out what kind of comedy you want to do." But there was another reason. Since New York was more tolerant than other cities, comedians were able to do comparatively tough racial humor. Pryor says that he and the other black comedians "killed whites because they were very masochistic in the early sixties. They liked it a bunch when you talked about them." By imitating Dick Gregory and Redd Foxx, he knew just how far he could go without going too far. However, Pryor says that road was a dead end. Foxx wasn't getting popular acclaim, and while Gregory was, Pryor admitted, "he's smarter than me. I don't like to read, for one thing, and I don't have the qualities to be an ambassador or nothing like that. My shit is more emotional, not intellectual." Besides, whites "got bored with that—fast" when riots broke out and cities began to burn. They no longer felt guilty enough to respond to bits about militants, the revolution, and integration. Thus, while the likes of Martin Luther King and the country's new President, Lyndon Johnson, took charge of civil rights reform, black comedians started leaving it behind.

(As of December 1982, only Dick Gregory was fighting as vigorously as before on behalf of human rights, getting himself arrested for praying in front of the U.S. embassy in South Africa as a protest against that nation's apartheid policies. Shortly before that, Pryor had also been in Africa, in neighboring Rhodesia, on vacation.)

Pryor was not surprised to see Cosby really take off in the backlash against militant comedy. "He is the only pure comedian around," Pryor said at the time. "His material is completely nonracial, nonpolitical, and, if you will pardon the expression, never off-color." Pryor also professes a great deal of admiration for what Cosby achieved. "He slipped up ... and walked away with everything," he says. "All society could do was go see him because they didn't have a chance in the world of stopping him."

Today, however, Pryor regrets having emulated Cosby, describing as "unnatural" the way he would go onstage and say, "Good evening, ladies and gentlemen, ha ha. You know, a funny thing happened, hee hee ..." and feeling guilty over the fact that Cosby would do a Noah "so I did Adam and Eve, it was that simple."

Having to be clean never bothered Pryor as much as having to be someone else. There were two reasons he was able to do it: he viewed the Cosby style as the road to success, and success the cure for his feelings of isolation; and he managed to convince himself that doing a Cosby act wasn't homage or compromise to the man, but holy war. Pryor copied Cosby in order to sneak up on him, to become, in his words "the only nigger. Ain't no room for two niggers." But, no matter how he tried to hide behind territorial bravado, Pryor was compromising and deep inside he knew it. He remembers an uncomfortable session in the office of Roy Silver, who used to manage Cosby. There, he says, an agent told him exactly the sort of persona he must project. "The cat said, 'Be the kind of colored guy we'd like to have over to our house. Now, I'd introduce *Bill* to my mother, but a guy like *you* ...'" Pryor pauses, shakes his head. "And I'm *buying* this shit. 'Don't mention the fact that you're a 'nigger,' don't go into such bad taste.' They were gonna try to help me be *nothing* as best they could."

Bill Grundfest, owner of the Comedy Cellar in Greenwich Village, points out that though Pryor resented this, he really had no choice. "In those days, if he hadn't done what we would consider not whitewashed material, 'Oreo' material, he never would have gotten to square one. The same was true of

Flip Wilson a little later. Compromise was a necessity of the times. Even if Pryor didn't like what some might consider the saccharine nature of the material, there was a benefit in doing it: performing even saccharine material allowed him to hone his craft. He didn't have Cosby's poise at the time, and, unlike a musician who can practice in a room and get better, a comic can't. A comic needs to practice in front of people.''

Actually, Pryor's act wasn't as tame as Cosby's, though Pryor thought it was. Pryor's characterizations, more stinging and adult than Cosby's Fat Albert, were of blacks in ethnic but nonaggressive situations, such as marital spats—taking both sides of the row—or at a Washington Street after-hours joint where blacks ''who knew their place'' fretted away their money, got sick from too much booze, or beat up one another. In short, he stuck to flavorful but uncontroversial topics. ''Every now and then I'd go for it,'' Pryor says. He would then come up with a remark like, ''I always wanted to be something else—but never white.'' While lines like these made him feel less of a turncoat, they were delivered in an offhand manner that no one could take seriously. And he would further declaw these remarks by adding an anxious comment like, ''Uh—hope I'm not outta line.''

Even with Cosby as a role model, it took a while for Pryor to feel truly at ease on the stage. He was pleased to get enough laughs that the people at the Café Wha? kept him on. ''I don't get to see me,'' he said. ''All I see is when I'm working they're laughing—thank God!'' However, his early work was still but a shadow of what it would become, and notices in the trade publications were often discouraging. The show business ''bible'' *Variety* caught one of his early twelve-minute routines and said of it:

> There is much in Richard Pryor's turn to re-
> mind of Bill Cosby. However, it seems to be natural
> rather than a consciously imitated mannerism. Col-
> ored comedian has strong and definite ideas on
> humor. He has an avant garde viewpoint, a healthy
> instinct for irreverence and a feel for expression.

However, there is still much for him to learn before he can go into commercial rooms. He is still in the coffeehouse stages as far as this audience was concerned on his opening night. He has the approach of an intellectual rather than an entertainer and writing seems to be for clever effect rather than laughs. Pryor needs a reexamination of his material best done with more forays in the offbeateries before moving into the uptown spots.

Most of the other critics dismissed Pryor's more provocative, ghetto-based humor and described him simply as having the potential to be another Bill Cosby. By and large, all of these critics missed an aspect of Pryor's talent that had really begun to blossom in New York—his ability to improvise.

Among Pryor's more astute critics was Louis Drozen, who would one day become the comedian's first record producer. Drozen asserts, "What impressed me, apart from his comic genius, was the obvious fact that Richard Pryor did not have a set routine. Anybody who's familiar with comedy could tell this. When he got up onstage he just started talking."

Pryor had never been a terribly disciplined performer. Improvisation had always been his way of keeping from getting bored, and the Village clubs were no exception. Because he didn't feel comfortable telling jokes and sticking to established gags, he did not, like Gregory and Cosby, wrestle with material until it worked. As time passed and his confidence grew, he took a concept and simply flowed with it.

An example of how Pryor works can be seen in the way one routine changed from telling to telling. Four different renditions of a preacher's first encounter with God gave four distinctly different interpretations:

"I first met God in 1929, outside a little hotel in Baltimore. I was eatin' a tuna fish sammich. And I heard this voice call unto me, and the voice said, 'Psst.' And I walked up to this voice and said,

'What?' And the voice got magnificent and holy and resounding and said, 'Gimme some o' dat sammich.' I said, 'God, make your own goddamn sammich. I don't mess with you, don't mess with me.' ''

The next time he did it, the routine went like this:

"I first met God—it was about 1929, in Baltimore. It was a little hotel. I was walkin' down the hallway and I see this man with blue eyes, eyes of flame, and I said, 'Are you God, you blue-eyed devil?' And he said to me, 'No, I'm not God. I'm the elevator operator.' So I kept on walkin'. Well, I got on the streets, and God was sittin' on the curb cryin'. And God said to me, 'Pssst. D'ya have a quarter? It costs a quarter t'get into heaven. I left my money in my other clothes.' ''

The third telling brought an entirely different slant:

"I first saw God in 1929 in Chicago. I was walkin' down the street on the south side, eatin' a sammich. And God come up to me and said, 'May I have a piece of your bread?' And I looked at God, I looked at God *good,* 'cause I was hungry. And I wasn't about to give up none o' dat sammich. And God said to me, 'He soever who touches knowest best his way in.' And it moved me—I kept on goin'.''

Finally, he put it like this:

"I first met God in 1929. I was walkin' down the street eatin' a tuna fish sammich, and I heard this voice call unto me, and I knew it was the voice of God for it came from without a dark alleyway as only the voice of God can come. However, I did not venture down that dark alleyway. For it might not

57

have been the voice of God but two or three niggers
with a baseball bat.''

In each case Pryor stuck with 1929 because it allowed him to
set the preacher's persona by thundering in a self-impressed
voice, ''nineteen twenny-*naaaaaahn*.''

Pryor stayed at the Café Wha? for a year. He was in no
hurry to hit the more prestigious uptown clubs such as the
Improv; he wanted to devote all his time and energy developing his characters to the point where they played well every
night. The close, dark atmosphere of the Village clubs helped
to empty him of everything but the people he was creating.
Pryor would stand behind a microphone or sit on a stool in
the center of the bare stage, the dinner menu scrawled on a
blackboard that often hung lopsided behind him, a glass of
water on a rickety table or chair off to one side. Bathed in a
single spotlight, he was able to forget Richard Pryor and
create one or more characters playing off each other in a
masterpiece of spontaneity.

These exchanges came naturally to Pryor because he
understood the characters he was playing. ''I love those
people,'' he said. ''They are real and have a need to *be*
somebody.'' Thus, the scenarios were real, gritty, and often
unpleasant, such as the classic wino-junkie dialogue in which
a street-historian drunk tried to tell a drug addict just what
was wrong with *his* life. This routine had long stretches
without a joke, but as long as the audience knew it was
coming, they'd hang on. As Pryor later explained, ''I like
to . . . take the emotion to a peak and then level it off . . . with
a nice laugh.''

Pryor's characters were usually not imps, like Fat Albert
and Weird Harold, but oddball misfits or swaggering bas-
tards. Pryor also used fantasy characters a great deal, taking
the movie myths he had adored as a kid and introducing them
to *reality*. Often he would combine the two approaches,
dipping into his memory for a kid who was too tough for any
human to push around, and pitting him against Dracula. That
would whittle the kid down to size (''Hope ya get sickle

cell,'' is all the violated youth can wail at the vampire), while at the same time wringing comedy from a towering figure of folklore by introducing him to ghetto reality. Pryor also had fun teaming Lyndon Johnson with Dr. Frankenstein and recounting the exploits of a black Superman called Super Nigger. If one or two characters made for good comic theater, five of them discussing evolution on a TV talkshow was even better. In this bit, with host Bob Bond introducing guests the Reverend Arnold T. Perkins, anthropologist Winston Stonewood, former junkie Miss Hazel Dumptree, and a relatively neutered black nationalist, it's difficult to decide who are the bigger asses, Pryor's characters or the real-life types on which they were patterned.

This brings up the quality that is the cornerstone of Pryor's genius. Whether he's using fantasy, tragedy, or any other means, he manages to pinpoint what is absurd or comical in human behavior. He doesn't rely just on punchlines or Looney Tune characters, like Mel Brooks and Carl Reiner did with their Two-Thousand-Year-Old Man, and Cosby did with much of his material. Even in absurd bits like the vampire attacking the tough kid, he creates something to which his audiences can relate. White audiences might not have known a Clark boy or a Captain Torsey or a Marie Bryant, all of whom appeared in Pryor's early routines, but they knew bullies, policemen, and grandmothers. Not only did this approach win Pryor his audiences' attention and, when he became a more polished performer, their sympathy, but it allowed him to improvise brilliantly. Mel Brooks was another great improviser, but his off-the-cuff material was outrageously silly; and Woody Allen, like Pryor, used reality as a springboard, but all of his comedy was written and carefully thought out. Of all the comedians of his generation, only Pryor mastered the art of playing from and responding to the heart.

After he had learned what audiences expected from him, Pryor ventured out selectively from the Café Wha? on his nights off to perform in other local clubs, such as the Living Room, the Village Gate, and the Bitter End, and occasionally played the so-called Borscht Belt clubs in the Catskills to become known by the older, more "establishment" audiences that had recently embraced Cosby.

By the end of Pryor's first year in New York, entertainment guide *Cue* categorized him as "sharp without being angry," his humor "rooted in his background but essentially nonracial in character." He had taken *Variety*'s advice and polished his act, and now felt ready to appear uptown in clubs like the Improv and Poppa Hud's. He played well before more mainstream crowds and was beginning to have hope for what had seemed like an impossibility not many months before—going on national television. One presumes that what "national" really meant to Pryor was having the people back in Peoria see him, for he had never lost the need to make them acknowledge his success.

The goal was closer than Pryor realized. Working back in the Village one night, he heard that a TV talent scout had just dropped in at the Bitter End. Pryor rushed over and persuaded the owner to let him do a short bit. The rep was impressed with what he saw. Aware of Cosby's wide following, the scout invited Pryor to meet with his boss, Rudy Vallee, who was host of a short-lived (July 1964 to March 1965) omnibus program called "On Broadway Tonight." Pryor was at his most charming when he met Vallee, and Vallee liked him enough to invite him to appear on the show.

As Dick Gregory defined show business, "In 1961 you were putting cardboard in your shoes to keep out the cold, and in 1962 you have more shoes than you'll ever need." Like Gregory, Pryor felt the shock. When he rubbed his sweating palms together after leaving the interview, he could still feel the dried paste with which he'd glued his name on photos of theater marquees. He still remembered his lines from *Rumpelstiltskin*, and when he closed his eyes he could see the Canadian lumberjacks clubbing one another over the head, and hear himself wondering aloud what the hell he was doing in this business.

He still wasn't sure. But whatever it was, he was doing it right, and that sent his spirits soaring—for now.

Chapter Five

The first time Pryor stood backstage to go before a TV camera, he had a serious case of stage fright. Despite his stated opinion that a comedian's fate is in the lap of the gods, that "a cat gets lucky and gets a laugh," Pryor knew that success or disaster on stage or on television came down to the matter of self-assurance. The act was good, but would *he* be good? What would happen when the camera went on? He knew from the rehearsals that he would feel naked and extremely vulnerable. Every part of him would be sent nationwide, not only the jokes but the wrinkles in his clothes; he'd be aware of every movement he made, of each time he blinked, of each bead of sweat on his forehead. Too, he realized that if he bombed, not only would he let himself down but he'd be laughed at by the folks back home.

But there was one saving grace. As Pryor waited to go before the cameras, he was filled with a sense of familiarity. Street corner, Carver stage, Harold's Club, the Café Wha? —it was still a stage; the trappings of TV had made this "adventure time," as he called it, but the people out there were still just an audience. They'd laugh at the same routines other audiences had enjoyed. That thought steadied him, and he went out and filled the spotlight like one to the manner born. Whatever Richard Pryor was feeling inside, outside he was a slightly hyper but otherwise very smooth hit.

Pryor enjoyed a gratifying sense of accomplishment. Through hustling, intelligence, and perseverance, he'd attained what few comics ever do—a spot on the launching pad to stardom. The satisfaction was heightened over the next few months as he became a regular fixture on television, appearing a total of five times on the "Ed Sullivan Show," costarring on the "Kraft Summer Music Hall," and doing stints on the

"Merv Griffin Show" and the "Tonight Show," both of which had not yet made the move to Southern California. He began earning decent money in the better clubs not only in New York but throughout the country, and had reached a point where he was very much at ease with audiences. Everywhere he went, program hosts and club managers praised him as "the next Bill Cosby."

Not surprisingly, the more they did this, the less Pryor saw it as praise. He became extremely sensitive to the comparisons and tried many times to put some teeth in his act. However, each time he tried to do bits about racism or punctuate his act with street language, his newly acquired managers and show-business friends, all the "beautiful people," would set him straight. " 'Hey,' " he recalls hearing, " 'you can't have that in there.' " Pryor complains that he couldn't even say *ass* without getting kicked there by some self-appointed censor.

Being told that he had to keep a damper on his style made him unusually testy. How he felt was typified by his response when Merv Griffin asked him if he changed faces by pushing buttons. Pryor's sharp reply: "There are no buttons to this cat, baby. I ain't no robot, you dig?"

Ironically, Pryor was no longer depressed about being lonely, although he still felt adrift in many respects. His career was rocketing through its various phases, and between his apartments in New York and hotel rooms on the road, he didn't really have a home. Nor had he been able to return to Peoria quite the conquering hero he'd have liked. He hadn't really expected parades or a Richard Pryor Day on his few return trips, but he had craved recognition from those who "knew him when. . . ." That didn't include Juliette Whittaker, whose pride, though heartfelt, was to be expected. What he really wanted was for his old pals to raise their sights from the pool tables and follow his rising star. But that didn't happen. He recalls a brief conversation he had with one of his friends, and while it may be apocryphal, it is close to what he was experiencing. The two met by chance on the street, and the young man said, "Hey, man, Richie—that you?" Pryor puffed and said, "Yeah, it's me." Nodding appreciatively, the other man said, "Hey, ya made it." Pryor grinned as if to say, *Yeah—now let's see ya treat me like a class clown*. Extending his hand, the friend asked, "Say, brother, lend me a twenty?"

The people of Peoria understood all kinds of odds except those that Richard had beaten, and that bothered the hell out of him.

Pryor's family gave him only slightly more satisfaction. He knew his mother and grandmother were proud, but it was Leroy he had wanted to dazzle. Unfortunately, Leroy apparently viewed him as little more than a trophy to show off around town. If he took pride in his son, Richard never seems to have felt it.

Pryor's one consolation—and it was an important one— was that he'd been accepted socially by people he'd met in the business. They embraced him for who he was and what he'd achieved, not just because, as in Peoria, he was good for a laugh. He spent time with people who he felt had some class and some awareness, never seeing them or himself for what they were.

"You get famous," he chides himself now, "you make a lot of money, you start hanging around with the hip crowd, the kind of crowd that looks at ordinary people going to work every morning and thinks, 'Look at those fools getting up going to work!'" That hip crowd snorted cocaine the way other people chugged martinis, and Pryor fit right in. The difference now was that he was using it not because he felt isolated socially but because he was frustrated professionally.

Pryor's feeling of confinement, of being trapped in banal comedy, was heightened by what was going on in the world around him. Everywhere he went he saw blacks with their backs to the walls. He came to the conclusion that being black was a series of "suicide traps," battles with bigots, police, and poverty. "If you're born black . . . you live around rats and roaches, and if you survive those bites and don't get rabies, you're lucky if you don't get brain damage from eating the lead paint."

Some of Pryor's newfound militance can also be attributed to living in New York. He felt that most New Yorkers were snobs, and took heart in going up to Harlem and "seeing all those black people. Jesus, just knowing there were that many of us made me feel better." It also made him angry, for while conditions were no better than in the Peoria ghetto, there were considerably more people living in Harlem. He was not prepared to go as far as Dick Gregory, who had virtually abandoned his career to march on the strongholds of segregation. But Pryor did feel that his work should acknowledge the movement, if not ideologically then culturally, and that he should be stumping for black dignity rather than hiding behind whitewash.

All these factors combined to alienate Pryor from his material. He did it, but his heart wasn't in it. He knew he had to make some changes. As one club owner who knew him in the mid-sixties recalls, "When he was coming into his black consciousness, Pryor actually looked down his nose at what he and Cosby were doing. I've spoken to Cosby about it, and he said that while he knew how Pryor felt, Pryor was so good at *whatever* he did that Bill couldn't help but have the highest regard for him."

Listening to his inner voice, Pryor disregarded the advice of his managers and set about changing his act.

But the voice that emerged from this turmoil didn't entirely reflect what Pryor was feeling. The material he began introducing late in 1965 and into 1966 was still comparatively restrained, the work of a part-time sniper rather than a full-time vigilante. Typical was "Black Ben," Pryor's skit about a play performed for the inmates of a Southern penitentiary. After one of the actors introduces this show about "a young Southern girl who falls in love with a black," a redneck jailor hurriedly cuts him off. Saying that the subject is too controversial, he orders the cast to leave, changing his mind only after the actor reassures him, "Uh . . . it's quite all right. The nigger gets killed."

(He isn't killed, of course; he not only gets the girl but establishes his own business. But Ben is a boob whose triumphs are accidental rather than militant, so he is at once a slap in the face of segregation without being objectionable to whites.)

Another of Pryor's bolder routines was the new, improved "Super Nigger," in which Clark Washington's X-ray eyes "enable him to see through everything except whitey." Once again, however, Pryor presents the character as something of a ne'er-do-well, a janitor and pot-smoking space cadet who may have super powers, but they're not directed against whites.

What prevented Pryor from acting fully on his convictions was a very real fear of losing the celebrity status he'd earned. He liked the women and the cocaine, the parties and the star treatment, and he reveled in the attention. He was assured by his associates that he'd continue to have all of these as long as he didn't go too far with his black schtick and stuck more or less to the middle of the road. And what they said was valid, from a commercial standpoint. Pryor's TV gigs earned him engagements at Las Vegas clubs, where his fee climbed to three thousand dollars a week. Though he would frequently blow his wages on five-thousand-dollar-a-pot poker, he was very impressed to be making more money each month than his parents saw in a year, and enjoying every penny of it.

So the disenchantment smoldered. He knew that what he was doing wasn't black but blackface, dishing up black people as whites wanted to believe they were; he wasn't Leroy Pryor telling it like it is, using the language in which it should be told. In his own words, he was "one-dimensional . . . locked up." But every time he felt tempted to break loose, something came along that made him withdraw.

He began to chomp at the bit again toward the middle of 1966, then put everything else on hold when he got an opportunity to do a motion picture; a movie producer had seen his act and wanted him for a small part in a minor film. Pryor didn't jump at the chance—he *flew,* and in October of that year started filming *The Busy Body* in Los Angeles. Sid Caesar and Robert Ryan costarred, Caesar playing a nebbish who is wrongfully accused of murder and becomes entangled with gangsters. While fleeing the mob, he stumbles in and out of situations that allow the supporting cast of comedians to strut their stuff, including Pryor as a rather ineffective detective and Dom DeLuise as a mortician, with Bill Dana, Jan Murray, and Godfrey Cambridge along for the ride.

The Busy Body was released in 1967 and did nothing for Pryor, save to whet his appetite for more film roles. He had done a poor job on this one, becoming stiff and inhibited when the cameras rolled. "I did every actor that I'd ever seen in the movies in this one role. I walked in the door like Steve McQueen, I took my hat off like John Wayne, even did some Charlton Heston. I had all these things, I'd rehearsed them all. I probably was real rotten, but I thought I was great, then." Fortunately, the thrill of seeing himself on screen didn't obscure the fact that in future performances he should just be himself. "I got it all out of my system in one role," he says of the emulations, and vowed to concentrate more on characterizations—provided anyone gave him another crack at making movies. Pryor just wasn't sure there would be much demand for someone who "wanted to be Marlon Brando, but was really Jerry Lewis."

Back in the real world, Pryor continued to wrestle with his material, with show business, and with his life in general. Despite having vowed to avoid disappointment in matters of the heart by "being my own family," he thought he needed the anchor of a woman. He married a woman named Maxine in 1967, and she gave birth to Elizabeth Ann that same year. Pryor wasn't producing children just for the hell of it: then as now, one of his greatest desires was "to raise a baby . . . and have him teach me and I'll teach him and grow together and be friends." In short, Richard wanted everything that he had missed as a child. He genuinely regretted not being with Renee and Richard, Jr., who were living with their mothers in Peoria, and he was looking forward to spending time with his new daughter. The problem was his career. He would later anguish over the fact that "I was never with any of my children from the beginning; I was out there doing what I had to do."

Rather than stabilize him, the marriage put all those old devils on his shoulders, and he ended this union as quickly as he'd ended the other two.

While he was reevaluating relationships, he also took a hard look at television. He was becoming so critical that he wondered if he could keep appearing in that medium. "It could be such an informative medium," he charged. "One week of truth on TV could just straighten out everything. One hundred and twenty-seven million people watch television every night; that's why they use it to sell stuff. It's just a business, that's all. It's just a place where you sell products...to perpetuate business. The top-rated shows are for retarded people." Needless to say, what he found personally abrasive were the restrictions placed on him by television. "They always say, 'Be clean.' They want you to be something that really doesn't exist at all. I do the shows, but I just get bugged."

Not surprisingly, Pryor's resentment of television finally reached a point where he stopped doing shows. The last straw was not a point of censorship but a talk show on which he felt that he, as a black entertainer, was being manipulated. The ploy, he says, was that "the host turns to you and says, 'Isn't America great, Richard?' and you're supposed to say, 'It sure is,' and then he says, 'See, guys, *he* did it—what's the matter with the rest of you?' I've gone along with that in the past, but no more." Pryor didn't dislike America; to the contrary, he once described it as "a beautiful country...I couldn't have done what I've done in any other country." His disdain was for television.

(By May 1979, Pryor would have done more than simply stop capitulating; he would have turned around and used the medium as a soap box. After a visit to South Africa, he went on the "Tonight Show" and stunned viewers by recommending, "If you're black...get a gun and go to South Africa and kill some white people." Host Johnny Carson was taken aback, but not nearly so much as many viewers, and in particular the National Federation for Decency, a watchdog group, which slammed NBC for airing Pryor's comments. "Such a statement could come only from a sick mind full of racial hatred," charged spokesperson the Reverend Donald Wildmon. "It was a tasteless, senseless, sick incident." NBC, whose censors apparently thought Pryor had been joking, made no comment.)

When Pryor finally made the break with TV, it left a bad taste in the mouths of many in that industry. Though his opinions were a matter of public record, it was the way he did the deed that offended people: he simply didn't bother showing up for an "Ed Sullivan Show." Instead, he stayed home and played with some 16mm movie equipment he'd bought. Professionally, he'd have fared better, might even have won grudging admiration, had he done the show and *then* quit, or at least given the producers adequate notice. Completely ignoring them was Pryor's way of "mooning" the television industry.

With no movie offers coming in, Pryor was limited primarily to clubs like New Jersey's Latin Casino and the Las Vegas nightspots, although it wasn't long before these began to annoy him too. "I made a lot of money being Bill Cosby," he says, "but I was hiding my personality. I just wanted to be in show business so bad I didn't care how. It started bothering me later because I was being successful at it. I was being a robot comic . . . repeating the same lines, getting the same laughs for the same jokes. The repetition was killing me." The bottom line, he says, was that he was starting to lose energy. Just like on the Carver stage.

Once again Pryor rebelled. At the Aladdin, he tried some routines that were angrier and certainly more off-color than usual, sprinkled with "motherfuckers" and "pussies." The management informed Pryor that the act was a bit extreme for the customers and asked him to tone it down. Pryor went out the next night and did the show exactly as before—compounding his sins, legend has it, by stripping, running into the casino, jumping onto the table, and yelling, "Blackjack!" He was fired the following morning.

Pryor had been looking for an excuse to move to Hollywood and make more movies; now he had it. Driven by the same enthusiasm as that with which he had taken to the road years before, he rented an apartment in West Hollywood. Using his name to open doors, he went on numerous interviews and read for many parts, but his success was marginal. Late in 1967 he was hired to play a soldier in John Wayne's superpatriotic *The Green Berets*. Billed as Richard "Cactus" Pryor—doubtless in homage to Wayne and the sagebrush adventures that had galvanized Richard's youth—he enjoyed working with his hero, who both directed and starred in the film. Wayne really was as big as he had always seemed onscreen, and because the two men had virtually no personal contact, Pryor didn't get to see the political side of his hero.

When *The Green Berets* was released in June 1968, Pryor also didn't get to see much of himself: his part had been trimmed to a few scenes of running and saluting—fortunate in this film whose claim to immortality is a scene in which the sun sinks slowly in the east.

Pryor fared much better in his third movie, the cult classic *Wild in the Streets*. Made shortly after *The Green Berets*, it was as dramatic a switch as any actor could hope for. Christopher Jones starred as a wealthy pop-singer/junkie who is elected President of the United States when the voting age is lowered to fourteen. Pryor had the featured role of Stanley X, the drummer in Jones's band, playing the part with an appropriate blend of hysteria and militance.

Pryor's film career did not exactly skyrocket, nor had he expected it to. At that time blacks were not making many movies, with the sole exception of Sidney Poitier. Thus, Pryor was content to take what came his way, supplementing his income with gigs at some of the less restrictive clubs locally and around the country. Though he worked more than most black performers, he did so in movies that ranged from bad to awful.

Hard on the heels of *Wild in the Streets* Pryor did *You've Got To Walk It Like You Talk It or You'll Lose That Beat*. He was cast as a wino and appeared in the first fifteen minutes of this otherwise forgettable film. Babbling bitterly about life and the establishment, he stumbles into a men's room and confronts Carter Fields (Zalman King), a middle-class character searching for a meaningful life.

Actor (now producer) King describes *You've Got To Walk It Like You Talk It or You'll Lose That Beat* as a picture that, because of its complex, often abstract narrative, "was never perceived as a film which would do well at the box office." Made in 1969, it was obviously perceived as far worse, for it went unreleased for two years.

King affirms that Pryor did the picture not just to work but because of "a very sincere love for making movies. Richard knew, as we all did, that we were making a fringe picture, but that didn't make him or me any less enthusiastic about it. I don't even think we were paid scale for it; we did it for the joy of doing it."

Pryor's love of film was also the reason he did *Dynamite Chicken*, a comedy compilation described by its producer as "a multimedia movie magazine inspired by the TV generation." In fact, it's a hodgepodge of alternately puerile and clever bits by the Ace Trucking Company, Ron Carey, Pryor, and others, with small parts by Joan Baez and John Lennon. Like Pryor's previous picture, this film, barely over an hour long, sat on the shelf for years before being given a very limited, unsuccessful release in 1972. A reissue in the summer of 1982, with Pryor misleadingly top-billed, initially did well on the strength of his name but quickly faded.

By 1969, Pryor was earning approximately $50,000 a year and enjoying himself enormously. Removed from the fights and self-reproach over television and Las Vegas, he felt good about himself and the slow but steady progress in his film career. "Making movies is as much fun as watching the finished product on the screen," he said. "I can spend hours watching people on the set do their thing. Take the makeup man. You'd think his work was the only thing seen on the screen. The same with all the people here. I guess that's why American pictures have the reputation of being so . . . perfect."

Movies *were* magic to him, and, as King suggests, Pryor took virtually anything that came his way. This included not only theatrical films and a week-long stint on the "Joey Bishop Show," but appearances on dramatic TV series such as "The Young Lawyers" and "The Mod Squad." He greatly enjoyed TV work, and even though it didn't have the glamour of movies, he could make an average of five thousand dollars for two weeks of interesting, challenging work.

Pryor's most distinguished project of this period was a 1969 made-for-television movie entitled *Carter's Army*. Produced by ABC, the World War II adventure was about a Southern officer assigned to defend a dam with a force consisting of untested black recruits. The late Stephen Boyd played the officer, with Robert Hooks, Roosevelt Grier, and Moses Gunn costarring. Pryor was extremely convincing in his role as a terrified medic, and for the first time he was genuinely pleased with his screen work.

"I played a coward," he says, "and that was the hardest thing I've ever done. But just having men like Stephen Boyd and Robert Hooks on the set each day was a tremendous psychological boost." He was particularly impressed with the fact that they were as concerned with his performance as with their own. "They have a great deal of experience and were always ready and willing to help me when I needed it." Pryor says he got so wrapped up in the film that when one of the actors didn't show up the day after his character had been killed, he had to stop and think whether the man had actually died.

Pryor was nothing if not committed to his new craft.

Chapter Six

For a brief time after making those films, Pryor felt good about himself and the fact that he had more control over his destiny than in previous years. He felt settled enough to give marriage a fourth try, and in 1969 his daughter Rain was born.

This marriage, like the others, was short-lived. Painfully reflecting on all his failed relationships, Pryor believed that he treated all his women like queens, "and if I treat a woman like a queen, she damn well better treat me like a king.'' He felt that he lived up to his part of the bargain but that they didn't. To his credit, he provided very well for his women; but on the debit side he was moody, often explosive, and was frequently on the road.

The pressures resulted in his women leaving and, as he saw it, ''taking something more with them than their clothes.'' What he lost each time was his chance to find happiness. But realizing that fact didn't necessarily enable him to do anything about it.

It's difficult to say how much of the disintegration of Pryor's most recent marriage, as well as subsequent relationships, was due to his increasing alcohol and cocaine habits.

Pryor makes no secret of the fact that at that time he was spending up to one hundred dollars a day on cocaine. Having been busted in 1967 for possessing an ounce of marijuana obviously hadn't fazed him; legal or not, these drugs were for him. He jokes that he was so hooked that not only was he snorting cocaine but was regularly applying it to his genitals. ''It was costing me six hundred dollars a day just to get my *dick* hard,'' he quips. He would frequently allude to cocaine in his act, one of his favorite routines being a fictitious confrontation with his grandmother. Pryor has her berating him for using the drug; being a dutiful grandson, he flushes it down the toilet. As soon as the deed is done, his grandmother, wide-eyed, leaps up and screams hysterically at him for having wasted sixteen hundred dollars' worth of good stuff.

There was always a good excuse to turn to cocaine. If it wasn't personal despair or professional frustration, it was something else. As a famous screenwriter and novelist who hung around with Pryor in the late 1960s relates, ''I've heard all that stuff about loneliness, and that *was* a contributing factor. But part of what made him run was facing up to the fact that he didn't like white people and white values very much. I don't know if that was a revolutionary phase he was going through, identifying with third-world concerns, or whether it was based solely on personal animus; I suspect it was a little of both.

''He had a number of white friends like me, but we were

not as close as his black friends. I think that the prevailing opinion—his then and mine to this day—was that disliking at least ninety-eight percent of the human race was a sign of sanity. In his case, disliking whites in particular may also have given him a sense of belonging. But dealing with that kind of *angry* sanity took extraordinary measures.'' Unfortunately for those around Pryor, many times the drugs and liquor didn't calm him but had the opposite effect. When that happened, it often meant that there was violence in the offing.

Most of Pryor's ex-wives won't discuss his reputed abusive behavior at home, but Pryor did lose control on July 26, 1967, when he punched out Fabian Tholkes, the desk clerk at his West Hollywood apartment, then attacked owner Wayne Trousper with a knife and fork. Pryor went to court in October of that year and was found guilty of assault with a deadly weapon, Superior Court Judge David W. Williams ordering him to pay damages of seventy-five thousand dollars.

Unable to exorcise his demons through humor or keep them quiet with cocaine, Richard Pryor let them loose on the people around him. When he wasn't assaulting physically he was lashing out verbally, breaking the ''eleventh commandment'' never to put down one's peers when he charged, ''Some people say there's no best in comedy. They're wrong. *I'm* the best. I don't mind saying that, because I worked hard to get where I am and because it feels good to say it.'' As though taking particular aim at the stubborn remnants of Cosby in his act, he added that the kind of character-heavy comedy performed by himself and Lily Tomlin (and later by Andy Kaufman and Robin Williams) ''transcends stand-up comedy crap.''

Writer William Brashler, a professional acquaintance of Pryor's, later observed in *Playboy* that Pryor could be ''instantly cruel, goading, unmerciful,'' then quoted another Pryor associate as stating that ''when the vodka and drugs take hold . . . he will go for your soul, just personally assassinate you.''

There were times, of course, when Pryor turned those demons on himself. He would go out of his way to tear down what he'd achieved, though it would be several years before he understood why. More interested now in movie-making and personal pursuits, Pryor became famous for no-shows at various clubs, and as a result found himself saddled with a string of lawsuits. Other clubs were understandably reluctant to hire him, and since Hollywood is nothing if not a tattletale, copycat town, it wasn't long before the film work dried up too.

Pryor pretended not to care. He became arrogant and snobbish, sticking to his ultrahip friends, getting high, and thumbing his nose at society. He even stopped paying taxes, not bothering to report the quarter-million dollars he earned between 1967 and 1969. (When Pryor was audited in 1974, his indiscretions earned him ten days in jail, three years on probation, a fine of $2,500, and a bill for $68,504 in back taxes.)

The death of Richard's mother and father in 1969 lifted him from his self-imposed seclusion, but it also placed another burden on his strained emotions. He was at Gertrude's side in Peoria's Methodist Medical Center during her illness, and it was extremely difficult for him to watch her drift away. (In contrast, Leroy was said to have died in the middle of a furious sexual encounter shortly thereafter. As Richard joked some time later, "He came and went at the same time.")

With his parents gone, Pryor was suddenly "promoted" to adulthood. He was truly on his own, and with that realization came another: that he had always needed to perform. He'd gone into show business for want of anything else to do, but he could have been happy in any situation that allowed him to be "on" for people. The money was important now, but it hadn't been the object when he started. Now that he had a chance to take stock of where he was going, he realized that from the start, "Making it had nothing to do with show business. The *it* that I've been trying to make is me."

Deciding that he had best start satisfying himself, he faced the fact that while he had come far in seven years, he was not where he wanted to be. Setting and attaining some goals became his top priority.

Pryor's good friend Lily Tomlin explains the kind of harsh self-evaluation through which every comic must go at some time. "The best material is always that which is funny and also has perceptions or insights, makes a comment without ridiculing and includes everyone in the comment. When I was first starting out doing stand-up, people used to say to me, 'You can't do the kind of thing you do standing up because it's not hard enough comedy, it's acting, or it's not this or it *is* that.' You can second guess yourself, but you must never doubt yourself. No one understands comedy better than a comedian, which is why you have to go to bat for yourself and say, 'Well, it's really a matter of sensitivity to the material, not what the material is about or who you are.' "

Pryor had always believed that intellectually, but he was beginning to accept it emotionally. He resolved to make his act more relevant, more personal, despite having been advised by his managers that it was a bad business move. He whipped up some very topical black street routines, and, to prove to his managers and himself that there was an audience for this kind of material, did a show in Los Angeles, to which he invited local black disc jockeys. They hated him, taking particular offense at his frequent use of the word *nigger.*

Devastated by the show's failure and disillusioned now in work as well as in love, Pryor became paranoid. He began to question the loyalty of his friends and associates, though in this case it was not entirely without justification. As soon as he had started making a lot of money, he became a target for the "would-be hip" people around him. Unemployed actors, struggling writers, waitresses looking for a break—all asked for favors or money. Pryor, who categorizes himself as "the softest touch in town," usually complied—until he realized that not one of these people gave a damn about him. "They finally nibbled at me so much and so long that there was nothing left," he complains. "I had no life to enjoy, really enjoy in peace. I couldn't say 'no' to them; I wanted to be everything they asked, even when I knew I couldn't do it or shouldn't do it."

But in 1970 he finally reached a point where he'd had enough of the compromises and the users.

It had been three years since his conflict with the Aladdin. Now, for a fee of six thousand dollars a week, he agreed to go back. But when he got to Las Vegas he felt like a traitor. For a long time he had genuinely hated his act—more accurately, hated himself for doing it—and knew, as he put it, "I was false . . . turning into plastic." He told himself to "fuck these people, man," thinking he would just take their money and do the show. But it was only when he said, "Fuck this way of living," that he actually felt better.

For once, the troubled Mr. Pryor took his own advice.

During his first show at the Aladdin Hotel, Pryor was doing his typical routines, talking about everything from fairy tales to army life, when suddenly he stopped in the middle of his act. Gazing at the audience and seeing nothing but the bright lights, he just "went crazy," as he describes it.

"I didn't flip out. I was just onstage, man . . . and I was *boring* people." Shaking his head, he yelled at the audience, "What the fuck am I doing here? I'm not going to *do* this anymore!" Leaving a stone-silent house in his wake, he strode from the stage. Unfortunately, Pryor happened to stride off the *wrong* side of the stage, from which the only exit was a passageway about eight inches wide. "This guy back there said, 'No, you can't go through there!' But I'm saying, 'Yeah I *can*.' I squeezed myself through it because I wasn't gonna have to walk back across the stage." Meanwhile, the audience sat quietly for several minutes before an embarrassed hotel representative came out and announced that Pryor hadn't been joking.

After leaving the stage, Pryor climbed into his car and drove away from the hotel. "It just came to me to do that," he would much later say of his departure. "It was like the gods or fate talking to me. I knew right away that it was a moment of judgment for me, and I knew I did the right thing." He adds without humor, "It was either that or I was going to become one of these tuxedo persons, arguing about who's going to appear with Sinatra at the Boffo-Boffo," then says more pensively that for years he "was young and naive and didn't know any better. And a young performer thinks he has to do these things till you realize it's all right to be who you are. It takes a long damn time for anybody, and that night I found it.''

Pryor drove straight to Los Angeles and packed up everything he owned. It would be years before he returned to the spotlight.

Chapter Seven

Some of Pryor's associates claim that he would never have walked away from earnings of more than $200,000 a year had it not been for the influence of drink or drugs. Pryor himself does not deny that when he got into trouble it was usually because he'd been drinking, smoking, or snorting to excess.

But not this time.

Pryor insists that what he did was what black people have always done when they've been pushed too far. ''Anytime you push that right button, he'll jump right to his stuff: 'Wait a minute. This meetin's over.' '' He maintains that there was nothing artificial involved in his decision to leave the stage—nothing artificial save for the people around him.

Surprisingly, Pryor had felt no animosity toward the predominantly wealthy whites in the audience. He didn't blame them directly for the kind of watered-down comedy he was being forced to do. Rather, he was tired of his partners and advisers, who cooed, ''Trust me, Richie baby,'' or, ''I'll take care of you, kid.'' Nor were his instincts about these people far afield.

''After I walked out on that engagement, I really got to know the people I was working with. I needed some compassion right then, but they were all thinking about themselves. They were saying, 'What are *we* going to do? What about *us*?' They weren't concerned about me. I was tired of that whole atmosphere, tired of meeting a parade of people I didn't like. They liked me, I guess, but I hated their guts. I would shake hands and look at them and see the devil—horns and all.''

Walking off the stage wasn't only an expression of Richard's professional discontent; it was also part of his ongoing battle with authority figures. For years these people had been telling him what to do. Now, in one brazen move, he had mowed *everyone* down. Part of him, at least, was satisfied.

Whatever the impetus behind Pryor's actions, he reached Los Angeles feeling reborn. Free of all responsibility, he decided to buff his tarnished talents and free himself artistically. It was time "to make changes, transitions . . . keep moving and growing and stretching to find out what you can do." There was only one rule he swore to follow, one thing he'd never do again, and that was to "kiss somebody's ass."

Closing up his home in Los Angeles, Pryor escaped to Berkeley, the seat of so much upheaval in the preceding decade. Though its time had passed, Berkeley was still the spiritual seat of iconoclasm and Pryor felt that the environment would allow him to grow his own way. In addition, he knew it would be easy to score cocaine there, which he knew he would need to see him through the difficult days ahead.

Like an Old Testament prophet, Pryor threw himself into deprivation and purging. He rented a $110-per-month efficiency apartment near the freeway, where he just "got naked . . . sat in my house and didn't come out until I was ready." He had only a general sense of direction, but he knew he needed to fill the gap left empty since 1966, when Lenny Bruce, age forty, died in his bathroom of a drug overdose.

There had always been more than a little Bruce in Pryor. Even though he wasn't familiar with Bruce's work, audiences in the Village had seen him in Pryor's delivery.

Bruce, like Pryor, had a remarkable talent for whistling up sardonic characters and jumping back and forth between them. The difference was that Bruce was less an observer than a debunker. The subject of his most famous routine, the Lone Ranger, *could* have been a target of Pryor's wit. But where Pryor might have replaced Tonto with a black man, Bruce went for Ranger Reid's psyche. Eavesdropping on a conversation between two townspeople after the Masked Man has departed, Bruce began with one of them griping:

> "What's with that putz? The schmuck didn't wait! Mama made coffee and cake and everything—what the hell is *with* that guy? I've got my hand out like some jack-off, he's on his horse already. The Lone Ranger. So what the hell does *that* give him? What an asshole. I'm gonna punch the shit out of him if I ever see him again."
>
> "Take it easy, Dominique—"
>
> "Take it easy my *balls*. Is that guy kiddin' me?"
>
> "You don't know about him? He's got a problem, goin' to analysis. He can't accept love."

Bruce's routines inevitably shaded into despair, as in the case when the Lone Ranger is revealed to be a pervert. No one in Bruce's world was psychosis-free, whether it was Tarzan finding Jane sleeping with Cheetah (Pryor, in his Tarzan bit, had a hip black man trying to understand the Jungle Lord's ape talk) or a timid musician apologizing to his bandleader, "I've got a monkey on my back," to which the Lawrence Welk sound-alike replies, "Oh, dat's all right. We *like* animals on the band." Bruce's material was the downtrodden looking down, not up.

There was still a dramatic difference in the styles of Bruce and Pryor even when the radically changed Pryor emerged from Berkeley after several years. Bruce was an autocrat who beat his audiences with irreverence and raped them with hard language. Pryor, even at his bluest and most vitriolic, couldn't molest an audience if he tried. He was a seducer who used his language and characters in a way that was charming and palatable.

After he went through the furnace of Berkeley, people stopped comparing Pryor to Cosby and started comparing him to Bruce. Pryor didn't resent this quite so much, though he never felt that doing characterizations and using foul language was any reason to be labeled "the black Lenny Bruce." A few years later, when Pryor saw Bob Fosse's award-winning film *Lenny,* he came to the conclusion that most people had missed what the two of them really had in common: a history of persecution. In Pryor's words, they had both "lived some life . . . paid some dues," factors that, regardless of the approach, gave their work the honesty to which audiences responded.

During this period, Pryor's sole and constant companion was his stereo, on which he continually played Marvin Gaye's "What's Going On." When he did go out, it was usually to bars and clubs, where he observed people; when he got home, he would tape-record his thoughts or throw out a few very rough bits.

Pryor also read voraciously, which he had never done before; his favorite topic was the life and writings of Malcolm X. After discovering the collected speeches of the black rights activist who had been murdered five years before, Pryor says he thought, "I'm not crazy . . . there's someone who thinks like I do."

What Pryor learned from Malcolm X was the *passion* to express himself. In heartfelt, powerful terms, Malcolm X stated the need for the black man to rise and assert himself against white society, establishing segregated states if necessary. (He generally excluded women, feeling that black men also needed to assert themselves against the dominant black matriarch. Given Pryor's own track record with women, he must have taken some solace in that.) As actor Ossie Davis noted in his eulogy after the activist's death, "Malcolm was our manhood, our living black manhood."

Pryor didn't want to see society overthrown, but Malcolm X helped him face what he had known all along: that whites needed a strong new look at blacks as they really were, while the strained relationship between black men and women could also stand some healthy parodying.

But Pryor didn't want to imitate the kind of hard-hitting racial material that Dick Gregory had made famous. The time for that kind of baiting and bitter comedy had passed. Ten years before, Gregory could sell a line like, "They asked me to buy a lifetime membership in the NAACP, but I told them I'd pay a week at a time. Hell of a thing to buy a lifetime membership, wake up one morning and find the country's been integrated." But by 1970, most of the civil rights and integration battles were being fought in the courts. It was no longer necessary or appropriate for comedians to call attention to it.

Pryor was more concerned with giving blacks entertainment and insights about themselves than with political or social movements. He wanted to use his characters to peel away pretension and expose the frailness underneath. After all, he had learned that from some of his favorites—Bob Hope, Lou Costello, and Daffy and Donald Duck putting on airs to cover their insecurities. He was simply going to apply this facade-busting to real people.

Despite the enormous failure of his Los Angeles disc-jockey concert, Pryor continued to follow his instincts about his material. He searched his experiences, shaping brutally honest routines from the disappointments, hopes, and hatreds he had felt or seen in others. Examining the minds of everyone from gays to street toughs was the same kind of challenge that creating characters had always been, but being able to do them the way he wanted, with all the quirks and street language, was heaven.

Whenever Pryor had developed a character or approach he wanted to test before an audience, he would go to a local club like Mandrakes or to Basin Street West in San Francisco. Working virtually for free, he'd try anything that would enable him to hone his craft. What he was doing might not make people laugh, but as long as it didn't bore them, and exacted an emotion of some kind, Pryor was content. More and more of the skits he performed were joke-free, as he learned to create humor through tension and pathos.

Pryor stuck primarily to ordinary people as characters, such as Mudbone, the brutally honest, naggingly practical ex-levee-worker (he didn't bother to tell the community that the levee had burst, feeling, "They were gonna find out sooner or later anyway"); the street-wise kids Weasel, Jesse,

Ronnie, and others (a typical, non-Fat-Albert exchange: "Hey, man, what you say 'bout my mother?'' "Shit, I didn't say *nothin'* 'bout the bitch!''); and a slave at the first Thanksgiving ("Are you thankful?'' "Yeah, massuh!''). At other times, he would experiment strictly with sounds, doing the outside world as heard by an unborn baby or exploring the two-dozen ways one could say *bitch*.

These extemporaneous bits were performed before well-integrated audiences consisting mostly of students and burned-out survivors of the sixties. All of them responded to what he was doing because, in his view, "People see themselves when I do a character because everybody talks the same kind of talk. That's what they'd be laughing at—themselves.''

Through it all, the real Richard Pryor was rarely seen. He would stick around long enough to break the ice with something outrageous, like looking at a predominately black crowd and saying to the few whites, "Whatsamatter, y'all stop fuckin'?'' Then he would disappear, to be replaced by one of his characters. Pryor would bob to the surface every now and then like a marathon swimmer coming up for air, introducing the next personality and then diving right into it.

Pryor loved every minute of what he was doing. "I felt free," he says of those days, "like I had just come out of a dungeon I had been in for years.''

One thing Pryor didn't do was use the stage to express his hatred of racism. White liberals were more frequent targets than the bigots he detested. Pryor portrayed the liberals as comic misfits—nasal, fawning, plastic creatures who couldn't tie their shoes without a map. In his view, they were liberal because it was as close to being black and cool as they would ever come. Pryor's references to racism or antiblack dogma were usually brief and oblique, as when explaining that the whole process of bringing Vietnamese to America was not the result of charity but because "white folk *tired* of our asses, have to get themselves some *new* niggers.'' He didn't want the artistry or sensitivity of his stage performances corrupted by vengeance.

Offstage and in private, however, Pryor lashed out at bigots and right-wing ideologists with a passion. Typical was the time Pryor was approached by a journalist from *The National Observer*. He answered the man's questions as obnoxiously as possible, claiming never to have heard of Charlie Chaplin and citing J. Edgar Hoover as his foremost comedic influence. Frustrated, the reporter finally decided to pack it in, at which point Pryor shot off, "Say hi to your boss Buckley." The visitor finally understood what the problem had been. He pointed out that noted conservative William F. Buckley was not the editor of *his* paper but of *The National Review*, and Pryor immediately apologized and gave him a real interview.

Pryor's anger was evident in his new hobby: collecting guns. He stressed to his few friends that he was not hoarding them for the revolution nor arming himself for protection. He bought guns solely for the aesthetics of owning them. However, as one Pryor intimate observed, if you were in his home and he became angry it was "best to back off and, if your face is white, to leave."

Pryor doesn't deny that he sometimes got carried away. Years later, he impulsively shot up his home and put a bullet through the center of his first gold record. He recalls, "The vodka was tellin' me, 'Go ahead, shoot something else!'"

As he worked out his new stage persona, Pryor would sometimes leave Northern California to do a small club in Los Angeles or some other city. Las Vegas, smarting from his behavior at the Aladdin, would have nothing to do with him. But that was okay with Pryor, who didn't care if he never saw a fancy nightclub again.

Critical reaction to the "new" Richard Pryor was mixed. Most of the critics mistakenly thought he'd gone militant with his emphasis on downtrodden black characters. An example of how easily Pryor could be misunderstood was his comment that back in Peoria, he and his friends were always being arrested because "the ugly white girls who couldn't get any say the niggers raped 'em." Focusing on Pryor's remark about the girls, many listeners missed his jab at the stereotype of the black as a sexual giant. By the same token, as quickly as he would deride Peoria's white police officers as stupid ruffians, he would have a cop turn to a black kid and growl, "No, nigger, I don't want to buy no radio." No sooner had he trashed a stuttering Chinese waiter then he would marvel, "But Chinese can eat with sticks, don't drop a goddamn speck. Nigger loose three pounds of food with a *knife and fork*."

Pryor had no patience with the critics who heard only what they wanted to hear. He lashed out, charging that none of them had had anything bad to say when he was pretending to be Bill Cosby. Now, however, "the time for being white is over. I'm not interested in diluting my conversation, diluting my feelings . . . I'm not interested in wasting my life compromising." Pryor wasn't disdaining mass appeal, he simply didn't see it as an end in itself. Pryor also suspected that some of this backlash was due to the way he had snubbed the establishment. "When they catch those of us who fly resting on a rock," he charged, "they pull off our wings." Pryor was not about to be grounded any longer.

Apart from the material itself, the most hotly debated aspect of Pryor's evolving act was his constant use of the word *nigger*, followed a close second by *motherfucker*.

To begin with, Pryor's definition of vulgarity wasn't the same as everyone else's. "Richard Nixon being allowed in Red China, that's very vulgar. That's vile. Vulgar, onstage, is colorful."

Many people disagreed. They felt that despite the new brand of societal comedy Pryor was creating, his profanity, as fellow comedian Robert Klein put it, "wears thin sometimes." But Pryor wasn't so much surprised by this attention as by the accusations that he was merely being sensationalistic.

People who had not grown up in the ghetto took *nigger* and *motherfucker* at face value, as defined in their dictionaries. But to Pryor these words meant many things. His *nigger* wasn't, as he described it, "the name they used for slaves, which made them less than human and justified in their own mind the way they treated us. You're a 'nigger' and you ain't a person. You don't have to talk to him, you don't have to feed him, you don't have to let him worship, you don't have to let him think—nothing."

In Pryor's routines, *nigger* was a catchall word. As in the ghetto, the speaker's intention was clear depending on the delivery: the set of his brow, his inflection, whether he was pointing or had thrown his arms stiffly behind him. It could indicate disparagement, kinship, authority, or pride. The difference is clearly illustrated in Pryor's 1977 film *Greased Lightning*. He is standing in a graveyard one night when costar Cleavon Little pops up behind him. Frightened, Pryor snaps, "That ain't funny, nigguh!" Later in the film, a white man tells Pryor, "Stay out of my way, nigger." Clearly, there's a world of difference.

Motherfucker was admittedly less versatile. It was limited mostly to insults and threats, though occasionally it was used as expression of admiration. Of it, Pryor said simply, "I find no other word can take the place of *motherfucker*," adding with disgust, "We seem to live in a society that lacks communication. When you try to communicate, you're called a radical, a communist, dirty, a Republican, or something to let you know you're not speaking their language. If you listen to everybody, you can usually judge for yourself what is good and what is bad for you. The words I use might be bad words, but you never know until it's open house."

The argument wasn't really whether the words were appropriate: they were. There was no way Pryor could create an aura of reality without using them. As he put it, "It's theater. I involve the audience in truth because everything is real. I'm possessed when I'm onstage." The real question was whether this was enough to keep him happy.

Chapter Eight

Pryor had evolved according to plan. He had found it easy to blame white people for the restraints that had been placed on him, and his language, his attitude, and his routines reflected his disgust for the society they represented. "I was becoming what I wanted to become," he boasts, "this kind of cult, mysterious person." The problem, he admits, is that "it was real hard living it," since the loud, public iconoclast had little in common with the quiet, less secure private man.

It would be several years before Pryor would change his outlook. Leaving a nightclub stage one night, he says, "This brother came up to me and said, 'How do you feel, man?' I said, *'Black!'* He said, 'Don't worry, you'll get over it.' It hit me, meant more to me than he'll ever know. It made me think, 'Why don't you stop this ridiculous anger bullshit. Just be funny.'"

The proof of the internal tug of war is that while Pryor willingly accepted exile from the fancier "white bread" clubs, he remained hopelessly smitten by the "establishment" glamour of Hollywood. He knew it was false, he knew it was very white, yet it was a part of him he couldn't let go of—the little boy who loved the movies. Accordingly, he would use any excuse to spend time in Wonderland, even if it meant acting in a terrible comedy like *The Phynx*.

The title of this low-budget 1970 film refers to a group of rock musicians who have been hand-picked by the government to put on concerts behind the Iron Curtain. There, the group's assignment is to rescue entertainers being held captive by a communist general, played by Michael Ansara.

Sight gags and one-liners abound, and, though they are eclectic—the topics range from the Ku Klux Klan to Madison Avenue to the Boy Scouts—most are awful. The film's one clever joke is uttered by Pat O'Brien, who rues that had *he* played "the other part" in that old Warner Brothers picture, he'd be in Sacramento "and Ronald Reagan would be here."

The actors who played the Phynx (read "Finks") were all unknowns; the film's name players, such as Pryor, Martha Raye, Butterfly McQueen, Dorothy Lamour, Guy Lombardo, Joe Louis, and Huntz Hall, appeared in cameros.

The film bombed. But Pryor wasn't upset, since his participation had been minimal. What discouraged him was that *The Phynx* was the only offer that came his way.

Pryor moved back to Los Angeles in 1970, the clubs in and around Hollywood being as suitable as those in San Francisco. He made the change because he felt that being close to the film industry would help him get better parts. He would be available to audition and felt that producers who saw his act might find something for him to do in their films.

There were, in fact, more parts being written for blacks than in previous years. Fred Williamson cavorted in *M*A*S*H*, James Earl Jones achieved stardom in *The Great White Hope*, William December Williams aka Billy Dee Williams became an overnight star in TV's *Brian's Song*, and the infamous black exploitation film cycle got under way in 1971 with *Shaft*. For Pryor, it was a matter of being dressed up and waiting for somewhere to go.

At this point Pryor received a call from recording entrepreneur Louis Drozen. Four years earlier, Drozen had left his job as an executive with a record company in order to establish Los Angeles-based Laff Records, the first exclusively comedy label. Drozen had seen Pryor in New York and now wanted him to cut some records. He felt that Pryor, old or new, would be an asset. Though Pryor had some misgivings about putting so much raw material on tape, he signed a multirecord deal in December 1970 for what Drozen describes as "a substantial four-figure advance."

The Laff contract was not Pryor's first with a record company. He had previously cut a drab album titled *Richard Pryor* for the Dove label, recorded live at the Troubador and issued in 1968. Tame in its language, the album is typical of the Cosby-like routines Pryor was doing in the sixties, containing jokes on everything from body odor to army life. Even the album jacket is a joke, with Pryor dressed as an aborigine, having taken the white man literally and gone back to Africa, where his expression and comfortable crouched pose show that he fits right in.

Drozen knew the Laff album would be different. For one thing, Pryor's act had changed in the last two years, the new material "hitting home with every black person," as Drozen saw it. Accordingly, Drozen decided to record Pryor at The Redd Foxx Club, a predominately black nightspot in Hollywood where "we knew we were going to get a good record."

Several shows were taped and extensive editing was done, Pryor getting more laughs on some nights and on others ad-libbing so extensively that it was necessary to cut and paste the tapes to make the best record. Hours of material ended up in Laff's library.

The first of Pryor's twelve albums for Laff was called *Craps (After Hours)*. It contains the best of the outrageous, seriocomic, streetwise Pryor on such subjects as wealth ("I've had money, but it never felt as good as when I come"), jail ("I was arrested in California—they be serious. They look all in your *asshole*. I say, 'What am I gonna hide in my ass, a *pistol*?' "), ("We fought the Indians too!" an offended black complains about historians who gloss over his people's contributions, only to be undercut by an associate who adds, "Shut up, motherfucker! You want the Indians to hate us too?").

Craps (After Hours) was released in February 1971. The jacket was a striking contrast to *Richard Pryor,* showing the comedian and some rather unsavory figures throwing dice in a back room. Inside and out, it was exactly how Pryor wanted to be perceived by the public. There was only one thing wrong: the record didn't sell.

Laff had an extremely modest distribution network, the lack of advertising didn't help, and Pryor's new act had an extremely limited market. Although the album is a top seller today, it hadn't been tailored like *Richard Pryor* to appeal to the middle-class whites who bought Cosby's records. The album was for blacks, and while Pryor may have been "hitting home" with them onstage, the records they bought were music, not comedy. The initial sales of *Craps (After Hours)* were so distressing to Drozen that he waited two years before releasing another Pryor album. Calculatingly titled *Pryor Goes Foxx Hunting,* it was not a tribute to Foxx's Hollywood club but an attempt to get some mileage out of Foxx himself, whose series "Sanford and Son" was one of TV's hottest new properties.

The *Craps (After Hours)* album was the only chance Drozen had to use vintage, grade-A material. Laff and Pryor ended up in court later in 1971 because Pryor decided that he didn't want to be bound to them exclusively. The result was that Laff released Pryor from his contract in November 1971 for "valuable considerations," which included Laff's right to package material gleaned from its tapes plus select material recorded subsequently. But the conflict would continue for years, Pryor ultimately trying to enjoin the Laff albums, which contained what he felt were awful, unpolished routines. Laff turned around and sued Pryor for $2.8 million after he used material from *Craps (After Hours)* in a film. The legal scuffles went on for years, Laff ultimately producing fourteen Pryor albums but otherwise making no copyright claims on the material.

Despite their subsequent troubles, Drozen remembers Pryor as a cooperative and enthusiastic young man, he was subject to frequent fits of self-doubt and discouragement. The producer says that Pryor's biggest problem was his reliance on drink and drugs, reporting that he had to keep a fifth of whiskey in his drawer for whenever Pryor would drop by. Pryor himself makes no secret of the fact that he used cocaine as freely as ever. "I'd take the dope and pretend I was Miles Davis," he says, perversely boasting that not only did he snort up Peru in search of a more satisfying persona, he could have *bought* the country with what he spent on its illegal export. The fact that he wasn't earning that kind of money didn't make Pryor give it up: when he was short he simply borrowed from friends and his new business associates. He wasn't comfortable about this, but his guilt was apparently softened by the belief that if these people cared about him, they would give him as much money as he needed.

Pryor was right, and before long he owed a half-million dollars. Worse than being in debt was the fact that he received no film offers during 1971. He continued to play the small clubs and managed to earn a devoted following there, his fame spreading locally as a brilliant "new wave" comic. But the clubs were a dead end. Although Pryor's future costar Jackie Gleason hit the proverbial nail on its head when he said, "I never knew a dramatic actor who became a good comedian, but I've known of several comedians who became good actors," Los Angeles already had more talent than it could use. And despite the changing trends, very few of them were black.

Pryor realized that the only way Hollywood would take notice was if word got back from New York and Chicago that he was someone with nationwide appeal. Veteran director Robert Wise draws this analogy: "Thousands of wonderful books may pass across producers' desks every year, but the bestsellers are the ones that get their attention." Pryor wasn't about to temper his new style; all he wanted to do was create a stir, generate big box office—become a bestseller.

Thus, eight years after leaving Peoria, Pryor once again hit the road—wiser, more experienced, but no less desperate than before.

Not surprisingly, Pryor took his act to almost exclusively black audiences. As he said at the time, "They're the only ones that have been where I've been, that know what I'm talking about." However, the black-oriented content was only part of the new Pryor. His delivery itself was geared to blacks, by his own admission an adaptation of the way blacks "say a whole lot of things underneath you, all around you."

Still, Pryor was "scared to death" that this first display of his new persona might not work. He'd been putting off just such a test in part because he wanted to stick around Hollywood, but also because "niggers will eat you up if your shit ain't right." If Pryor couldn't sell blacks on his views of life, love, and intolerance, he was prepared to make yet another radical change. No more Berkeley or Los Angeles: "I'd have to go to some ghetto to live . . . I'd have to go live with my people." After having been false for so long, he was convinced that the only way he would achieve personal and professional satisfaction was to pursue truth in his work.

One of Pryor's first and certainly the biggest test of his new material was playing the Apollo Theatre in New York's Harlem. The Apollo was the largest and best-known black showplace in the world, and Pryor was in awe of the fact that he would be on the same stage as such legendary black entertainers as Pigmeat Markham and Stepin Fetchit. "I was tense and scared," he admits, and went "right to the real stuff: you didn't have time for the bull," black audiences being in his estimation the least patient crowds on earth. Fortunately, the audience at the Apollo responded with thunderous approval, and Pryor says, "I was fine after that, wherever I went."

The box-office receipts bear him out. Pryor won raves for concerts in Chicago, Detroit, and other centers of black culture. "People felt good," Pryor declares, "and to see people laughing at each other and not being so serious, that made me feel good."

Ironically, Bill Cosby happened to be in the audience at one of these engagements, and commented on the change in Pryor: "Richard took on a whole new persona—his own. In front of me and everyone else, Richard killed the Bill Cosby in his act, made people hate it. Then he worked on them, doing pure Richard Pryor, and it was the most astonishing metamorphosis I have ever seen. He was magnificent."

Based on the results of these early engagements, it began to seem that Pryor might never attract more than a very limited following among white audiences. Although young whites, the "radical" college kids, did attend his shows, an informal survey pegged his audience at eighty-percent black.

Months after the tour began, Hollywood was no more impressed than when Pryor was among them. One-third of all movie audiences were black, but they were content with the same movies the whites liked. Hollywood felt there was no need to give them Richard Pryor, who had no appeal among the other two-thirds of the moviegoing public.

Pryor was disappointed, though his spirits were bolstered by the popularity of his concerts. Having dwelled on the white side of the fence for so long, he found it exhilarating to reach his people with the likes of Mudbone and Super Nigger. "Maybe that's my lot," he said. "Twenty-five million black people. That's enough for me."

But it wasn't enough for another young black, who had already set the music business on fire and felt it was time to do the same for motion pictures. Ironically, it would be a singer and a comedian who helped him do it.

In 1959, former boxer and assembly-line worker Berry Gordy, Jr., had founded Motown Records with one goal: to showcase black talent and see to it that they were not cheated in the process. Within five years he had built an empire by recording such stars as the Miracles, Stevie Wonder, and Marvin Gaye. Eager to branch into other media, he established a Motown film division in 1969. His first project was a movie about one of history's greatest black artists, jazz singer Billie Holiday, based on her autobiography, *Lady Sings the Blues*. It was Gordy's feeling that a good movie about blacks would have no trouble pulling in a sizable white audience, which his costly new undertaking would require.

First published in 1956, the book was not upbeat material for a debut film. Born in 1915, Holiday spent her childhood in brothels, first as a maid and then as a prostitute. She later managed to improve her lot by becoming a singer, but the pressures of performing and overcoming racial barriers turned her to drugs; she died a heroin addict at the age of forty-four.

When Gordy went west, his working knowledge of film and the film business was virtually nil. Accordingly, the industry was betting that his stay would be brief. But Gordy understood deal-making and financing. He managed to set up a coproduction deal with Paramount Pictures, which put two million dollars toward his production and agreed to distribute it. The industry was impressed, but their admiration turned to outright horror when Gordy announced that the part of Holiday would be played by one of his recording artists, pop singer Diana Ross.

The skeptics pointed out that Ross had no acting experience and that even as a singer she had neither a vocal range nor a style even remotely similar to that of "Lady Day." But Diana Ross had more going for her than people realized. Like Billie Holiday, she had grown up in a Detroit ghetto from which the only way out was show business. Teaming with high-school friends Mary Wilson, Barbara Martin, and Florence Ballard, Ross formed a singing group called the Primettes. In 1960, Gordy hired them as backup singers for what was then called the Hitsville label. Sensing potential in the teen-agers, he taught them how to dress and perform with style, and commissioned material for them. When Martin quit to get married, he renamed the trio the Supremes.

In 1964, after a few moderately successful records, the Supremes recorded the single "Where Did Our Love Go?", which sent them on their way to becoming the second most successful group of the decade, surpassed only by the Beatles. But the Supremes' music, like Pryor's early humor, was comparatively mainstream. And because Diana Ross was a more visible figure than Pryor, blacks frequently called her a "sellout." Stung by this rejection, she sought publicly to embrace a black identity. Gordy, leaning more toward his role of lover and mentor than shrewd businessman, had bought the rights to *Lady Sings the Blues* with this in mind.

Hurt but not daunted by her critics, Ross spent months listening to Holiday albums, adopting the singer's style and inflection, pushing her own voice to its limits. Even her harshest critics would have to admit that she did an extraordinary job.

Meanwhile, it looked as though the doomsayers might be right about Gordy. Paramount quickly became disenchanted with him. They were never really comfortable with the thought of Ross in the title role, and they were also dissatisfied with the script, which hopped unevenly through key events in the singer's life, beginning with her early teens and concluding with a triumphant concert at Carnegie Hall. Paramount was even more concerned at the amount of money

Gordy planned to spend recreating the 1930s and 1940s. He insisted that the ambiance be *right*, from the cars to the club interiors to a suitable wardrobe for Diana's screen debut.

Finally, the studio and Gordy parted ways. However, Paramount did agree to stay on as the picture's distributor—if the producer could still get it made. Gordy thanked them and returned their two million dollars. Rather than drop the project, he postponed it for a year, during which he managed to raise the money on his own.

As sure as Gordy had been that Diana Ross would star, there was never any question in his mind about who would costar. *Brian's Song* had become the most popular made-for-television film in history, due largely to the talent and sex appeal of star Billy Dee Williams. Gordy signed him to play Holiday's sponsor and husband Louis McKay, a character built from various figures in Holiday's life. As McKay, Williams would strut more charisma across the screen than most actors before or since, and he would become known as "the black Clark Gable." For the part of Piano Man, the nightclub musician who discovers the singer and sticks with her through thick and thin, Gordy passed over Motown's awesome stable of musicians to go after Pryor.

Gordy had followed the comedian's career since its inception, and it wasn't Pryor's limited ability at the keyboard that attracted him. He wanted Piano Man to be a blend of humor and pathos, and he had never seen anyone meld the two as expertly as Pryor. "Berry Gordy came up and said, 'I need somebody to do a little comedy,'" Pryor relates. "Then John Wayne died and I took over."

Piano Man is an amalgam of characters with whom Holiday worked, from the piano player who discovered her in the first club she played, to her road accompanist Bobby Tucker. As written, it was a pivotal but decidedly supporting role with only three major scenes: forcing Billie to sing when she fails her audition as a nightclub dancer (an event taken from Billie's book); arguing bitterly that her pusher in Harlem has a reputation for peddling cut stuff, ending with Billie and Piano Man crying over the death of her mother (Pryor's hysterical reaction was entirely ad-libbed); and procuring drugs for Billie in Los Angeles, where Piano Man is hunted down and beaten to death by gangsters for taking off without paying.

Pryor could have played Piano Man as written—a honky-tonk figure who lives in Billie's shadow. Instead, he turns him into a poignant, fidgeting harlequin whose mumbled words are less important than his expressions. Pryor almost makes him a mime, communicating primarily with exaggerated hand movements and facial contortions. On another level, Piano Man serves as Billie's alter-ego. Because the singer's mood shifts are understated and Piano Man is just the opposite, Pryor *directs* his agitation, making his character a mirror of Billie's hidden fears. It is fitting that Piano Man is killed procuring drugs for her, Holiday's addiction literally slaying a part of her.

Despite the heavy melodrama, there are still a wealth of Pryorisms. When the nervous Billie is heckled during her first-night performance, Piano Man snarls at the man, "Want me t' put my foot in your ass?" Later, when gangsters come pounding on his door for their money, he stalls them by sputtering, "We just hafta . . . uh, flush the toilet!" the sort of line young Richie Pryor might have tried on the police back in Peoria.

Newcomer Ross was understandably concerned about playing opposite Pryor and Williams. However, she found them both very helpful throughout the forty-two-day shoot and performed admirably in the role. Ironically, her weakest moments are those in which Billie has money and happiness: that's when Diana Ross comes through. Ross is most convincing when she is Holiday at her worst, whoring and high on heroin, suffering withdrawal and screaming in rage at the Klansmen she and her musicians encounter while on tour.

The picture was released in October 1972 and was immediately dismissed by most critics as trite and superficial. ("Valueless as biography but okay as soap opera" was how one reviewer put it.) Regardless, the public loved it. As Gordy had hoped, the film drew a huge crossover audience, and his profits were in the millions. Pryor got what he wanted, too: excellent notices for his work. *Newsweek* praised his Piano Man as the only "memorable part" of the picture, *Women's Wear Daily* agreeing that Pryor's performance was "show-stealing." And, although Pryor was inexplicably overlooked at Oscar time, he was genuinely pleased to see Ross win a Best Actress nomination. (She lost to Liza Minnelli, amid rumors that Motown had tried too hard to "buy" her the Academy Award. In fact, Motown had mounted a massive print campaign extolling Ross's performance, and this turned off many Academy voters. The picture also mounted losing battles in the categories of Best Screenplay, Set Decoration, Scoring, and Costume Design.)

But Pryor was still delighted. The combination of his own superb reviews and the staggering popularity of *Lady Sings the Blues* all but assured him of a successful career in motion pictures. He did a few clubs and college campuses, averaging $300,000 per year and keeping busy while waiting for the phone to ring. Unfortunately, he waited in vain.

Chapter Nine

Pryor was stunned and disappointed when Hollywood didn't want him to appear in more movies. However, he quickly realized that the problem wasn't with him: rather, his timing was off. He was pushed aside by the so-called "blaxploitation" films, which featured cool, powerful black men or women handing whitey his head. The popularity of these films was predictable backlash against years of oppression onscreen and off and a natural outgrowth of the "black is beautiful" phenomenon. The mass-produced quality of these movies was no less predictable, black and white filmmakers alike taking a hard look at Pryor's "twenty-five million blacks" and realizing that formula movies tailored to this audience guaranteed tens of millions of dollars at the box office.

The blaxploitation craze was unprecedented in terms of the numbers of films produced, the percentage of profit they generated, and the overall lack of quality. Even the low-budget horror films released from 1979 to 1982 don't compare in any of those categories to the superhuman adventures of Shaft and Superfly, of athletes-turned-actors Jim Brown and Fred Williamson, and others. More honest films such as *The Learning Tree* and *Sounder* were rare compared to movies in the action-reactionary mold of *The Spook Who Sat by the Door*, *Three the Hard Way*, *Cleopatra Jones*, *Boss Nigger*, *Stud Brown*, *Black Hooker*, and even horror-blaxploitation efforts like *Blacula* and *Blackenstein*. It wasn't that the good films did poorly at the box office: they simply required more effort to make. Then as now, artists of the quick-buck variety far outnumbered talented filmmakers in Hollywood.

From the beginning of the cycle in 1971 to its demise three years later—which is the average lifespan of a film fad—establishment Hollywood denied the blaxploitation films, more gifted black filmmakers damned them, and civil rights groups protested the way the blacks were portrayed as violent and vengeful. However, the protestors' efforts only worsened the problem, calling attention to those elements that jaded black audiences were hungry to see.

Aesthetics aside, blaxploitation films hurt the black film industry in two ways. First, by providing so many black crew members and creative people with their first screen credits, they relieved Hollywood of the pressure to find creditable work for them. When the cycle fizzled, there was nothing like today's affirmative-action policies for these black artists to fall back on. Equally serious were the limitations these films imposed on black actors. No one was likely to take the tough stars of a *Black Gunn* or *Cleopatra Jones and the Casino of Gold* and cast them in *Network* or *The Goodbye Girl*.

Pryor worked in blaxploitation films, as did virtually every other black performer in the business. But Pryor survived the death of the fad because the characters he played were never in the foreground. After his role as Piano Man, Pryor was regarded as ideally suited to play the sordid, lowlife characters who popped up now and then in blaxploitation films.

As much as he craved more serious assignments, Pryor publicly defended the blaxploitation genre. He said, "I don't think any of these films are going to hurt the moral fiber of America and all that nonsense. The black groups that boycott certain films would do better to get the money together to make the films they want to see, or stay in church and leave us to our work." Privately, however, Pryor didn't care for the films, though he was careful to keep his opinions off the public record lest he offend the people behind the only game in town. But more-established stars had no such reservations. Sidney Poitier, the most successful black actor at the time, spoke for many of his peers when he condemned the films for providing "momentary satisfaction" when "their actors had a bigger responsibility to represent the community on levels more important to its existence."

Though Pryor tried to turn the characters he played into figures that were real or at least sympathetic, the films undermined his efforts. *The Mack*, made in 1973, featured Pryor as Slim, a pimp who is swept up in the war between an Oakland pimp (Max Julien) and the underworld. Better-acted was *Hit!*, made that same year with Pryor and Billy Dee Williams. But it too was undermined by poor writing and an overreliance on action, Pryor playing a small-crafts specialist in this story of a narc's search for the drug dealers who caused his daughter's death.

It was beginning to seem that Pryor's film career succeeded even when he failed. He was so good at playing characters like Piano Man that he got more of them. When he did break away from the type, no one noticed him. Typical were two interesting roles he managed to land in the middle of the blaxploitation craze.

Some Call It Loving was a low-budget film shot early in 1973 and released in November of that year. Based on John Collier's short story "Sleeping Beauty," it's about the romance between jazz saxophonist Robert Troy (Zalman King) and two women, one a carnival "sleeping beauty" (Tisa

Farrow), the other a wealthy Californian (Carol White). Pryor was featured as Jeff, Troy's biggest fan and a drunk who dies of self-abuse halfway through the film.

King remembers that just as in *You've Got To Walk It Like You Talk It or You'll Lose That Beat,* the cast of *Some Call It Loving* was striving above all to create a work of art. "That's why I used whatever clout I had to *get* Pryor again. I thought that he would enrich this film as he had the other, and the people I was working with felt the same way. I think we succeeded to some degree in making an interesting and unusual film, though I'm sure we all wish it had been seen by more than the cast and crew and their families."

King found Pryor to be like many actors with whom he's worked—extremely reserved off-camera yet coming alive once a scene got going. Unlike other performers, Pryor got so totally into the character that he kept throwing in his own dialogue. "What was unusual about that was the way Pryor proved to be much more gifted than anyone around as a writer and as an actor, in terms of knowing what was best for him and what was funny." Twenty years later, King says fondly, "It was really a thrill to work with him, and he absolutely deserves his success."

The offbeat but ponderous *Some Call It Loving* came and went. Pryor had barely more luck in his own milieu, appearing as himself in the omnibus movie *Wattstax.* Filmed in August 1972 at an outdoor festival sponsored by Stax Records, the picture featured performances by artists such as Little Milton and Isaac Hayes. These sequences were intercut with views of life in Watts, the Los Angeles slum that had exploded with violence over a year before. Pryor's scenes, shot in a bar, showed him going through his repertoire of characters new and old—the wino, the junkie, a minister, a pimp, and a frightened ghetto child, among others. The film was not widely seen, though it is valuable today as an example of the black-oriented routines he was performing at that time.

As the blaxploitation films ran out of steam, they left behind one positive element: quality now had to be the cornerstone of any black project that hoped to find financing.

But Hollywood still feared that audiences wouldn't be able to distinguish between good films and bad ones, and for a while *all* black films were considered the kiss of death.

One film that was made during this transition period actually straddled the old and the new, adding characterization and humor to the proven action/ethnic elements of the dying craze. To get it produced, its director and star, Sidney Poitier, had to use every ounce of influence he had. As it turned out, *Uptown Saturday Night* was the surprise hit of 1973, an underworld comedy starring Poitier and Bill Cosby as good-natured opportunists who go searching for stolen money and end up battling the black Godfather, played by Harry Belafonte. Pryor was selected by Poitier to play detective Sharp-Eye Washington. This comparatively brief, straitlaced part didn't allow him much range, but at least it was a change from the sleazier roles he'd been doing. Of course, despite its being a better part, there wasn't much room for it in the spotlight, which doted on the somber Poitier and the endearing Cosby.

The fact that the film was a solid moneymaker would have meant more to Pryor's career had he been allowed to appear in the two sequels, *Let's Do It Again*—which made twice as much money as the first film—and *A Piece of the Action*. But these were Poitier-Cosby vehicles and, as the saying goes, two's company....

Despite the fact that 1972 and '73 were discouraging in terms of movie roles, Pryor was prospering on the nightclub circuit. He had made his way into some of the better clubs, even though he was still doing exactly what he'd done since the retreat to Berkeley. But now people were really listening to what he was saying, and deciding that he wasn't really as militant as he seemed. It was a two-way learning experience: as Pryor put it, their applause and the encounters such as the one he had regarding his "blackness" made him realize that while in one sense he was doing black humor, "it was human humor, too. And human beings were liking it. I'd get confused to see more and more whites in the audience. What was happening was that they were saying, 'Hey, we're people. We enjoy something good.'" He still shunned TV for the most part and shied from interviews, preferring to build his audience primarily through word-of-mouth, which no other comedian of his generation had done.

One film project that held extraordinary promise came to Pryor's attention early in 1973. Comedian Mel Brooks had been approached to direct a spoof of Hollywood westerns, and he went to Pryor for help in writing the script.

Brooks, a former writer for Sid Caesar's classic TV series, "Your Show of Shows," had come into the public eye teamed with Carl Reiner in a series of albums featuring the mock-sage, raucous philosopher the Two-Thousand-Year-Old Man. Before long, the duo had added to their act such lesser-known characters as the frenetic Two-Hour-Old Baby and stuffed-shirt filmmaker Frederico Fetuccini.

Like Pryor, Brooks had always wanted to make movies. To date, he had made two inexpensive comedies: *The Producers* (1968), the tale of a Broadway producer's plan to defraud his investors by staging a sure flop called *Springtime for Hitler*—which, of course, was an enormous hit; and *The Twelve Chairs* (1970), about a nobleman's search through Czarist Russia to find a chair in whose cushion is sewn a fortune in gems.

Both of Brooks's pictures won loyal followings, *The Producers* even nabbing an Oscar for Best Screenplay. However, neither film did well in Peoria. The western comedy would be Brooks's last chance to pitch his bellicose Jewish humor to a wide film audience.

The idea of doing a western spoof wasn't Brooks's but was the brainchild of writer Andy Bergman. Bergman had submitted a screenplay titled *Tex-X* to Warner Bros. As originally written, *Tex-X* was a comedy about a black man in the Old West, a story full of clever but restrained humor. A studio executive was intrigued by the possibility of doing a more outrageous sendup and passed the screenplay to Brooks. The production VP suggested that Brooks work with Bergman, but Bergman wanted to gather a team of writers and, in sweatbox sessions like those that had produced the finest humor on "Your Show of Shows," hammer out an insane collaborative work. His plan made sense to Warner Bros., and they gave Brooks the green light. He hurriedly assembled a staff consisting of himself, the comedy team of Norman Steinberg and Alan Uger, and Richard Pryor, who, in Brooks's view, was "a black person of outré imagination."

Pryor was happy to be onboard, not only because the vehicle would allow him to make cynical comments about prejudice but because in their early meetings Brooks insisted that he wanted Pryor to star. Though no promises were made, Brooks saw no reason why the Warner brass, who had the power to veto any and all casting, would deny him his choice of star. The chance to play a western hero in an innovative screen comedy excited Pryor greatly.

For nine months the team worked doggedly to polish the script, which had undergone a title change from *Tex-X* to *Black Bart*. Before the script was completed, it would go through additional title changes, including *She Shtupps to Conquer*—a reference to the Marlene Dietrichesque seductress Lili von Shtupp—before *Blazing Saddles* was finally decided on.

"We went all the way," Brooks boasted of his crew, "especially Richard Pryor, who was very brave and very far-out and very catalytic in writing heartfelt stuff about white corruption and racism and Bible-thumping bigotry." The story they concocted followed the misadventures of a slick young black named Bart who is pulled from a chain gang and named sheriff of a corrupt town, where the governor (played by Brooks) and his henchmen hope that he will be unable to control their lucrative criminal operations. But not only does the sheriff outfox them, with the help of a washed-up gunfighter named the Waco Kid, in a rousing finale he chases Hedley Lamarr (Harvey Korman), who is the real power behind the inept governor, from set to set on the Warner Bros. lot before galloping into Hollywood for a showdown at the Chinese Theatre.

As expected, the racial jokes flew like slingshots. Given Brooks's penchant for the ribald, it's not surprising that many of them focus on the stereotype of the black sexual goliath. One of Pryor's most memorable contributions to the script occurs when the newly arrived sheriff stands before a crowd, reaches into his pants, and cracks, "Let me just whip this out!''—then withdraws nothing but his orders as the populace sighs with relief. Brooks wrote an equally memorable exchange in which Lili von Shtupp asks the sheriff, "Is it twue vot zey say about how you people are built?" A zipper then grinds open and she gasps, "Oh, it's twue! It's *twue*!" Cut from the film was the sheriff's embarrassed retort: "Excuse me, ma'am. I hate to disillusion you, but you're sucking my arm."

For the most part, Warner Bros. loved the completed script. The only reservation they voiced pertained to a campfire sequence in which bean-eating cowboys break wind across the prairie. The studio felt the sequence was in bad taste and wanted it deleted. Brooks argued that if he was going to spoof Hollywood westerns, he was going to do a thorough job of it. "In every cowboy picture," he said, "the cowboys sit around the campfire and eat 140,000 beans, and you never hear a burp, let alone a bloozer." He was adamant, and Warner Bros. capitulated. They paid Brooks the agreed-upon fee of fifty thousand dollars for his work, the other four writers receiving approximately ten thousand dollars each. Brooks was also given one hundred thousand dollars to direct the film. However, the studio wasn't as agreeable in the matter of casting. In a meeting with Brooks, they made it short if not very sweet: they did not want Richard Pryor to star.

Brooks reacted angrily. He didn't deny that Pryor was somewhat off-center. As he later remarked, "In order to be free and rich and as emotionally abandoned as Richard is, you have to give up certain safeguards; you risk bananaland, and he risks it every day. He gives himself to each moment in life, totally, without a governor. Dumber people don't have many choices, so they pursue their goals more easily than Richard does."

Even while acknowledging Pryor's mercurial nature, however, Brooks dismissed the studio's decision as cavalier. The studio answered that it was nothing of the sort; they simply felt that Pryor was too undisciplined a performer and might ruin the film by failing to stick to the script. Brooks sensed a smokescreen and said so, pointing out that since parts of the script had been written by Pryor, anything he might ad-lib would be well worth listening to. The Warner brass countered that Pryor lacked leading-man experience and had no track record for holding an audience ninety-plus minutes. Brooks reminded them somewhat disgustedly that Pryor had damn near stolen every film in which he had appeared. There was dead silence, after which the truth came out: they were concerned about Pryor's reputation for no-shows. Warner was remembering what had happened at the Aladdin three years before and the other clubs in which he'd performed disappearing acts. There was nothing to ensure them that he wouldn't for some reason walk off their set, thereby stalling the multimillion-dollar film or, worse, forcing them to reshoot everything he'd done.

Brooks didn't believe that that would happen and pointed out that the situations were entirely different. Pryor had made a deep emotional commitment to the film and would see it through, he said. But the decision was out of his hands. Though Brooks had risked all to retain a "bloozer," he had no choice but to get himself another sheriff.

Brooks was not at all pleased, since his admiration for Pryor knew no bounds. "He does characters fuckin' right on; I mean, that's it. He gets all the nuances; he gets the breathing right. You say, 'I know that guy, that's true.' And that's blindingly brilliant and amazing." But if Brooks was upset, Pryor was inconsolable when he learned of the decision. Yet, as upset as he was, Pryor feels he'd have handled it better had he heard the news from Brooks rather than finding out in an extremely humiliating fashion. "I was in the car with Cleavon [Little, who got the part] and Billy Dee Williams, and we were going to a nightclub. They asked what I was doing. Naturally, I said I was going to do *Blazing Saddles*." There was an awkward silence, Pryor recalls, during which Little and Williams exchanged pained looks. Williams finally looked away while Little informed Pryor that he had just signed to do the part.

While it's true that Pryor didn't get the bad news from Brooks, Cleavon Little maintains that things weren't quite the way Pryor described them. "That's a distortion of the story, and I think that Richard or whoever interviewed him mixed the time up. The night Richard refers to took place a year before I knew about *Blazing Saddles*. I'd come to Los Angeles to see about a TV series, "Temperature's Rising." Richard and I and Billy had gone out to the Lighthouse to listen to some music. Richard and I had done a "Mod Squad" earlier, which was where I'd first met him, but that evening at the Lighthouse was the first *and* last time I saw Richard for some time. A year later I was interviewed for the role in *Blazing Saddles*. I knew Richard was one of the writers, but that was all I knew. I had two interviews with Mel Brooks and then I did a screen test; that's how I got the part. I didn't know that Richard had even been up for it, and I have no idea how he learned the part had gone to someone other than himself. But his implication that I was sitting in the car and knew that I'd gotten the part is incorrect. I would never have done something like that."

According to an associate of Brooks, although Pryor's feelings were hurt, there had never been any intention to mislead him. The director's aide says that Brooks was simply following protocol, allowing Pryor's agent to bear him the bad tidings.

Regardless of how it happened, Pryor has nothing but angry words for Brooks. "That movie wasn't funny when I first got there," he said. "*I* told Mel Brooks to put in the farting and shit." As for the part itself, he says, "I didn't want it originally, but I was told I was going to get it. After that I wanted it. I didn't think Mel Brooks was the sort of man who would lie. You get your hopes up. That's the thing that hurt me the most. He hurt me . . . didn't have the decency to call me up and tell me I wasn't going to star in *Blazing Saddles*."

Unhappily, after Little got the part, his relationship with Pryor soured. "There was some animosity between us," Little allows, "though I'd never understood it. It may have been that I'd done something wrong from Richard's point of view, but I never felt that I had. Regardless, I was sorry to see it happen." Pryor felt the same. It wasn't that he blamed Little per se; he was simply unable to dissociate the two. The strain was lessened when Little and Pryor costarred in *Greased Lightning* some years later, though that's the only time they've been together since the debacle of *Blazing Saddles*.

Blazing Saddles opened in February 1974 and became one of the most-popular films ever. Pryor's bitterness was heightened because he felt cheated by the subsequent publicity the film received. Virtually every item gave the impression that the script was solely Brooks's work, minimizing the contributions of Pryor and the other writers. Brooks didn't do this intentionally; in fact, in *Playboy, The New Yorker,* and other forums he gave lavish praise to his coworkers. But he was the man in the public eye, and his was the name that was linked with the film.

(There is an ironic postscript to the saga of Mel Brooks. The following year he collaborated with Gene Wilder to write the equally successful *Young Frankenstein*. However, none of Brooks's subsequent pictures fared as well at the box office, including *A History of the World, Part One*. Reinforcing the irony is the fact that Pryor was to have costarred in that picture but then had to cancel when he was burned; his presence might have insured much heftier box-office receipts, though the press probably would have given Brooks the credit.)

Pryor obviously survived losing *Blazing Saddles,* though the same cannot be said for Little having made it. Critics who originally hailed his performance as "suave" and "slick" have since downgraded his work in light of how much better it's *assumed* Pryor would have done. Typical is Pauline Kael's comment that Pryor would have made the sheriff "crazy, threatening, and funny both."

Little scoffs at such comments. "I don't think it's fair to conjecture with hindsight; we just don't know what would have happened. If Richard had done the film, he would have been directed to give fundamentally the same performance." That would not have allowed Pryor to showcase any of the sassy humor that would win him fans in later films. On the other hand, Little concedes that director Brooks might not have been able to force Pryor into the mold in which Little so effortlessly played. It's impossible to know whether Warner

Bros.' fears might thus have been realized, or whether Pryor would have created the same kind of panic-stricken intensity with costar Gene Wilder that the two later generated in such megahits as *Silver Streak* and *Stir Crazy*.

Brooks refuses to speculate, though he does make one interesting observation. Considering the way Pryor's films have reaped fresh fortunes through video cassettes, *Blazing Saddles*, though popular in that medium, would have done phenomenally better as one of the handful of films in the Richard Pryor catalog. "And boy," Brooks reveals, "is Warner Brothers sorry now."

As for Pryor, he sums up the experience as "a thorn in my heart." The only word he has ever uttered on behalf of the film is an offhanded, "I liked Gene Wilder in the movie; nice choice."

After this fiasco, Pryor stayed away from movies for two years. He won a pair of prestigious honors for his contribution to *Blazing Saddles*, awards from the American Academy of Humor and the American Writers' Guild. Pryor accepted the awards graciously, though he probably would have preferred to see both groups divvy up the script line for line and read publicly the percentages of authorship.

But Pryor's disappointment in Mel Brooks wasn't the only factor that kept him from the screen. He would have considered any part that he felt had some substance, but the demise of the blaxploitation fad caused a temporary collapse of the entire black film industry. Even Poitier's projects, with the exception of his comedy trilogy, smoldered on the launching pad or were dumped into the marketplace without fanfare.

Oddly, it was in the rubble of black moviemaking that the seeds for Pryor's superstardom took root. In order to continue making movies, black actors and filmmakers had to reach beyond their traditional audience and tap into the two hundred million white moviegoers. Stars like Jim Brown and Fred Williamson were doomed, having been typecast in the antiwhite action films. As recently as 1981, Williamson was still churning out these movies at the rate of one every two months, writing, producing, directing, and starring, and breaking even because he spent under a million dollars on each picture. But the films grossed only a small fraction of what they would have a decade before. Black Hollywood had to court a crossover audience before Pryor, Cosby, Paul Winfield, Lou Gossett, and others were able to find work and begin reshaping the black film identity.

In Pryor's case the climb took longer because, first, the other studios knew about the Warner Bros. decision. They saw that *Blazing Saddles* was a hit and assumed that the reasoning about Pryor had been sound. Second, in his soured frame of mind, Pryor returned to his nightclub routines. Creating them was a solo experience, of which he felt, "Bad, good, or indifferent, at least it's mine."

But not everyone in Hollywood was wary of Pryor. Even as Cleavon Little was stepping before the cameras as Brooks's sheriff, a number of people whom Pryor had known for years and respected enormously felt that their projects would benefit from Pryor's talent. Pryor knew that it wasn't pity but his ability that compelled them to solicit his help, and he gladly accepted.

Chapter Ten

During this bleak period, Pryor's sponsors were Redd Foxx, Flip Wilson, and Lily Tomlin. All were appearing on television and worked hard with their staffs of writers.

In addition to scripting, Pryor made guest appearances on the "Flip Wilson Show," ending his four-year hiatus from national TV. Although his former white middle-class constituency barely recognized him, his portrayals of a timorous aerialist and especially of the pool-hustling Peoria Stroker won him excellent notices. He was also cited by Wilson for making contributions to his own bag of characters, such as the Reverend LeRoy of the Church of What's Happening

Now and private eye Danny Danger. These characters were similar enough to Pryor's own preacher and film detectives that he had no trouble sliding right into their personae.

Pryor's writing for Redd Foxx's "Sanford and Son" was somewhat more restricted due to the format of the program. However, "Sanford and Son" had only just premiered in 1972 for a five-year stay, giving Pryor a good deal of freedom to help Foxx develop nuance for the crusty, lower-class junk dealer and the burgeoning cast of supporting characters. His major complaint was the laugh track, and he says he complained to the producers. " 'Don't you think people are sophisticated enough to enjoy something without being told when to laugh?' " he asked. They didn't agree, and as he bitterly told a reporter, canned laughter is nothing more than a way of coercing viewers. "The laughter is in yourself. If you don't want to laugh, you don't have to laugh; you could just be enjoying something. You don't have to laugh because somebody in the audience is laughing."

The best work Pryor did during 1973 was for Lily Tomlin's special "Lily." Tomlin said that of all the talent she had met since coming to Hollywood for "Rowan and Martin's Laugh-In" in 1970, "Pryor is the one that has the most instant rapport with his audience." Aired in November of that year, "Lily" featured skits that were more sophisticated than those on Flip Wilson's show, ranging from the Beverly Hills ban on fat people (filmed in news-documentary style, its classic sequence occurs when police raid a home as its occupant vainly tries to flush a pizza down the toilet) to religion. Not surprisingly, there were run-ins with the censors; in particular, Pryor says, they clashed over a skit involving little kids talking about their bodies. Pryor was playing a little boy who was to have said to Lily's little girl, "I have titties bigger than your titties. First boys have titties, *then* girls." But the censors cut that, leaving Pryor to despair rather poetically, "The earth of it was cut away. As it was growing, someone had these shears. Snap, cut, cut. It was like silly shit that they cut. It was a waste." Pryor won an Emmy for his contributions, and the show itself was honored by the television academy as Outstanding Comedy-Variety Special.

Unlike his previous writing awards, the Emmy meant a great deal to Pryor, reflecting a collaborative work that had been uniquely and uncharacteristically rewarding. Immediately after accepting the statuette, Pryor impulsively flew to Peoria and presented it to someone whom he felt truly deserved it—Juliette Whittaker, the woman who had made his career possible.

Pryor was relatively pleased with his TV work, having always regarded writing as another facet of performing. "It's all the same," he said, "everything is improvisation." But Pryor was first and foremost a performer. Acting wasn't work; it was his very life. If the mood struck him, he could crank up bits and go on for hours. His record was a nonstop barrage at a pool party hosted by Hollywood costume designer Sally Hanson, who says, "He started in just doing Richie during the late afternoon and didn't stop until four-thirty in the morning."

But the time and the people had to be right. He was always uncomfortable just jumping into his stuff, especially on television. One couldn't simply tap his madness, as with Dick Shawn or Mel Brooks. Pryor needed time to build up to it, whether it was onstage or portraying a hernia-bound weightlifter on the "Tonight Show." The few talk shows he did to promote his records, films, and stage appearances were doubly intimidating because, as always, he had no desire to talk about himself. Appearing on the "Mike Douglas Show," he said exactly two lines: that he had met fellow guest-star Martha Mitchell once before, when he portered for her onboard a train (a joke); and that his kids had no respect for any of his achievements, save for the time "I admitted I was their father" (no joke).

Conversely, on another Douglas show, Pryor became so nervous that he couldn't shut up. Comedian Milton Berle was plugging his autobiography and discussing his lovers when Pryor indelicately wondered aloud if Eleanor Roosevelt had been one of them. His comment cued the following hostile exchange:

BERLE: "Maybe I better tell the story another time."

PRYOR: "I'm sorry, Milton. I was out of line. [To himself] Richard, shut up now. The man's trying to tell a story."

BERLE: "Let me just tell you something, baby. I told you this nine years ago and I'm going to tell you on the air in front of nine million people . . . pick your spots, baby."

PRYOR: "All right, sweetheart. I'm sorry . . . honest, I'm just crazy."

BERLE: "No, you're not crazy."

PRYOR: "I'm just having fun here. I wasn't laughing at you. I apologize because I don't want to hurt your feelings. But I don't want to kiss your ass."

BERLE: "[To Douglas] If you want to cut here, it's okay with me. I'd rather not discuss it anymore."

Douglas took his guest's advice; after the break, the tension had been sufficiently defused for the show to go on.

Despite his claims about writing, Pryor was hungry to perform. This need was particularly strong when he had to sit in the wings and watch Tomlin or Foxx perform material he'd helped to mold. Finally he wrote a screenplay, running a western motif through the grinder with the classic chiller *White Zombie* and coming up with *Black Stranger*, the story of a black cowboy who dabbles in the occult. Pryor planned to raise money for the picture and make it independent of the studios that had "blacklisted" him. But, as the saying goes, he couldn't get himself arrested where the film industry was concerned. Even though the budget on *Black Stranger* would have been modest, Pryor was unable to get the project off the ground.

The stage was Pryor's only real creative outlet, and here at least he was in top form. He kept breaking in new material and was hitting his stride with it more quickly than ever.

What's more, he was clearly having fun. He did more routines about things he enjoyed, giving audiences his perspective on everything from none-too-bright boxers ("George Foreman just come out when the bell ring, say, 'Which one the referee, 'cause I'm gonna kill the *other* motherfucker!' ") to movies ("Nigger woulda handled *The Exorcist* differently, woulda walked in the house, 'Bitch, what's wrong with you? Get up outta bed and wash your ass, girl, you're stinkin' up the whole motherfuckin' house. And get the cross outta your pussy.' ")

In one of those ironies unique to the entertainment industry, early in 1974 Warner Bros. asked Pryor to cut an album on the Reprise label. Fortunately, Pryor has a sense of humor and didn't punch out the executives. However, while he had no desire to work with the company that had all but traumatized him a year before, they were waving a sizable sum in his direction and he needed the money. There were old debts to pay, he was still supporting his cocaine habit, and he had always felt that "it's better to have money and not need it than need it and not have it."

Pryor's first Reprise album was titled, flamboyantly enough, *That Nigger's Crazy*. It was taped at Don Cornelius's Soul Train in San Francisco, and, in industry lingo, it went through the roof. What was astonishing about its climb up the charts was that it took only months, rather than the years it took for the Laff albums to see any kind of profit. Furthermore, the people who bought *That Nigger's Crazy* did so entirely on the recommendation of friends. There was no advertising whatsoever, and the album contained nothing a disc jockey could play on the radio. What impressed the people at Reprise even more, however, was that not only blacks were buying the album; young whites were picking it up as well.

That Nigger's Crazy won Pryor the Grammy Award as Best Comedy Recording of the year. It also earned a gold record for generating one million dollars' worth of sales, then quickly surpassed that and earned a platinum record for selling one million albums. Pryor's share of the take was over a quarter of a million dollars.

In the wake of *That Nigger's Crazy,* Pryor did not want for concert engagements. He had more requests than he could handle and accepted dates in San Francisco, Detroit, and in Los Angeles at the *very* legitimate Shubert Theatre. However, at no time did he appear at a mainstream "white" club at the expense of playing to blacks. Since turning his back on the Aladdin, Pryor never again considered the personal benefit of one outlet versus another. He went where he was wanted, where he was loved, and most of all where he felt he could do some good. This philosophy extended beyond concerts. While he loathes having his privacy invaded by reporters, he gave interview after interview to *Ebony* magazine, while repeatedly dodging *Playboy,* which boasts four times the readership. It wasn't a matter of trusting the journalists of one over the other, since *Playboy* interviews are usually conducted by well-respected writers. Rather, he wanted to do what he could to help the sales of *Ebony.*

Not surprisingly, Pryor's benevolence extended in other directions. He didn't enjoy celebrity tennis matches—he detested losing and didn't like being a bad sport in public—yet he participated when he felt the causes were just. He also did what he could to reach children. While he wasn't the only star who did solo segments on the PBS series "Sesame Street," he was one of the few who played to the kids as though he were their best friend and not a stodgy adult. Talented performers including Burt Lancaster, James Earl Jones, and Madeline Kahn have gone on and recited the alphabet, but Pryor and only Pryor brought it to life. "V was *W,*" he snarled, then assured the kids that "X had it covered. Y?" he shrugged. "'Cause that's the *Z* of the game." The letters became language and the language told a story. Performing totally unrehearsed, Pryor, who had been thrown out of junior high school, showed the educators what teaching is all about.

Pryor did other solo segments of the popular PBS program, one of the most memorable portraying a confrontation among three kids in the street. Pryor assumed all three parts, playing a tough kid, a friendly kid, and a wishy-washy kid interacting on a playground. Again ad-libbing, he promoted the virtues of sharing while capturing the essence of youthful values ("You guys have to hold first," one child orders, "because it's *my* jump rope!").

(The "Sesame Street" performances are interesting not only as examples of Pryor's craft but as comparisons of his work with that of Bill Cosby, who was a regular "crosstown" on PBS's "Electric Company." Cosby created delightful variations of his grinning, head-bobbing little-boy character, and children had no problem identifying with that. However, in episode after episode Cosby gave more or less a one-note performance, while Pryor crammed astonishing versatility into his two-minute segments.)

Pryor's concert tours were sellouts. He played to a large, predominately white audience at the prestigious Avery Fisher Hall in New York, where he stuck with crowd-pleasers such as the wino and the junkie, Dracula in the black neighborhood, and his preacher's encounter with God. Conversely, in a return engagement at the Apollo, he tossed in more social asides than usual, particularly about Richard Nixon. Pryor describes his appearance before the jammed, wildly appreciative house that night as "the pinnacle" of his career. He also sold out the Kennedy Center in Washington, where no one left even when the sound system failed. ("Can you hear me?" Pryor screamed to the people in the third tier. When they called down that they could not, he shouted back, "Then how the fuck did you hear *that*?")

In contrast to his bad luck in Hollywood, Pryor *was* able to "get himself arrested" elsewhere—literally as well as figuratively. During June of 1974 he did a ten-day gig in Los Angeles County Men's Jail when the Internal Revenue Service caught up with him for the taxes he neglected to pay during 1967–1970. Even though he felt that the government didn't deserve his money, and woke up each morning expecting the judge to "come down and apologize and let my ass out of there," he had no complaints about his visit. "I was treated with kid gloves," he explains. "They kept me in 'protective custody' so I couldn't mingle with the other prisoners. Said they were afraid the other prisoners would take me for a ransom so they could escape." The special treatment made

him uneasy because everyone else suffered from what he considered dehumanizing conditions. Thus, on the last day of his stay, Pryor talked Flip Wilson into putting on a benefit show for the three hundred inmates. Pryor took the true-to-life part of prisoner 2149-875, Wilson playing Deputy Sheriff Geraldine Jones, and the comedians performed for forty-five minutes. Pryor says he did the show to be sure that he had the inmates' fullest attention when he gave them this heartfelt message: "When you get out, please *stay* out."

Pryor fared slightly better with the law in August of that year during an appearance at the Richmond Coliseum in Virginia. Aware of Pryor's reputation, the police ordered him to clean up his act. He ignored them and was arrested. However, the officers waited until he was finished with his act before moving in. As Pryor observed, "They were going to arrest me *during* the show, but with twelve thousand niggers there enjoying themselves, they had second thoughts." He was charged with disorderly conduct, a court date was set, and he was then released on a five-hundred-dollar bond. However, the charge was soon dropped, at the request of the prosecution, which apparently was unwilling to weather the expected minority backlash.

The success of the record album and concerts was satisfying, but Pryor remained painfully aware of movies. "I'd like to be a big star," he confessed at the time. Indeed, he wanted to be a superstar, a Brando or a Cary Grant, "just become pure light and go off into space." At the time, he considered himself only "a booty star, which is what you got to be before you get to be a movie star." *Boot* was a ghetto term used to describe shoeshine boys and generally included all black men who were low on the professional totem. In other words, Pryor viewed himself as only just starting up the ladder.

With a year of TV and touring behind him, and a good deal of money in his pocket, Pryor felt that it was time to make another assault on the mountain. He began writing another script, called *This Can't Be Happening to Me*. The script is clearly autobiographical, and Pryor's feelings of futility and neglect are revealed in the following scene where the character Richard, dying, has a chat with his prostitute mother. She is busy entertaining a white man, her husband peeking through a keyhole, when Richard approaches and asks:

"Why is this happening to me?"

"Life is like that, Richard. That's the way life goes. Sometimes things just go down that way."

"Is it really good?" interrupts the unfeeling john.

"Oh honey," his mother coos, "there ain't a white man in the world can fuck as good as you."

Tucking what he thought was newfound clout under his arm, he made the rounds of the studios, intending that he would star in this Cinderella story or it simply wouldn't be made. A year later, that tack would work with an unknown actor who wanted to star in the script he'd written, *Rocky*. But what Sylvester Stallone was able to pull off didn't work for Richard Pryor. He was inclined to ascribe these setbacks to the fact that white executives didn't understand him, and he was probably right. However, the overriding problem was that there was still little market for black-oriented films.

Early in 1975 Pryor cut his second Warner album, ...*Is It Something I Said?*, recorded live at the famous Latin Casino in Cherry Hill, New Jersey. Since he had lightened his concert schedule to work on the film project, Pryor went to the Comedy Store in Los Angeles every night for six weeks, working on the characterizations until they glowed. After only a few nights, *New West* magazine stated that the characterizations "were so perfect that he could throw away the original stories, improvise madly, and still have it come out right every time."

Pryor's stars in this outing were the ever-popular Mudbone discoursing on the headaches of posing as a Chinese to get work on the railway; a preacher turning biblical text into something very Motown; Richard Nixon and his cellmate, an ineffective white lawyer; wounded husbands; vicious wives; and cocaine users. Yet, more than the album itself, the record jacket best typifies the comedian's view of himself. Lashed to a tree, kindling spread around his feet, he looks imploringly at the buyer as hooded torch-bearers approach him through the mist. It's Pryor at the Inquisition, not fighting for his life but seeking even at the bitter end to understand the crime he has apparently committed against society.

As *New West* implied, Pryor was completely in control of his material. Of particular interest is the way the street language is integrated into the flow of the act. He uses it frequently, of course, but by emphasizing it less, delivering it with finesse as well as anger, Pryor liberates the rest of his material from its shadow. Explaining the change, he says that it was a result of learning how to govern his energy levels. "By the time I get to the mike, the energy is so high I wouldn't care if a dude in the audience has a heart attack. All they could do is carry him out because I'm going to finish." Instead of channeling this fire into his language, he was learning to spread it around. In doing so, Pryor didn't sacrifice the side of him that was angry and volatile, he simply explored new facets of himself, particularly those that could be as smooth as a Cary Grant . . . or Cleavon Little.

Pryor won another Grammy and numerous other awards for . . . *Is It Something I Said?* and had a second smash seller. Against all odds, in the space of two years, he had not only turned his life around but was making a great deal of money doing material the way *he* wanted to do it. In the process, he was also reestablishing himself as one of the foremost comics of the decade. Like Muhammad Ali, whom he greatly admires, Pryor was making a habit of comebacks. Then, as he had done five years before when things were looking up, Richard Pryor dropped out.

It's easy to dismiss Pryor as a man bent on self-destruction, always managing to climb to prominence and then pulling himself down. But that drive really embraces two distinct causes. David McCoy Franklin, the man who would serve as Pryor's manager for five years, explained one of those problems: "Pryor is a supremely gifted and talented person who does not believe he should be. That is the root cause of a lot of his problems." It's certainly one facet of his Jekyll-Hyde behavior, the strong need to perform followed by guilt for having done it so well and so effortlessly. According to Pryor, nothing in life should be easy, yet this was; the only way to feel better was to tear it down.

"I had to find some trouble every now and then or I wouldn't feel connected," Pryor explained. "Most of my life I spent feeling bad; I'm used to pain. When I'd wake up in the morning feeling good, I'd think something was wrong . . . that really scared me. There was this thing that if you were a comic, you didn't go get healthy because you weren't able to get funny."

But there was another, less esoteric side to his self-destructiveness. Pryor is an impatient and impulsive man, and people or circumstances that fail to satisfy him are not long for this world. It isn't cruelty but simply, as he puts it, "a low tolerance for bullshit." Needless to say, his definition of *bullshit* may not have jived with the one held by the rest of the world, but Richard Pryor didn't care. He lived by his own rules and took the consequences.

Both factors influenced his latest act of professional suicide. While Pryor didn't hate the concerts and records the way he'd hated what he was doing at the Aladdin, he had achieved his goal and now it failed to fulfill him. "I don't really want to go around the country playing clubs, seeing cities," was how he expressed his feelings after turning down a tour guaranteed to earn him one million dollars. It was movies he wanted, and now that he had replenished his fame and finances, he vowed to do nothing else until it was movies he *got*.

Opening an office in Hollywood, Pryor staffed it with secretaries and front-office personnel, then sat back and waited for the phone to ring.

Chapter Eleven

Except for an occasional fluke, as in the case of Stallone, there are really only two ways to get into movies. The first is to have had an enormous hit. That assures you another turn at bat, and as long as you keep hitting the ball you're a moviemaker. The second is to be an insider, chummy with the decision makers and power brokers. Pryor was neither, and he had a poor reputation to boot. All the talent in the world couldn't get him over those hurdles and into quality motion pictures.

Rather than sit around hoping for offers, he accepted a costarring role in one of Fred Williamson's films. He did this in part for the money but primarily to squelch his insecurity about his future in film. This is indicative of the paradox about knocking himself back to "Go" every few years: Pryor brought on the misery willingly, then immediately scrambled in any direction he could to get away from it. Thus, at a time when he should have been changing his image among the Hollywood elite as an actor of little discernment, Richard Pryor took the first job he could find.

The picture was *Adios Amigo,* one of the most amateurish and incoherent films ever made. It was one of the seventeen pictures Williamson produced, wrote, directed, and starred in between 1974 and 1983, and was an attempt to branch into westerns.

"I'd thought that *Blazing Saddles* was a silly film," Williamson contends. "I wanted to make a comedy western without the extremes of showing Gucci saddlebags and other anachronisms, a down-and-dirty, dusty western whose comedy came about from the presence of Richard Pryor."

The story is meager at best. Williamson stars as Big Ben, who is chased from his land by hostile whites. After shooting up the white leader's house in retribution, Ben is arrested and carted to prison in another county. En route, he is freed when a thief and con man named Sam (Pryor) Spade robs his captors. Thereafter, Sam gets himself and/or Ben into numerous tight spots from which Ben must rescue them. These include a showdown with a knife-throwing killer, a chain gang in a mine, a fistfight with a local Goliath, and entrapment by a huge posse. Incredibly, there's no payoff for the whites who hounded Ben in the first place.

The adventure sounds more exciting than it was. Williamson doesn't disagree that the film didn't live up to his expectations, though he feels that this was due largely to his unexpected difficulties with Pryor.

"When I first thought of the film, I wanted to be able to maintain my straight-man figure to Richard's con man, still be tough and do my fight scenes—but just have someone floatin' around me like a butterfly to provide the comedy. Richard was perfect for that, for getting me into situations that required physicalness on my part to get out of.

"But I had a problem: I only had a twelve-page script. Going into this film, I was counting heavily on him to improvise; I wanted to give him an idea, a concept, then just turn the light on him and let him do whatever he wanted. You know what they say about comedians—that you can just open the refrigerator door and the light comes on, the jokes roll on out. Well, Richard's light didn't come on. We'd be on location or on the set and he'd keep turning to me and saying, 'What do you want me to do, what should I say?' I'd look at him and answer, 'Hey, this is *your* scene, Richard. Here's what I'm trying to do with the story; all you have to do is get us from this point to that point.'

"So Richard would nod, and then he'd get in front of the cameras—and do thirty seconds at most. He'd walk off, and I'd be staring at him and say, 'Man, what are you *doing*? I need *more,* go and *do* it.' But he'd stop and tell me he was nervous about it. There was no getting him to do what I wanted, so every night I'd have to sit and write eight or nine pages of dialogue. My twelve-page script ended up being a regulation script, but it kept me up a lot of nights. What kills me is that I *know* how great Richard is—he's probably the funniest man on earth. But as many movies and television shows as he'd done before, in this movie the pressure of having to ad lib just closed him up.''

Pryor's hangup with *Adios Amigo* was that as much as he wanted to be in movies, what he really wanted was the chance to act. It was not his ambition to do on camera the kind of work he'd done onstage.

Pryor's apathy wasn't the only problem Williamson had with his costar. ''Richard also couldn't ride a horse,'' he shakes his head, ''and I should've known better when he told me, 'It's okay, I can do it.' Every time he got in the saddle it was a runaway. We had this pinto for him, and that kind of horse is a little extra-frisky. But Richard let the horse know he was frightened, so whenever he'd get on the pinto it would look back at him as if to say, 'Okay—I got ya now,' and take off, running zigzags at a mile a minute. Richard always hung on, too scared even to scream. We spent, no exaggeration, half our shooting schedule chasing Richard Pryor on that damn animal.''

Adios Amigo was shot in nine days. Released in 1976, it made back its money and kept Williamson's Po' Boy Productions solvent. But Pryor didn't like the film and quickly disavowed it: ''Tell them I'm sorry,'' he said to one reporter. ''Tell them I needed the money.''

Williamson had palled around with Pryor for years before they worked together, and when he heard of Pryor's statements, he felt betrayed. He had provided Pryor with a part close to his heart, a Lash LaRue role, at a time when no one in Hollywood was offering him *any* work. Williamson feels that Pryor's reaction is an example of his immaturity. ''Richard is a strange person, and strange people have strange attitudes. He does things sometimes just so that people will react to them, for impact or humor, and I'm sure that was the case here.'' Williamson doesn't hold it against him, but he wishes Pryor had shown a little more sensitivity for the feelings of his fellow moviemakers.

Williamson considers *Adios Amigo* Pryor's ''thrust'' picture, the movie that propelled him into the major leagues. It was that, but only because the experience was so dreadful that Pryor vowed never again to do a film of such low caliber.

He faced the fact that one of his biggest problems was a lack of objectivity, though he didn't know what to do about it. If something felt or sounded good, he did it without a second thought. Professionally, he could no longer function that way. "I'm good," he would say, "I'm *good*. I don't know if I'm great but I'm better than the stuff I've done, I know." This was true enough, though a few more films like *Adios Amigo* would destroy his chance of escaping the rut in which he was trapped.

The direction that Pryor needed was provided when he met David McCoy Franklin, who was to become the most important and controversial figure in Pryor's professional life.

Franklin is an Atlanta-based lawyer who also maintains an office and residence in Los Angeles. Franklin was not licensed to act as an agent in California, but he considered that a technicality, claiming not to have solicited work per se for his clients but merely to have fielded offers that came their way. In this capacity he handled such stars as Cicely Tyson and Roberta Flack, while in Atlanta working as an attorney, with United Nations Ambassador Andrew Young among his clients.

A short, stocky, no-nonsense man, Franklin, who is black, met Pryor through mutual acquaintances. He showed an immediate perception of Pryor's needs and knew the kinds of problems he was up against. Franklin said that because blaxploitation films had left black Hollywood dependent on the sympathy of white Hollywood, "ninety percent of the black artists are getting ripped off today. The best service I could give them would be to take a machine gun and wipe out all the people around them and start over."

That kind of thinking made a believer of Pryor. "I like David's energy and his creative ability," Pryor remarked at the time. "He's much smarter than anyone he's dealing with and he's not afraid of white people. I knew he was serious when he asked them for more money." He hired Franklin as his attorney and manager, and together they set about remaking not only Pryor's career but his life as well.

Richard Pryor in *Silver Streak* in 1976 (*Wide World Photos*)

Richard Pryor and former girl friend and
actress Pam Grier in *Greased Lightning* (*Wide World Photos*)

Richard Pryor and Diana Ross dancing at Studio 54
(*Wide World Photos*)

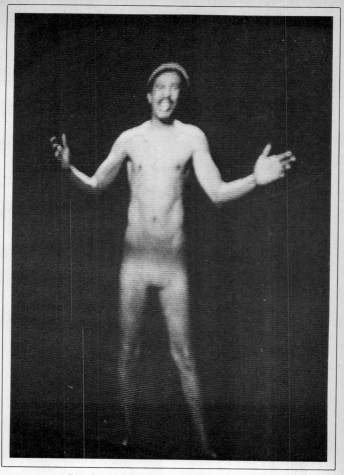

Segment of *The Richard Pryor Show* cut
by NBC censors (*Wide World Photos*)

Richard Pryor speaks at press conference concerning censorship of his NBC Special (*Wide World Photos*)

Richard Pryor and former wife Deborah
enjoying their wedding cake (*Wide World Photos*)

The three faces
of Richard Pryor in
Which Way Is Up
in 1977
(*Wide World Photos*)

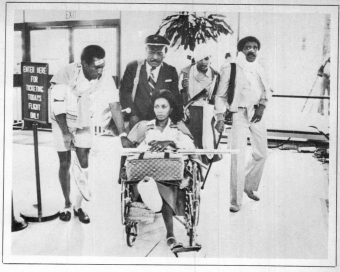

Embattered tennis
players,
Richard Pryor
and company
in *California Suite*
(*Wide World Photos*)

Richard Pryor
with
Jennifer Lee
in 1979
(*Wide World Photos*)

(*Right*) Richard Pryor showing scars from his accident in 1980
(*Steve Schapiro/Sygma*)

Pryor's ex-wife and daughter awaiting
the news of his condition at the hospital (*Wide World Photos*)

Barbara Walters interviews Richard Pryor
six weeks after his accident (*Wide World Photos*)

Richard Pryor on the *Tonight Show*
with Johnny Carson (*Wide World Photos*)

Richard Pryor and Gene Wilder
in a frenzied scene from *Stir Crazy*
(*Wide World Photos*)

Richard Pryor in front of the all wood house
he built in Maui (*Steve Schapiro/Sygma*)

Richard Pryor in Maui with his dog (*Steve Schapiro/Sygma*)

(*Left*) Richard Pryor relaxing at home in Maui
(*Steve Schapiro/Sygma*)

Richard Pryor, star of the concert feature
Richard Pryor Live On The Sunset Strip
released in 1982 (*Wide World Photos*)

Comedian Pryor in *Richard Pryor
Live On The Sunset Strip*
(*Wide World Photos*)

Villainous Richard Pryor salutes
Christopher Reeve in *Superman III*
(*Wide World Photos*)

Professionally, one of their first projects was to incorporate Pryor, which meant, he said, "I don't have to pay a lot of taxes." Pryor was slightly bemused by the whole thing, snickering, "Only in America. I've gone full circle, from underprivileged kid to imperialist, incorporated conglomerate pig." But at least he hadn't lost his perspective: conglomerate or not, he said, "I *still* can't get a cab to take me to Harlem."

In addition to seeing that Pryor's record royalties were paid on time and in full, Franklin expended much effort trying to get him to stop using cocaine. Franklin had informed him at the outset that under no circumstances was he "interested in representing a junkie," although his ambition was more sensible than practical. Pryor was admitting to friends that he shouldn't do cocaine a lot because "it messes my life up," and hard on the heels of joining with Franklin he announced publicly, "I'm through actively messing with my body." Pryor told one reporter, "I love drugs, I really do," but that he was an adult, not a kid, and was equipped to make the break.

Pryor intimated that he changed when Franklin entered his life, but the change was illusory. He made a few career decisions, nothing more, and all his attempts to turn his back on cocaine failed. Franklin apparently wasn't surprised. In the short time they'd been together, he had to have realized that Pryor would never straighten himself out until he was free of the albatross of self-destruction. Franklin wasn't sure how to achieve this, though a sensible first step seemed to be to help Pryor cross the line from "booty star" to movie star.

History was repeating itself in more ways than one.

Pryor had been helped from his last voluntary exile by Berry Gordy, and the young man from Detroit was about to come to the rescue again.

Gordy had made a number of films since *Lady Sings the Blues*, among them *Mahogany*, starring Diana Ross and Billy Dee Williams, and *Scott Joplin*, also starring Williams. Gordy's reliance on Billy Dee wasn't surprising, since Williams had signed a seven-year contract to make movies only for Motown and was collecting $200,000 a year whether he acted or not.

Pryor had not been offered a similar deal, because Gordy's funds were limited and, talent aside, there was question as to which performer was the more photogenic.

What brought Pryor to mind were the staggering sales of *That Nigger's Crazy*. Being in the record business, Gordy was aware that the same youth market that buys most of the albums also attends most of the movies. And there just happened to be a part in Gordy's new film that was ideal for Pryor. There was only one catch: Pryor didn't want to do it.

The film was *The Bingo Long Traveling All-Stars and Motor Kings*. Based on a book by William Brashler, it is a story about baseball's Negro National League during the Depression. Billy Dee Williams was already set to star, along with James Earl Jones. The part for which executive producer Gordy and producer Rob Cohen wanted Pryor was that of third-base player Charlie Snow, an athlete who wanted to get out of the Negro league and into the major leagues. In those days, before Jackie Robinson broke the color barrier, that wasn't possible. Nonetheless, as the All-Stars traveled through the Midwest, the intrepid athlete played as hard off the field as on, alternately pretending to be a Cuban or an Indian— anything to get into the majors.

Pryor, refusing to read the script, had made his decision based on a synopsis. As he explained to Cohen, he'd had his fill of being a costar or featured player. Though Pryor could have used the approximately fifty thousand dollars Gordy was offering, he wanted a starring role. He wasn't being self-destructive this time. He knew that character bits had done nothing to advance his career in the eight years since he'd made *The Busy Body*, and he feared that each new one he did would further cement Hollywood's perception of him as a supporting player.

But Gordy wanted Pryor, and so, script in hand, Cohen drove out to the comedian's house to pitch the project in person. He appealed to Pryor's sense of black heritage, emphasizing the fact that the film would be re-creating a slice of black history that was largely unknown to the general public. It was a calculated argument, but it touched a nerve. Pryor read the script and was impressed with the honesty of the treatment. What moved him even more was the alternately silly and tragic nature of Charlie Snow; he could identify with the man's desperation. Although the role wasn't the lead, there was, as there had been in Piano Man, at least enough in it for Pryor to mount a showstopping display. He agreed to do the film.

The Bingo Long Traveling All-Stars and Motor Kings was filmed in July 1975. The cast and crew traveled to Macon, Georgia, where Gordy's scouts found settings that resembled the impoverished locales described in Brashler's book.

The trip was an eye-opener for Pryor. It was the first time he'd been in the South for an extended period, and he was upset by the conditions under which the blacks were living. The big-city ghettos, for all their flaws, were at least part of the current decade; but the small towns in which the film was shot were unchanged since the height of the Depression. And the Southern blacks were not only poor but were pathetically complacent to be so.

Pryor doesn't like mingling with outsiders when he's making a movie. "When you're working," he says, "you can't waste your time doing that—you need all the extra moments you have to concentrate on what you're doing." However, in the early shooting on this picture, he watched the local people from the sidelines and before long found himself drawn to them. The feeling was mutual. Though Pryor wasn't the star of the film, he was the star of the set. The locals had seen him on television, read about him, and heard his records; and they were far more excited about his presence than that of Billy Dee Williams.

Pryor didn't visit with these people when he was working, but at night. Rather than go back to the hotel, he would stay and do his routines for them, often into the early morning hours. "You look at them," he said once of common folk everywhere, "some brothers and sisters who can't read, some who may have their combs sticking in their heads, or a big fat black woman with her hair going every which way—but when you live with them and hear them talk, you know that they are some of the smartest people on the planet." Producer

Cohen describes it as a "real joy" watching Pryor enjoy himself. He told interviewers Fred Robbins and David Ragan that the few times he overheard Pryor and his fans, "they would get going into the black dialect so thick that . . . I couldn't follow it. It just got going quick. Every once in a while, he'd go blah-blah-blah and there would be this huge burst of laughter." Pryor was back in the streets again, and he hadn't been so much at ease in years.

Unfortunately, that fraternal experience was virtually all that Richard Pryor took from *The Bingo Long Traveling All-Stars and Motor Kings*. The specialized picture did well at the box office, managing to earn over half the money grossed by the far more commercial *Lady Sings the Blues*. Pryor's work won him his best notices since that last Motown film. However, the performance critics reviewed was not quite the one Pryor had given. It had been hacked to the bone in the cutting room, the producers using Pryor for his name value but opting to cover their bets by giving the bulk of screen time to sex symbol Williams. So much for his part in boosting black heritage.

Pryor was more hurt than disappointed. But, reassured by Franklin that his time would come, Pryor was determined not to let the system beat him.

Yet, as much as Pryor was sinned against, he also remained a sinner. Author Brashler, who interviewed Pryor for *Playboy*, experienced firsthand the two Richard Pryors that friends and associates were always talking about—the "berserk angel" (the title of his piece) and the shy, reticent little boy.

"When I contacted his office about doing this piece," Brashler wrote, "Pryor personally phoned me and said he'd be glad to talk, though he preferred not to be subjected to a long interview. I told him that was fine and, in almost inaudible tones, he thanked me. He often thanks people." Brashler was instructed to fly to Hollywood to meet with Pryor. After waiting for several days to see him, the author learned that his subject had flown to Hawaii, Pryor aides informing Brashler that this sort of behavior was nothing new. "He is likely to remain incommunicado for days," the author was told, "cancel appointments, renege on personal commitments, or simply go off somewhere."

Brashler left Los Angeles as curious as he was disgusted. One month later he received a call from Pryor. Without apologizing or even mentioning the incident, Pryor gave him an hour-long phone interview. The somewhat schizophrenic portrait of Pryor that emerged whetted the publisher's appetite for a feature interview, but Pryor still refused to allow anyone to probe that deeply into his private life.

The Bingo Long Traveling All-Stars and Motor Kings was released by Universal Pictures. Like Gordy, Universal had seen box-office potential in Pryor's youth appeal, and even before the baseball film had gone into the marketplace the studio offered him a part in an omnibus comedy called *Car Wash*. It was a way of testing his appeal without committing an entire film to him.

The nominal plot of *Car Wash* featured cars rolling in and out of a car wash, with musical and comedic interludes by George Carlin, Garrett Morris of "Saturday Night Live," the Pointer Sisters, Professor Irwin Corey, and others. Pryor was offered the part of Daddy Rich, founder of the Church of the Divine Economic Spirituality. Advocating the worship of money instead of God, Daddy Rich practices what he preaches by wearing expensive jewelry and driving around in a gold Rolls-Royce.

Pryor was not at all keen to do the picture. Even in the telling, the role was superficial. Besides, this was 1976: years had passed since the days of *Dynamite Chicken, Wattstax,* and *The Phynx*. He didn't want to do a picture in which he was just part of an insane ensemble. However, experience had taught David Franklin that steady exposure in major studio releases was a good way to work up to better parts. Though Pryor was unhappy with the role, there was no denying that the picture would do him more good than harm. Pryor more or less sleepwalked through the picture, but once again he was cited by most critics as being the best thing about the film. Indeed, *New York Times* film critic Vincent Canby wrote that with Pryor's obvious talent, it was only a matter of time before he would "suddenly become a star on his own."

Pryor's faith in *Car Wash* as an artistic disaster was upheld by filmgoers, who sent the picture limping back to Universal with grosses that didn't reach even the modest level achieved by *The Bingo Long Traveling All-Stars and Motor Kings*. But the theory of acting even in low-grade mainstream films wasn't wrong. It was simply a matter of paying dues and waiting for a better vehicle.

Chapter Twelve

Pryor wasn't a movie star by anyone's definition. What he had was a large following and impressive reviews in every film he had ever made. However, by the middle of 1976 he had one thing more.

Pryor was shooting a movie for Twentieth Century-Fox, which he had agreed to make because, although he was not enamoured of the part, it was larger than any he had ever been offered before. But he and the film's director had hit it off perfectly, there was something magic going on between Pryor and his costar, and word around the lot was that Fox would have a blockbuster at Christmastime.

The scuttlebutt wasn't lost on Universal. Richard Pryor had always *seemed* to them a good bet for stardom, since he had proved that he could make an impact in minor roles. Now, as he was allegedly working wonders in this new film, they were more convinced than ever. And they were willing to back it up with their checkbook.

At the studio's request, Franklin set up a meeting between himself, Pryor, and Thom Mount, executive vice-president in charge of production at Universal. The site Franklin chose was Pryor's new home in Northridge. The location itself told Franklin that Universal was eager, for the studio deal maker was abandoning his home turf, where he'd have been infinitely more at ease. But Franklin didn't necessarily want the Universal representative at ease: he wanted to make the best deal possible for Pryor. Thus, while Pryor stretched out on a white sofa and only half-listened, Franklin and Mount hammered away at each other over the career they hoped Pryor would have with Universal.

Hours later, the men had agreed in principle to a deal unparalleled in Hollywood history. Universal would pay Pryor nearly one million dollars a year for four years, for which they would receive the first right of refusal on six films Pryor might wish to make. Pryor didn't even have to appear in these movies, though if he did he would be entitled to a hefty share of the profits. As part of the agreement, Universal committed itself to develop projects on its own for Pryor, buying novels or screenplays that they felt were suited to his talents. In any of these projects he chose to undertake, Pryor was guaranteed complete creative control.

Remarkable as this deal was, the most astonishing concession was that Universal would allow Pryor to star in films for other studios. In allowing him this freedom, Universal felt certain that Pryor would want to star in films of his own creation, and since they got first crack at those, they didn't doubt that they'd be getting the best of Richard Pryor. They were taking the chance that no other studio would offer him a project as desirable as one he would design himself.

It was the first such contract in the half-century history of Universal Pictures. Explaining why they made so many concessions to someone with a good but not unblemished record, Mount said at a press conference that because "Richard tells the truth about the human condition . . . we believe it is possible to make money on class-A pictures that not only star black people but are made by black people." Mount also felt Pryor would find a broad crossover audience. Pryor heard Mount out before responding with typical paranoia, "I guess that means if these movies don't make money, a whole lot of niggers gonna be in trouble."

Bill Cosby had never doubted Pryor's crossover appeal. He said that in Pryor's audience one was likely to see "dudes with blue blazers and penny loafers sitting next to a cat who has just taken a needle out of his arm." What that meant in terms of box office, said Cosby, was that Pryor would be "a twenty-ton elephant." Mount and Franklin were no less confident—though Mount was nervous while Twentieth Century-Fox put the finishing touches on Richard Pryor's first big-budget, costarring vehicle. If it was a hit, he'd have beaten the rush to Richard Pryor. If it fizzled, he might well find himself in the unemployment line.

A year before, *Silver Streak* had been one of the "iffier" projects on the Twentieth Century-Fox production schedule. Gene Wilder had been signed to star, but that put no one's mind at ease. Wilder had not done well in December 1975 with *The Adventures of Sherlock Holmes' Smarter Brother*, of which he had been both star and director. Because it fell so far short of Wilder's previous two films, *Blazing Saddles* and *Young Frankenstein*, Hollywood felt that he was a potent box-office draw only when teamed with Mel Brooks. Compounding doubts about *Silver Streak* was the fact that the director, Arthur Hiller, hadn't had a hit since *Love Story* five years before.

There was precious little else going for *Silver Streak*. Costar Jill Clayburgh was a fine actress but unknown, and the film's other star, Patrick McGoohan, was certainly not a box-office draw. Pryor was the ace in the hole.

Hiller had seen Pryor in a local nightclub and, having admired his film performances, approached him through Franklin. Pryor was inclined to do the film even without reading the script. Hiller's 1975 film version of the play *The Man in the Glass Booth* was one of Pryor's favorite movies; though it had been a commercial flop, he had seen it more than fifty times. Franklin cautioned Pryor to read the script just the same.

A meeting was held at Hiller's office at the studio, and the director recalls, "It was one of those really satisfying meetings where everyone was liking each other and the project very much." Though the script itself hadn't taken Pryor's breath away, it was reminiscent of Hitchcock's classy mysteries, wherein an ordinary man is thrust into extraordinary circumstances involving theft, murder, and blackmail.

130

Pryor felt that *Silver Streak* could be a solid hit, and while he would not be playing the Cary Grant part, at least he wasn't consigned to the background. In fact, once he had been cast, the script was reworked to give Pryor's character more to do.

In Colin Higgins's scenario, publishing executive George Caldwell (Wilder), traveling the Silver Streak from Los Angeles to Chicago, strikes up a friendship with fellow passenger Hildegarde (Clayburgh), who is accompanying her art-professor boss on a book-promotion tour. That night, the professor is murdered, and Caldwell, who has seen the body, is thrown off the train. He survives but, worried about Hildegarde's safety, manages to intercept the Silver Streak at a later stop.

Hildegarde seems oddly distant to him, but, more surprisingly, the professor is alive. Caldwell subsequently learns from an FBI agent that the man who he thinks is the professor is actually someone impersonating him to discredit the book. It seems there are findings that will ruin the career of an art critic named Devereau (McGoohan), who has been authenticizing fakes for his own monetary gain.

Devereau learns that Caldwell is onto him. Caldwell, battling a henchman atop the train, is knocked from the Silver Streak by a signal light. At the nearest town, he falls in with a petty thief named Grover (Pryor), who helps him get back onto the train where Caldwell is captured and locked with Hildegard in Devereau's cabin. Enter Grover, dressed as a porter. He pulls a gun on Devereau; in the ensuing gunfight, Grover and Caldwell are forced to jump from the train.

Later Caldwell and Grover hop aboard again and find Hildegarde. But after Devereau kills the engineer and is himself shot, the Silver Streak becomes a runaway. Its three surviving passengers manage to unhook their car before the train slams into Chicago's Union Station.

The additions made in deference to Pryor were insignificant in terms of the narrative. The film is still fundamentally the romance between Caldwell and Hildegarde, wrapped up in the Devereau intrigue. However, the changes may have made all the difference in terms of the film's ultimate appeal.

"Originally," Hiller says, "Pryor did not return with Wilder to the train the second time. After they are rescued by the FBI, Grover said, 'I want to go home,' and did—and that was the end of him. But once Colin and I talked to Pryor, we got so enthused with *his* enthusiasm that we decided he had to come back. So Colin rewrote the script.''

As a result of the changes, the film took on a different flavor. For the first half of the film, Wilder played his typical bubble-headed persona. The picture was fun but shallow. In the second half, the unique balance between the frantic Wilder and the cool but explosive Pryor gave the film its vitality and interest, which, helped along by the clever murder mystery, made *Silver Streak* much more than the sum of its parts.

There are two scenes for which the film is best remembered, sequences in which Pryor is so good that it's quite possible that they alone made him a star.

The classic bit is one in which Grover and Caldwell must sneak past G-men at one of the Silver Streak's station stops. Approaching a black station attendant, Grover buys some brown shoe polish, a radio, and a cap. Taking Caldwell into the men's room, he helps him black his face, shows him how to hold the radio to his ear, and gives him a crash course in "acting black." The uptight Caldwell gripes that it'll never work, but gives it a try. He emerges from the men's room a spastic, ludicrous figure who, on his own, never would have made it past the agents. Though Grover is painfully aware that the impression stinks, Pryor's grim expression gives the bluff a veneer of credibility. His solemnity tells the agents, *Yes, this guy is crazy, but* I've *got things under control*. It isn't just the brass of the maneuver that makes the ploy—and the scene—work, but the chemistry between the two characters. The agents, dumbfounded, are unable to focus on either of them and merely take in the dizzying whole.

More of a showpiece for Pryor is his attempt to pass as a porter in order to save his friends. Director Hiller sets up the scene masterfully. A black porter serves Devereau his breakfast and leaves. As Devereau advises Caldwell that he is soon to die, a black porter returns, his features unseen. The camera dwells on Caldwell's gloomy expression, which brightens when a familiar voice asks Devereau, "Coffee, mister?" Cut to Grover, smiling impishly.

Pryor does a fine job playing a thief trying to act the domestic, at the same time stalling until he can get the lay of the land. When he makes his move and spills the scalding coffee, Devereau calls him a nigger and Grover blows his cool. Yanking a pistol from his jacket, he shrills in vintage Pryor, "*Say,* man, who you callin' a *nigger,* huh? You don't *know* me well enough to call me a nigger! I'll slap the taste outta your mouth! You don't even know my *name*. I'll whoop your ass, beat the *white* off your ass."

Yet, except for the chastising of Devereau, Pryor did no ad-libbing whatsoever. It wasn't necessary, because director Hiller understood Pryor's range and had communicated this to author Higgins for the rewrite. "Tailoring the script to him was a matter of distilling what Pryor did in his act and fitting it carefully in our story," explains Hiller. "When I had seen him on the stage he was just magnetic, but if you watch any of his films he's a different performer. No less magnetic, but more controlled; it's what people mean when they talk about his skill. He gives audiences emotional feelings because he exudes so much warmth and compassion. Even when he plays a heavy, he's full of humanity." Pryor brought his unique delivery and pace to the perfectly molded script, leaving Hiller to marvel, "If it's not true that there isn't anything Pryor can't do, it's pretty close to true."

Hiller reports that throughout the length of the shoot in Calgary, Pryor was extremely cooperative. "I've heard things about Pryor misbehaving on other pictures, about arguments and fights, not showing up, and that sort of thing. But on this film we had no problems like that at all." Pryor was never late, always knew his lines, and didn't miss a single day of shooting. "All of us really enjoyed it," Hiller says, "and a lot of that is due to Gene Wilder. Gene is very giving, very easy to work with." Pryor had been predisposed to like his costar if for no other reason than that Wilder was the only member of the *Blazing Saddles* team by whom he did not feel betrayed. But it was Wilder's patience, good humor, and generosity as a performer that really won Pryor over.

As *Silver Streak* was assembled in the editing room, the film began to look like a winner. Pryor felt the electricity, and the director says he seemed to be in heaven, "at ease with all of us, full of fun." Hiller elaborates, "I remember we went to dinner one night in Calgary, about fifteen of us. Suddenly the waiters were coming at us with a cake and singing happy birthday to me, which was very sweet—except that it wasn't my birthday. Richard had set it up, and it didn't matter to him that he was a half-year off. It was just his way of being friendly and amusing."

Pryor did indeed work hard on the film, feeling that if *Silver Streak* worked, he would continue to work. Yet, when the film was in the can he claimed to have had no affection whatsoever for the project. "I put myself in *Silver Streak* but I didn't do it with my heart. It was a business decision." His criticism didn't stop with mere disparagement. He went on to say, "I was looking to hustle and I got hustled," meaning that while he intended *Silver Streak* to be his vehicle into top-quality films, everyone else was using his contributions to their own advantage. He represented himself to the press as the well-meaning black who had been taken by whitey once again, singling out the blackface sequence as a perfect example of how he had been used: "They felt that having a real black actor in the movie would sort of make it all right."

Nothing could be further from the truth, according to Hiller. "The only thing that troubled Pryor was the *way* we did that scene. We completed the first day of shooting, did most of the scene, and that night Richard called me. He was very calm, very polite, but a little upset because he felt that some of the things were maybe a little antiblack. I said, 'Well, you have to tell *us* that,' since it was obviously something he would know better than we. Anyway, I told him, 'Let's do the scene again tomorrow,' and I promised that we wouldn't use any of that day's work. That's exactly what we did, and he was happy with it." Hiller says that when they watched the second set of rushes—the footage that had been reshot—he asked Pryor over and over if he was satisfied. Pryor said that he was. According to Hiller, Pryor was extremely appreciative for the chance to have settled his

134

qualms over the scene. "To be honest, though," Hiller concludes, "there was very little difference between the two versions that I was aware of." All Pryor had done was make Grover a little less tolerant of Caldwell in blackface, torn between necessity and the fact that that makeup traditionally has been used to degrade blacks. The change in his attitude signaled to the audience that Pryor and his character, Grover, had accepted the disguise only as a clumsy attempt to *be* black, not as a visual gag mocking blacks.

While Hiller is confident that "during the making of the film the lavatory scene was *all* that disturbed Pryor," that isn't quite accurate. There was an incident that bugged Pryor more than anyone ever knew, and that was when they were back in Hollywood, shooting the interiors, and Mel Brooks came to visit Wilder on the set. In the course of running around and doing his loud, bad-boy schtick, Brooks locked his arm around Pryor's neck, holding him and yelling to the other cast members that Pryor was "wonderful and talented" despite the fact that he wasn't Jewish. Pryor laughed uproariously through round after round of Brooks's wisecracks. He did so not because he thought any of comments were funny, but because it would keep him from crying. When Brooks departed with Wilder, Pryor stalked off to his dressing room, fell onto the bed, and tried in vain to prevent the years from peeling away, the hurt from rushing back.

No one connected with *Silver Streak* believes that Pryor really felt the way he says he did, and certainly it was no one's intention to use him. Hiller had capitulated beyond duty's call regarding the blackface bit and insists, "You couldn't have asked for a better group" on either side of the camera. Pryor was simply repeating the scenario of *Adios Amigo,* protecting himself against potential criticism by damning the film himself. Pryor's comments were also his way of apologizing to blacks for having "abandoned" them to do a mainstream "white" film.

There is no question that it galled Pryor to have to smile at people he didn't like or ask for changes in a script. He didn't enjoy putting on airs, and he didn't want to hurt other people or be disliked as a result of having done so. Only when such circumstances were past him would Pryor get angry and mouth off, and then with excessive force because he was disgusted with himself for having been dishonest in the first place. Few people understood this, of course, fueling the popular impression that Pryor had an extremely bad temper.

Happily, Pryor and his coworkers were amply rewarded for their efforts on *Silver Streak*. The picture returned nearly thirty million dollars to Twentieth Century-Fox, making it one of the top fifty grossing films in motion-picture history. At the same time, it earned Pryor extraordinary reviews. Overnight, his dream had come true: he was a hot box-office commodity. "I like it on top," he said. "I got here myself. I earned it. I love it." In the wake of achieving stardom, he said he'd "drive down the street, roll up all the windows, and yell at the top of my lungs, 'Yahoo!'" It also gave him pleasure to make others happy. He donated regularly to numerous charities—from muscular dystrophy to Kwanza, a society of black actresses—not small sums but $100,000 at a clip; he was also a great gift-giver, buying a $52,000 Rolls-Royce for Franklin and a diamond pinkie ring for his record producer Biff Dawes, regularly giving money or presents to all the messengers and secretaries who worked with him on films, and, as always, lending money to anyone who needed it. The cynics said that he gave so much because he wanted to ensure support and respect if ever the chips were down, but Pryor paid them no attention. Success meant that he didn't have to listen to anyone but himself. Fittingly, his would prove to be the most critical voice of all.

Of course, it also meant that now Thom Mount could rest easily, knowing he'd made a good deal.

Chapter Thirteen

Chronic worrier that he is, Pryor would probably have been anxious about the fate of *Silver Streak* after its completion, had there been time. But he jumped right into a new project, his backbreaking schedule no doubt inspiring at least some of the hostile remarks he was making about the film.

Pryor wasn't one for leisure activities, though the first half of 1976 had been especially demanding and he could have used a rest. Even mere diversions were few and far between, but Pryor embraced them whenever he could. Typical was the day he heard someone on the *Silver Streak* set comment that Muhammad Ali was going to be thrashed by Japanese wrestler Inoki in their hoked-up exhibition fight. Upset at the prospect of his hero losing, Pryor purchased sixteen tickets to the closed-circuit TV broadcast at the Hollywood Palladium, inviting friends along just to give the champ "psychic" support. The fight ended up being so dull that there were more jeers than cheers, though Pryor did come to life when Ali called his foe a "mother" into the microphone. For the rest of the night all he could talk about was how that "that word" had finally been beamed off a satellite in outer space.

Pryor's new project was a record that would be his last entirely original album to date. A cynical tribute to the craze that possessed America for over a year, the album was titled *Bicentennial Nigger.*

Bicentennial Nigger was recorded in Los Angeles at the Roxy in July 1976, a few days after Pryor finished *Silver Streak*. He had twice postponed the recording because the picture wasn't yet finished, and was inclined to put it off yet again, since he was leaving to shoot another film in less than

137

a week and wouldn't have time to polish the new material before a number of audiences. But after doing it at the Comedy Store for three days, he decided the show was as ready as it would ever be and gave Warner Bros. Records the green light.

The Comedy Store interlude was important to Pryor because, more than just the chance to do a dry run, it was a reminder of his standing among other nightclub comics. When word reached the Comedy Store that Pryor was on his way to break in some new material, an employee phoned Freddie Prinze, Pryor's self-described biggest fan. Sitting at the bar with other comedians, Prinze watched Pryor do his show, muttering to himself, "He's the best, he's the goddamn best. If I could get *five* minutes like any of his stuff, I'd come for months." There were times when Prinze got so excited watching Pryor that he would start punching people in the arm.

The adulation of Prinze and the others flattered Pryor. Before, his attitude had been one of suspicion. "Nice that they say they love me," he snickered, "but I see it like the western movies, just the young gunfighters waiting for the old man to show up." But this night was different. Pryor no longer felt threatened or especially competitive, and he needed all the encouragement he could get.

On the night of the *Bicentennial Nigger* recording, Pryor was a psychosomatic wreck. His back was sore, his legs were stiff, and he was nauseous. He confided to a friend backstage that he was afraid he wouldn't be funny, and his state of mind very nearly caused that to be a self-fulfilling prophecy.

Onstage, after a seemingly endless shower of applause, Pryor began talking about race, about cocaine, and about the recent Ali-Inoki bout—subjects that drew appreciative but subdued laughter. He was uptight and the audience knew it; he could hear people talking to one another and shifting restlessly in their seats. Pryor wanted to go off and hide somewhere, but his peers and friends were in the audience, entertainers like singers Smokey Robinson and Minnie Riperton. Pryor didn't want to walk off a performance in front of another black artist.

Pryor plugged on until, several minutes into the show, someone yelled out, "Get crazy, man!" This was followed by cries of "Right on!" and Pryor just stood there, stunned. Then, as though reacting with a delayed fuse, he stomped forward and shouted, "What you *talking* 'bout, nigger? You wanna *fight*?" The challenge brought the house down, and the break loosened Pryor up, sending him on the way to one of the best and most irreverent performances of his career.

In *Bicentennial Nigger,* Pryor's preacher no longer brags about meeting God. In fact, he more or less throws mud in His face when explaining that he's heard there will be an end to oppression "when an angel come up out of the sea. He will have seven heads and a face like a serpent and a body like a lion." The preacher assures his listeners, "I don't know 'bout you, but I don't want to *see* no motherfucker look like that. And if I see him come up out the water, I'm gonna shoot him in the ass." Later, explaining his ministry's policy toward healing, the holy man roars, "I like to say to the cripple peoples that come here—can't you find *another* church to go to? Goddamn, you come in knockin' shit down and breakin' up furniture and shit. And you deaf and dumb motherfuckers, we don't *need* you here! All that 'hooo-haaa' shit—kiss mah *ass*!"

Not even Pryor's good friends were sacrosanct. Actress Rosalind Cash was in the audience, and while he's quick to praise her performances on the screen, Pryor can't resist adding that in the bedroom it's a different matter. "Bitch won't give me *no* parts of the pussy, babe. I have begged for the pussy for seven years. 'Please, Roz, just let me smell it.' " Blacks as a whole also come under unusually harsh fire. Mudbone bemoaning how "niggers ain't made outta what they used to be made outta. You could stab a nigger four or five times and it wouldn't hurt him. Nowadays you cut a nigger and he shit on himself."

Once in a while Pryor gets around to addressing the Bicentennial theme of the album, as when he remarks at how far blacks *haven't* come since the Revolution. "I went to see a movie about the future, *Logan's Run,* and there ain't no niggers in it." He lets audiences in on the obvious conclusion: "White folks ain't plannin' for us to be here." He also delivers a stinging, very serious monologue by the "Bicentennial Nigger," who was reduced from being a king in Africa to a slave in America, had his life expectancy shortened from two hundred to fifty-two years, watched his family sold and divided, and can look forward to another two hundred years of the same.

The material isn't all quite so embittered, balanced between jabs at Shakespeare, white women, and Hollywood. His characterizations are particularly inspired, especially when the audience calls for their favorites and Pryor ad-libs them.

Bicentennial Nigger won the recovered Pryor a standing ovation, not to mention his third Grammy. Like the Warner albums before it, this one went gold, and Pryor's take from the sales swelled his bank account by one million dollars.

Pryor's transition from recording star to screen star effectively put an end to the former. However, that didn't put an end to the albums—only to those featuring new work. With the exceptions of *Wanted, Richard Pryor Live in Concert* in 1978, which consists of material he developed for his first concert movie, the soundtrack of his film *Live on the Sunset Strip* two years later, and the album of his 1983 concerts, virtually everything came from the files. Earlier that year a small label called Tiger Lily, which had been allowed to tape one of Pryor's dates at P.J.'s in Los Angeles, hurried out an album titled *L.A. Jail*, while Laff issued *Richard Pryor Meets Richard & Willie & the S.L.A.*, consisting of "filler" by the popular ventriloquist.

Laff has since issued ten additional records: *Are You Serious???* in June 1977; *Who Me? I'm Not Him* in November 1977; *Black Ben the Black Smith* in March 1978; *The Wizard of Comedy* in September 1978; *Outrageous* in July 1979; *Insane* in February 1980; *Holy Smoke* in August 1980; *Rev. Du-Rite* in May 1981; *The Very Best of Richard Pryor* in April 1982; and *Super Nigger* in the spring of 1983.

To keep its own sales force busy during Pryor's hiatus, Warner Bros. served up *Richard Pryor's Greatest Hits* in 1977, consisting of material from both his Laff and Reprise albums as well as a previously unreleased cut about Muhammad Ali. Apart from this, the only other album in the Pryor log is *Richard Pryor Live,* which came from World Sound Records in 1977 and was reissued in 1982 by Phoenix 10 Records. Since the original *Richard Pryor Live* had been produced as part of a tax-shelter deal, never to be rereleased, the Phoenix 10 record was withdrawn from the market.

In light of Pryor's recent success, Universal wasn't the only studio eager to get Pryor's name on a contract. In fact, while *Silver Streak* was still in production, Twentieth Century-Fox had been busy scouting around for another project. What they came up with was a black version of *Cyrano de Bergerac,* with Pryor playing the swordsman-poet role, which had won José Ferrer an Oscar. The studio was prepared to send cast and crew to exotic locations in Haiti, but the project fell through because Pryor and Franklin weren't happy with the man who had been chosen to direct the film. "He wanted to experiment on us," Franklin charged after meeting the novice director. The attorney didn't want anyone learning his craft at Pryor's expense, and the aspiring director was quite annoyed. Since he also happened to be a business manager at Brut Productions, which had agreed to cofinance the film with Fox, the project was canceled.

However, Pryor didn't have time to mourn. While Universal was kicking around potential properties, including an adaptation of George Orwell's *Animal Farm,* a remake of *Arsenic and Old Lace,* and a sequel to *The Sting* costarring Lily Tomlin (none of which were ever produced), Warner Bros. offered Pryor a screenplay that they'd optioned with him in mind. Actually, they wanted Pryor for more. Less than three years after they considered him not good enough for *Blazing Saddles,* they suggested that this new film be part of a package deal. After several hours of negotiations with Warner executives, Pryor and Franklin brought home yet another multimillion-dollar deal. This one was for four films to be created jointly by Warner Bros. and Richard Pryor Entertainment, Inc. In short, Warner would develop projects for Pryor and would have dibs on whatever Pryor films Universal decided not to make.

The industry was impressed, though Pryor remained humble enough to point out that if the first film flopped, "it'll become a *one*-picture deal."

The picture in question certainly didn't have a lot of popular appeal. Called *Greased Lightning,* it was the true story of Wendell Scott, the first black to become a championship race-car driver. Like *The Bingo Long Traveling All-Stars and Motor Kings,* it was set in the heart of repression and poverty.

Greased Lightning gave Pryor his first chance at a dramatic leading role. That appealed to him enormously, of course, but equally important was the fact that he understood Scott. Pryor describes him as "special kind of people," and obviously saw a lot of himself in Scott. "When he was a kid, they told him the rules. They said, 'You can't cross that street over there until the light changes.' And he said, 'I understand all that, but excuse me.' And he went and crossed the street. And he didn't get hit by no car—nothin' happened. So he made the rest of the kids feel stupid for listenin'." Pryor's portrayal of this independent yet ingratiating character was excellent, particularly when he expressed the man's boyish love for automobiles, which was a variation on a theme Pryor well understood—the bond between a cowboy and his horse.

Pryor worked hard on the shoot, which lasted into the fall of 1976. Again he spent several weeks in the South, this time in Madison, Georgia. Unlike his last visit, there was little time to mix with the locals, since Pryor appeared in virtually every scene of the film, and when he wasn't shooting he hung out with Scott, consulting with him or studying his walk, his mannerisms, and his inflections.

"I had a very good relationship with Richard," Scott says affectionately. "I would tell him how to do these things, and he was very cooperative. And he never did use one word of profanity the whole time we were making the movie. I'm a little old-fashioned, and so they'd warned me that the guy would be cursing. But I guess he respected my feelings. Also, he was a very serious actor. Maybe he felt that not cursing would make him closer to the kind of man I am."

The film's best moments are those in which Scott blows

off steam. This happens only twice: when bigoted judges rob him of a clear victory, and when he and his white friend Hutch (Beau Bridges) dine at a segregated restaurant, Scott's scrappy sidekick keeping an angry throng at bay by using the Confederate flag as a lance.

Scott relates that these and other scenes of confrontation are only suggestive of his real life, claiming that he was never as docile as Pryor portrays onscreen. However, the producers felt it best to restrict the flareups to Beau Bridges's character so that their hero wouldn't be unlikable. Pryor defends this approach by describing *Greased Lightning* as "a light drama...a fun-time kind of movie without any wrath-against-the-world stuff." Scott grudgingly concurs that the film is "good entertainment," but feels it would have been more accurate to show a bit more of his hostility toward his oppressors.

As much as Scott enjoyed working with Pryor, in retrospect he is bitter about the project. He was hired as technical adviser, but he says that except for Pryor, the filmmakers rarely took his suggestions. He was particularly disturbed at the way the characters of Hutch and his mechanic, Linwood Carter, were changed. "Hutch," says Scott, "was really a great big guy, not small like Beau—and I was *lucky* he was big because he and I had to fight our way out of the race track a lot of times." The mechanic was turned into a brooding mechanical wizard by singer/actor Richie Havens. "They should've used that character for comic relief. Linwood was perfect for that: he was so stupid he could barely change a tire. But he was the best I could do for a pit crew, and you never got that from the movie." (Scott adds that Carter "was even too stupid to get excited about the movie, though he never got to see it shooting because he lit up a cigarette in bed one night and died three weeks before they started filming.")

Even more distressing to Scott was the delay of several weeks before he was allowed to make any creative contribution to the racing sequences. From the beginning, the sixty-three-year-old Scott wanted to be Pryor's double, driving for him in the long shots. Justifiably, he felt that he could do it better and more accurately than the stunt personnel who had been brought in. But, not being part of the Hollywood family, he was kept on the sidelines. Compounding Scott's frustration was that when he arrived on the set, he saw that the man who had been hired to do the driving for the character Beau Welles (Scott's fictionalized nemesis) was "a man who had really been one of my worst enemies on the race track. I couldn't believe they were using him and I was real displeased, though I found out why they did it. He had been in some movies before and had connections." Scott concedes that the man was a good choice for the job, but he is bitter because the man not only collected a hefty fee for his stunt work but "helped them fix a lot of the cars and made more money out of the movie than I did."

Scott eventually got his wish and was allowed to double for Pryor, but only because the filmmakers found themselves in trouble. "It was Richard's idea to hire me because the movie people didn't know what they were doing. The stuff they shot wasn't realistic, and Richard knew it." Director Melvin Van Peebles was fired, replaced by Michael Schultz of *Car Wash,* and Scott says, "they finally put me behind the wheel, after doing about five or six weeks of filming that they had to throw away." Scott's footage was intercut with actual film from his races, making for authentic action sequences.

The film saga of Wendell Scott ends with Pryor lofting the checked flag at the Grand Nationals, but Wendell Scott is a loser where *Greased Lightning* is concerned. While he is disappointed that he and Pryor haven't had any contact in the six years since the film premiered in Atlanta—"I thought we would've stayed in touch, even thought I would have been asked to do stunt driving in some more movies"—Scott holds that he hasn't "been treated fair about the film, financially."

Nor is Wendell Scott the only one who attaches unpleasant memories to *Greased Lightning.* Adding a twist of irony to Pryor's first starring role is the fact that Cleavon Little originally thought he had the part. "But after it was offered," Little says, "the producers decided that I wasn't right for the character." Instead, they offered him the featured role of

Peewee, Scott's partner in moonshining. Little turned them down, opting instead to star in a different Warner Bros. project, which was to have been directed by Robert Altman. The studio said that Little could do the Altman film if he played Peewee, and Little agreed. But shortly thereafter the Altman picture was canceled, and Little, having agreed to do *Greased Lightning,* found himself in support of Pryor. "It was fun working with Richard," Little says, though he'd have preferred a reunion that left him feeling less manipulated.

Chapter Fourteen

Greased Lightning performed very respectably at the box office, considering how different it was from the kind of work that Pryor's fans expected. Certainly Pryor gained a lot from it in terms of honing his craft. He says he learned a lot from Beau Bridges, who "was wonderful. I'd watch him in a closeup and want to kill him, he was so good. He taught me a lot about acting in front of the camera."

A good portion of the success of *Greased Lightning* can be attributed to the fact that it followed *Silver Streak* into the marketplace by a matter of weeks, enabling it to cash in on that film's phenomenal popularity. However, neither picture had yet been released when Pryor decided on his next project, his first of the Universal pact. He made his selection with the understanding that it would be best to follow the comparatively straight racing film with a comedy, to keep his fans happy.

The property he began developing in the fall of 1976 did two things for him. First, since it was a remake of an artistic classic, Lina Wertmuller's 1974 film *The Seduction of Mimi,* it appealed to his sense of irreverence and mischief. Second, it gave him an opportunity to play three characters in one film: a naïve young man who gets into personal and professional trouble; the youth's cranky father; and—it was only a matter of time—a posturing preacher.

The film was *Which Way Is Up?*, and it went before the cameras in December 1976. Though the screenplay is credited to black author Cecil Brown and *Jaws* scripter Carl Gottlieb, Pryor was paid a screenwriter's fee for his contributions, not the least of which was creating the three featured characters. Anyone who doubts Pryor's contributions has only to compare the names of the characters to some of the people Pryor has known.

Which Way Is Up? is nothing more than a vehicle for Richard Pryor. Every twist and development was created to show off Pryor doing the kind of material that made his albums bestsellers, the Reverend Thomas and Rufus being identical to Pryor's pompous preacher and Mudbone.

No film before or since has given Pryor so fine a vehicle for his comedy. He has had better roles in terms of drama and emotional range, but *Which Way Is Up?* showcases Richard Pryor, comedian, at his best. Accordingly, while this was a movie about blacks, for blacks, Pryor drew young whites in astonishing numbers. Produced for under three million dollars, *Which Way Is Up?* put nearly nine million dollars into Universal's coffers. Suddenly, Hollywood began to wonder whether those were the top numbers Pryor could be expected to generate on his own, or if they were just warmups for some kind of blockbuster main attraction.

Though Pryor's career was finally moving in a satisfying direction, he wasn't happy. As Steve Krantz, husband of author Judith and producer of *Which Way Is Up?*, put it, "He's a wonderful man but deeply troubled. He needs emotional help."

Pryor's biggest problem was cocaine. He was still seesawing, telling one reporter that he was "sick of it," announcing to ex-offenders, "Dope is for dopes. I get high on myself," yet still relying on it for an emotional pick-me-up. Pryor was also depressed by the state of his personal relationships. Since the collapse of his last marriage nearly seven years before, he had dated a number of women, and the fatality rate was high. Pryor's attitude toward women hadn't changed over the years, underscored by his sincere desire to remake Lina Wertmuller's *Swept Away* starring himself and Cybill Shepherd. "I like it because it's cruel," he said of the idea, "and that's sexy." But the constant break-ups were not entirely his fault. Pryor's friend Budd Friedman, owner of the Improv, suggests, "I think maybe the women were doing a number on him," exploiting Pryor once again for his money and connections, and he wouldn't tolerate that.

During this period his most successful relationship was with actress Pam Grier, who had played his wife in *Greased Lightning*. "It's a very big thing," he said. "I like her very much, and she likes me." They went to various industry functions together, such as the Grammies, and in November 1976 became engaged.

Pryor was Grier's kind of man, someone who isn't macho but has sex appeal and "hides it, cherishes it like a jewel." According to him, she was no less ideal. It didn't matter to him that she stood four inches taller and had a successful film career; as he put it, "I love strong, smart women." Nonetheless, intelligent, independent women made him "feel inadequate." It took a while before this catch-22 affected his relationship with Grier, but when it did it was a lulu. The proverbial last straw came during a tennis match. Pryor has never been more than a mediocre player, and he was crushed when Grier beat him on the court. Then she tried to help by giving him some pointers, which caused him to explode, "I'm supposed to take instructions and have you beat my ass *too*? No way!" He insisted on a rematch, playing game after game and battering away at Grier until she literally fainted. Annoyed that now he wouldn't have a chance to even the score, Pryor ignored her plight and strode from the court. The wedding was canceled even before a date had been set.

Pryor went from his romance with Grier into an even shakier relationship with actress Lucy Saroyan, daughter of novelist William Saroyan. Within two weeks they were engaged; in less time than that they were disengaged. As Pryor would later comment, "Yeah, I get women. I can't *keep* 'em, but I get 'em."

None of Pryor's personal ties was made in heaven, but there was one professional bond that was absolutely made in hell.

Pryor had never been enamored of TV. However, it had been enormously helpful to him throughout his career, and he yearned to have the medium at his disposal. Certainly the numbers of people he could reach were staggering: in one night, more people watched any given TV show than went to the most popular film of the year.

Since reworking his act, Pryor's TV appearances had been restricted to the late-evening programs like "Midnight Special" and "Saturday Night Live." These were experiments for him, an attempt to see whether his material could rise above the mundane levels through which he'd suffered in the past. Despite being deprived of his street language, he managed to be true to Richard Pryor on the air, particularly with the "Saturday Night Live" program he did on December 13, 1975. Not only was it a fine showcase for guest host Pryor, it gave him a chance to interact with comedians whose irreverence was similar to his own, the original team of Chevy Chase, John Belushi, Dan Aykroyd, et al.

Pryor saw firsthand that TV didn't have to be a wasteland. His two monologues consisted of some of the more offbeat material from his act—the wino-junkie dialogue; a drunk insisting he's not inebriated (while vomiting all over the floor); and a black man's first acid trip. He also costarred in a number of skits, which were typical "Saturday Night Live": Pryor and Belushi as samurai hotel bellhops; Pryor as talk-show guest Junior Griffen, who'd disguised his face with shoe polish in order to write the book *White Like Me* ("It was spooky . . . I'd apply for jobs and get accepted eight out of ten times!"); Chase interviewing Pryor for a job by playing word association, which degenerates from dog–tree, fast–slow, rain–snow, to colored–redneck, jungle bunny–honkey, spade–honkey *honkey,* nigger–*dead* honkey; and a classic retelling of *The Exorcist* with Pryor as a terrified priest.

Fueled by the ratings of his guest appearances, NBC had been after Pryor to do a prime-time special, but Pryor had been loathe to do so. As much as he'd had to prune his act for late-night TV, a slot between eight and ten o'clock would have meant laundering it even further. But there were two compelling reasons to do the show. First, it would bring his comedic work to tens of millions of viewers, and would inspire a sizable share of that audience to go and see his movies. Second, NBC offered what he describes as "so much money you can't refuse," and he agreed to appear on a special that would air in May 1977.

"The Richard Pryor Special" was written by Pryor and a team assembled by himself and producer Burt Sugarman. Pryor themes abounded, from a slightly crazed evangelist urging people to send "big bucks" to his ministry (the phones only start to ring when he announces that the money will be used to send blacks back to Africa), to a drunk staggering home from a bar to his alternately angry and sympathetic wife, played by writer Maya Angelou. The new material and the few new characterizations he whipped up with a limited amount of rehearsal—such as Idi Amin ("I love the American people. I had two for lunch.") and a blues singer sharing a tune with guest-star John Belushi—prove that while spontaneity may have sapped his confidence, it didn't hurt his ability. These portrayals were right on target.

Before turning the show over to NBC, producer Sugarman wanted an objective opinion of its merits and arranged to have it broadcast over cable stations in San Francisco, Seattle, and other cities. Since most of the cable subscribers were white, he was shocked when the viewers gave the special higher marks than any other show ever tested in NBC history. The audience for the NBC broadcast in May was equally enthusiastic. National ratings convinced the network that Pryor had an audience that would develop as his film career blossomed.

Not surprisingly, NBC put another hefty sum on the table and asked for a second special. Pryor snapped up the offer, though he advised the network that they would have to wait until he could fit them into his schedule. NBC wasn't the only one with an investment in Richard Pryor.

Eager to get some mileage out of Pryor's name and talent, Universal decided to pitch him an offbeat picture being developed by writer/director Paul Schrader. It was one of those "prestige" pictures the studios make occasionally, a film with little commercial appeal but loads of PR value; the kind of movie a studio will use to justify dross like *Jaws 2* or *Airport 1977*, by claiming that some of the profits from those films are being applied toward art.

The picture was to be the first directed by Schrader, who would somehow survive and graduate to *American Gigolo*, *Cat People*, and others, as well as writing such movies as *Raging Bull*. Titled *Blue Collar*, this was the story of union corruption in the automotive industry. Unlike Pryor's other union film, *Blue Collar* was dead serious. As the somewhat disconcerted Pryor noted after reading the hardhitting script, "It deals with violence, unions in Detroit, and racism—everything that makes Disney popular."

Like most of Schrader's work, *Blue Collar* is not an upbeat film. Assembly-line employees Zeke (Pryor), Smokey (Yaphet Kotto), and Jerry (Harvey Keitel) are finding it difficult to provide for their families and, worse, are getting no help from their union. Contacting underworld connections, Smokey learns how to get through the security system at union headquarters. Persuading Zeke and Jerry to join him, they break in and crack the safe, only to find it short on cash. However, they uncover a ledger that details illegal use of union money. They take the book and offer to sell it back to the union.

When the union pressures the three to return the book, each man reacts differently. Smokey defies them and is murdered; Jerry goes to the police; and Zeke accepts a union position, bribed into silence. The film ends with Jerry, who is preparing to testify, running into Zeke. Jerry calls Zeke a coward, Zeke calls his ex-friend a traitor, and the two men lunge at each other in the final fade out.

Schrader's film may be ambiguous, leaving the viewer to decide who is right and who is wrong, but it pulls no punches when it comes to sifting through the men's troubles at home and on the job. The theme song sets the stage for what is to come ("I'm just a hard-working, fucked-over man . . ."), and it's downhill from there. As Zeke observes when condemning the union early in the picture, "The plant is just short for plantation."

The biggest problem Schrader had was that Pryor, Kotto, and Keitel couldn't get along. The actors, says Schrader, "were at approximately the same stage in their careers . . . and they were all determined to assert themselves in this movie." Schrader's objective was "to keep them working . . . under pressure," in order to simulate the characters' emotions in the story. But the actors were suspicious of the director's motives. They misread him, each actor believing that he had personally been singled out for punishment by Schrader. Pryor felt that he was being played as an Uncle Tom–like sidekick to Keitel; Keitel thought Schrader was using *him* as a straight man for Pryor; and Kotto believed that *he* was working in the shadow of the other two.

Every day was hell for Schrader and the cast members. If one of the actors improvised a line, the others would complain that it shifted the emphasis of the scene to that person; if the lighting or camera angle favored one, the other two complained. Before the film was completed, neither Pryor, Keitel, nor Kotto was speaking unless the cameras were rolling.

Pryor appears to have had the most serious problems of the three. Not only was his ego on the line, but he had grave reservations about the part. "People are going to come in expecting laughs and they'll see this different side of me," he worried. "I don't want to be used to bring in the black audience and then to have them devastated. I don't think I could stand the rejection." Not surprisingly, Schrader turned a deaf ear to Pryor's fears, explaining that he told him, "'Look, you want to be an actor, you be an actor, you play a character. If you want to be a public personality, you shouldn't be doing this movie.' "

But Pryor knew that it was something he should do. He acknowledged that "nobody can stay the same unless he's Plastic Man," but doing it and liking it were two very different things. He was hung up on the way his character betrayed his friends by capitulating to the union, and confirms that "it was really hard living with that every day for ten weeks, knowing what he was going to do."

It was no less trying for those around Pryor. Apart from being testy and vulgar, he became violent on occasion and threw props at Kotto, then punched both him and Keitel. But that was mild compared to what happened when actor George Memmoli said something to which Pryor took offense. He slugged the actor, then grabbed a chair and hit him over the head. Memmoli ended up with a fractured skull, Pryor with a one-million-dollar lawsuit. What astounded everyone who worked on the film wasn't that Pryor did these things but the fact that hours later he could be the sweetest man alive.

Pryor doesn't deny that he was uncontrollable at worst, unpredictable at best, but feels his actions were justified. "It's an emotionally violent movie and I felt pain when I made the film. The energy of the work brought me down." Schrader agrees that this was probably true, though he also believes that the movie was an outlet for Pryor's insecurity in other areas. "The more successful he is in the white world, the more resentful he becomes, the more afraid that he's not being black enough." That, says Schrader, compels him to do "something very pathological and very dramatic to remind everyone that he is black first and big second." Then, having alienated his white associates, he quickly becomes, in Schrader's words, "fearful that he's no longer going to be big, that he's only going to be black." He gets back in everyone's good graces by giving gifts, making small talk, and acting concerned about everyone—which makes him feel less black and starts the cycle anew.

Aesthetically, Schrader welcomed Pryor's personal unrest because it helped create realistic tension between the characters. Pryor agrees. "It depressed me to make it, and I think I hate Harvey Keitel, Yaphet Kotto, and Paul Schrader today because of that movie.'' Professionally, however, the director describes the making of the movie as ''putting three bulls in a china shop and making sure that none of them got out . . . certainly the most difficult film experience I've had, and, I suspect, that I'll ever have.'' He adds that he was only able to finish the picture thanks to one of Pryor's employees, Rashan Kahn. Kahn had been hired to serve in the rather unusual capacity of both spiritual and athletic adviser, and several times a week would box and jog with Pryor to keep his body fit, then discuss faith and philosophy to get his spirit in shape. Kahn was constantly on the set; whenever Pryor would get upset, he'd take him aside and try to soothe him.

Shot during May and June 1977, *Blue Collar* was released in February 1978. It garnered fine reviews, many of them singling out Pryor's change-of-pace performance. He holds his own against trained actors and brings a pathetic quality to this noble man who is ultimately beaten by the system.

The box office, as expected, was dismal: the film earned only four million dollars. But Pryor was proud of his work, content that he hadn't simply been ''used'' for his box-office draw, that he had actually brought some depth to the part. As he says, ''I carry no negative shit about that movie,'' he said in retrospect. ''I knew while we were doing it that we were doing something very good. The energy was right, and the actors are superb in terms of their art. There was a lot of pressure, and it was the hardest work I've ever done, but it came out well.''

Chapter Fifteen

More than ever before, Pryor was hungry to be in charge of a project. That was the legacy of *Blue Collar*—the need to be free. That oppressive film was the one of the three reasons he ignored the advice of friends and associates and accepted NBC's offer to do a regular prime-time variety series.

NBC had come to him with a relatively straightforward deal: they would pay Pryor two million dollars for the exclusive rights to his services on television over the next five years, whether he appeared or not. They wanted a minimum of two sixty-minute specials each year, his creative input on a third, and first rights to any series he might conceive. If he chose to star in that series, there would be more money for him. NBC assumed that he'd want to go on as frequently as possible, a spokesperson stating, "Once we get him on the air, the audience will recognize him as the star he is and he'll keep going and going."

Pryor didn't want his film work to be disrupted, but, again describing himself as "greedy," he grabbed the big money and agreed to do a series. That was the second reason. The third, according to producer Steve Krantz, who watched from the sidelines, was "his lack of self-confidence." Pryor wanted something in his back pocket in case he suddenly soured on the screen.

Whatever his motivation, Pryor insisted on certain provisions. He didn't want to be in the so-called family viewing hour from eight to nine, and he didn't want the censors tampering unreasonably with his material. NBC said that if he would commit to ten one-hour shows, they would air them on Thursdays from nine to ten. Pryor accepted, leaving it to his representatives, including Franklin, to figure out how he would get all his film and TV work done. Gathering up his four children, Pryor flew to Europe for what he thought would be a vacation. He describes the trip as a "mistake," more exhausting than work. "There was just not enough daddy to go around," he discovered, and was glad to return to the "sane" world of Hollywood.

While Pryor was gone, NBC inadvertently made the scheduling job easy for his team. Once the basic agreement had been made, the network decided to shift the show to Tuesday nights from eight to nine. Their feeling was that young people would watch the "Richard Pryor Show" at that time, turning from "Happy Days" and "Laverne and Shirley," which were dominating that time period. When Pryor found out, he was furious. Not only would the early hour limit the amount of adult material he could do, but he was probably more than a little anxious about going against the two highly rated shows.

Pryor was also faced with the fear of coming up with good material on a weekly basis. He used the new time period as a reason to get out of his contract, becoming "so busy" that doing the show was impossible. But the network refused to capitulate. Pryor was in a bind. He'd worked hard to dispel his reputation as unreliable, and didn't want to become tangled in a contract battle. Furthermore, his staff was complaining. Many of them had turned down more lucrative jobs to be with Pryor, which they made graphically clear by hiring a plane to circle Pryor's house with a banner that read: SURRENDER RICHARD. Pryor decided to compromise, suggesting to NBC that he be required to do only five shows instead of ten.

NBC was not in a position to bargain. They were consistently below the other networks in the ratings and were already touting the Pryor coup to advertisers as a sign of renewed life. Rather than engage in a bloody and expensive legal battle with their hoped-for savior, NBC accepted the new deal. They put on a cheerful public face in announcing to the press that ten shows, five shows, it didn't really matter. "We are delighted that Richard Pryor has joined NBC," a spokesperson gushed, insisting that getting Pryor "even for half of what he was supposed to do" would benefit them. NBC still had high hopes for the limited series. They were convinced that public reaction would be enthusiastic, just as it had been for the special, showing Pryor "how big a star he is to the television audience" so that "he won't want to stop."

The network's statements failed to mollify Pryor. But he kept a relatively open mind, since he had a lot of people to help him. There were his headwriter and lesser writers, a producer, musical director, casting director, and numerous other directors. For Pryor's convenience, many of the script meetings were held at his home, in the upstairs study, often beginning late at night after a busy day and continuing long into the morning. Pryor would flop behind his desk while the writers sprawled on the huge sofa or on the floor and threw out ideas. "I don't just let people write it and I go out and do it," he said. "I'm involved from day one." Fielding ideas, Pryor would cut off the writers if they were missing their mark. Often he would throw out ideas of his own, which no one would criticize, causing him to yell that they should "stop sitting around nodding and smiling." Sometimes he would pace around the room, stopping at the window to stare down at the roof of the lower level of his house.

Once the show got under way in August, Pryor's mood shifts at the Burbank Studios were reminiscent of those on the set of *Blue Collar*. On the days when Pryor felt that everything might work out, he was very expressive and very giving, constantly meeting with the writers or working with the actors, or improvising with his typical genius and incorporating that material into the skit. He even threw in $85,000 of his own money to cover things which hadn't been allowed for in the budget of the first show. According to one of the series' regulars, stand-up comedienne and Laff recording artist Marsha Warfield, when Pryor was in these moods he "was personally very helpful" to everybody. "For example, I have a lot of trouble with cold readings, and when I'd get a script I wouldn't be able to get a handle on it. But he never worried that I couldn't see it right at that moment, never gave the piece to somebody else. He's suggest things, say, 'Take your time and work with it.' That kind of freedom is unusual in TV, but with it I'd take the script home and kick it around." She says he ran the show as if they had all the time in the world, and when they suddenly ran out of time on the day of the taping, "and the cameras came on . . . everybody was fine."

Acting with Pryor was equally comforting, Warfield recalls, and she praises his ability to "play to the audience and camera both, yet make the other actors feel as though he were playing to them."

On the bad days, however, Pryor felt like an inmate on death row. He seldom directed his animosity toward NBC, for network representatives rarely stopped by the studio to look over his shoulder. They knew better. Although Warfield notes, "I'm sure he'd rather have been freer, doing the kind of things he did at clubs or on records," most of the time "he seemed content to take TV to its limits."

Most of the time.

On the off days there was no consoling him. He'd abuse himself verbally for having sold out to TV. He'd pause in the middle of a conference or rehearsal and spit out remarks like "I can't do this—there ain't no art," or, "I can't go to Burbank, to NBC, every day . . . I bit off more than I can chew," even announcing to his staff that their crusade to revolutionize the medium would leave him "with my brains blown out . . . I'm not stable enough. I don't want to drink and I don't want to snort and I can't do it no other way . . . I knew this was wrong after we finished the special."

But between the mood swings he did produce the series, whose irreverence is legend, despite network TV's restrictions. And, as if being protective, he kept most of his regular characters away from this enterprise, which he was certain would be a disaster. As a result, audiences were exposed to a new breed of characters, which, because of their one-shot nature, could be as quirky or experimental as Pryor wanted.

Typical were the characters of the first show, which opened with the memorable Big Ed skit, about a Southern attorney prosecuting an accused rapist in Mississippi. Given Pryor's soured view of justice, it's no surprise that the defendant is innocent, counselor Ed and half the people in the courtroom having slept with the plaintiff on the night of the alleged crime.

From there, Pryor moved easily through portrayals of a guru in an African village, the lead singer of a rock group named Black Death—he machine-guns the audience at the end of his concert—a samurai, and other figures.

Hesitantly, NBC left the first show intact and aired it as a special before the new season got under way. Their thinking was sound: they would familiarize audiences with the show and its format while the competition was still in reruns. The ploy apparently worked, for the special got impressive ratings, leaving NBC eager for the head-to-head confrontation between Pryor and the Fonz.

The first show of the regular season was literally Pryor's finest hour on TV. It opened with Pryor insisting to the audience that he'd "given up absolutely nothing" to get his act onto television—the camera pulling back to show Pryor obviously emasculated in a flesh-colored bodysuit. Next was a brilliant *Star Wars* spoof, Pryor tending bar at the Sky Wars Bar, where alien creatures congregate for refreshment. Pryor acted as though there were nothing unusual going on, discussing baseball with his patrons, and at one point exclaiming to an extraterrestrial, "Hey, man—you look just like a nigger I know from Detroit."

Back on earth, Pryor was the fortieth President of the United States; he wastes no time showing his true colors, ignoring white reporters, announcing the appointment of Huey P. Newton as head of the FBI, and admitting that he dates white women. The other sketches ranged from broad comedy—a construction worker stripping while he sings "I've Gotta Be Me"—to the bittersweet, Pryor playing a soldier who looks up an old girlfriend in a Harlem nightclub where she performs as "Satin Doll." (In real life, Satin Doll was the name of a sixty-year-old performer who befriended Pryor at the Youngstown, Ohio, club where he had to pull a pistol on the owner to get paid.) To Pryor's credit, he stays in the background while singer Paula Kelly and the rock group the O'Jays poignantly evoke the 1940s when black nightclub entertainment was in flower.

The mixed bag had something for every taste. There was one notable exception, however. The press release from the network read: "NBC Broadcast Standards made the judgment that one sketch was inappropriate, and a brief edit was made." The scene in question was, ironically, the opening of the show with Pryor castrated. To no one's surprise, when he learned that he'd been censored he went berserk, ranting that the network executives were "Fascists" and saying it was nonsensical to think that any censor's opinion "is better than the creative people who put the show together."

To vent his fury, Pryor called a press conference at the

Burbank studio on September 12, the day before the show was to air. There, facing journalists with none of the reserve characteristic of Pryor interviews, he blasted NBC for having "retained about six thousand people to do nothing but mess with my material," and charged them with "stifling my creativity," perpetrating "a violation of an artist's right," and committing "an offense to our mentality." While agreeing that his contract *did* give the network the right to edit his show, he snidely observed, "That's why they're number three." Pryor then vowed that if they tampered with the second show, he would not be able to continue. He promised to fight "that okey-doke pressure thing," and never give audiences "the same old stuff."

For all of Pryor's harsh words, NBC wasn't greatly upset. Temperamental stars rebelled often; it meant little, when weighed against the publicity value of having a controversial, must-see show. NBC simply reiterated its pleasure at having Pryor in their stable, and defended their editing by saying that they wanted "to protect the children" who might be watching. They failed to address the crucial issue of why they had put Pryor in the family hour in the first place.

Ironically, more people saw the deleted clip on the evening news than would have seen it on Pryor's show.

NBC might have left the show intact, for all it mattered. Fonzie's trip to Hollywood for a screen test easily overwhelmed Pryor's show.

No matter how much he told himself that TV just wasn't mature enough to accept him, Pryor's ego was bruised. However, to his credit, he didn't pack up and leave, as he had at the Aladdin. He did the four hours remaining in his commitment, and though the material tended toward lunacy, it was still innovative by television standards. Indeed, as a writer for *Ebony* put it, it kept viewers "perched on the edge of your seat, ready just in case Richard at any moment did something that would make it necessary for every Black person in America to suddenly drop whatever he or she was doing and run like hell!" Among the highlights of subsequent weeks were a wino meeting Dr. Jekyll just as he's becoming

Mr. Hyde, and Pryor as a Japanese cook preparing a meal in front of the diner—in this case, a woman taking a shower.

Subsequent programs fared no better in the ratings, and Pryor turned his attention to other matters. Among these was taking his fifth wife, twenty-five-year-old actress/model Deboragh Denise McGuire. The show was still in production when the couple wed on September 29, and, still wearing his white wedding suit, the groom sped from the ceremony to a 10:00 A.M. taping.

Pryor had pursued Ms. McGuire on and off for three years. He tied the knot when he realized that Deboragh was the one reality in a land of facades, the one source of love in his life. "Debbie is my life force," he had concluded. "This is the first time I've been married—in my heart." The new Mrs. Pryor was less categorical with her affection, commenting that being with Richard was like having an emotional smorgasbord. "There are many facets and stages to Richard, and I think I know each of his little roles. I have to sort of get into each personality of his, which . . . keeps you on your feet."

The second thing Pryor did was accept an offer from Universal and Motown, both of which had been after him to take a part in their coproduced film version of the hit Broadway musical *The Wiz*. As much as he didn't want to be part of an ensemble that featured such heavyweights as Diana Ross and Lena Horne, he did the film, for a number of reasons: first, he was offered the part of the all-powerful Wizard of Oz, a distinct change from the sniveling or nasty characters he'd played in the past; second, it was an all-black film and he felt dutybound to lend his support to the project; third, he was eager to work with director Sidney Lumet, whose many distinguished works include *Serpico, Dog Day Afternoon* and *The Verdict;* and finally, the picture was shooting in New York. That may well have been the most important consideration, for it would give Pryor a chance to put some distance between himself and the scene of his TV activities while NBC evaluated each week's ratings.

The floundering TV series wasn't the only reason Pryor felt he had to get out. In September, showing signs of the strain of his television regimen, he caused such a scene at a

Hollywood rally called "A Star Spangled Night for Rights" that he made news from coast to coast. The rally was organized by local gay leaders and the American Civil Liberties Union to raise money to combat Anita Bryant's antihomosexual crusade. Staged at the Hollywood Bowl, it featured Bette Midler, David Steinberg, Lily Tomlin, Paul Newman, Olivia Newton-John, Robert Blake, Valerie Harper, and others, addressing or entertaining the crowd of seventeen thousand.

The concert took in $350,000, the audience—composed predominately of white males—having paid twenty dollars each. Pryor arrived in good spirits and patiently waited backstage for his spot in the second half of the show. However, the man who went onstage was a different Richard Pryor.

Pryor had been drinking heavily before his arrival, and while standing backstage he noticed two groups of dancers preparing to go on, one white and one, the Locker Dancers, black. As they got ready, it was apparent to Pryor that a concert coordinator was showing the white troupe far more courtesy. "When the white dance act went onstage, every damn body and his brother went to fix the lights," he later said. "They didn't do shit for the Lockers. Then a fire marshal started to reprimand a black youngster, and all the white folks simply turned their backs and ignored what was going on. I got mad as hell." The outrage was still with him when he went on. Pryor told the crowd in earnest that he'd once had a gay experience and didn't like it, but the dialogue seemed to stick in his throat. "I'm the only person connected with this thing who has actually come out and admitted having a homosexual experience," he went on, people bristling when he tauntingly referred to it as "fucking a faggot." Then, no doubt emboldened by alcohol, he turned on the crowd and yelled, "Where were you when Watts was burning?" There was a sudden, shocked silence. "When the niggers was burning down Watts you were doing what you wanted to do on Hollywood Boulevard—fucking and didn't care a damn. You are not concerned with human rights, you're just concerned with *fun*."

Pryor proceeded to deride the audience for claiming to

support rights and freedom when really they were concerned only with their own cause. "Fags are prejudiced," he declared. "The Locker Dancers came backstage dripping with sweat but all you could say is, 'Oh, that was nice.' But when the ballet dancers came out dancing to that funny music you said, 'Wow, those are some bad mothers.' Stirring from their stupor, many in the audience booed and some cried, "We want Bette!" but most sat silent, hoping that Pryor's outburst would pass as quickly as it had come on.

After a few minutes, Pryor's inexplicable anger did seem to wither, and he laughed that he had been "testing" the audience to see how thick-skinned they were. He went on to his routine—but not for long. Without warning, Pryor renewed his attack, assailing the audience repeatedly. "How can fags be racists?" he wondered aloud. "This is an evening about human rights and *I'm* a human being. I just wanted to see where you was *really* at, and I wanted to test you to your motherfucking *soul*. I'm doing this shit for nothin'. But I wanted to come here and tell you to kiss my ass with your bullshit. You understand?" He advised them they'd all be better off pursuing honesty rather than sexual freedom, getting "out of the closet with *everything*, with your entire self."

Running out of steam after fifteen seemingly interminable minutes, Pryor turned his back on the audience and did something that uprooted whatever seeds of truth he may have planted. Tugging down his pants, he invited the audience to "kiss my happy rich black ass" before stalking abruptly from the stage.

The concert jolted to a halt, though the audience was less astounded than Pryor's coworkers. The crowd, said singer Helen Reddy, at least "tried to ride it out with him." But Pryor's coworkers were dumbstruck. Lily Tomlin, who had been instrumental in getting Pryor to do the show, was mortified, ineffectively shrugging off her embarrassment by commenting that when you ask for Richard Pryor that's what you get, for better or worse. Others were less forgiving.

Trying to kick the proceedings back into gear, Aaron Russo, Bette Midler's manager-lover, and the prime mover behind the gathering, went out and apologized for Pryor's behavior. He doesn't know how he got through the speech, and backstage admitted, "I'm still in a state of shock." While he allowed that "Richie has the right to say what he feels, he deflated a lot of spirit" of the show. His explanation for the outburst? Pryor was seized with panic. "I wanted Richard on the show very badly. I think he's a genius. But he lost control of the situation and had to go to those lengths to save himself from the fact that he was bombing."

Reporters accepted Russo's story, and it was several years before Michael Schultz, Pryor's director on *Greased Lightning,* broke his silence to tell reporters Fred Robbins and Dave Ragan that Pryor had merely been reacting to "blatant racism," the fact that the show's representative was "definitely giving the black group second-class treatment and talking offensively to them. Anybody else would have . . . tried to rationalize it. But Pryor came out . . . and told them how upset he was and exactly what was on his mind."

Lashing out at gays in Hollywood is tantamount to slamming jazz in New Orleans. Though he quickly stated in public that his comments may have been ill advised, and apologized to everyone who took offense—not because he felt he was wrong but simply because he agreed with his detractors that the concert "was not the right place for a debate" —blacklash was severe. The most stinging repercussion came from a group of gay actors, who took out an ad in *Variety* several days later. Addressing Pryor, the ad read, in part, "All of us who have made . . . contributions to the cause of civil and human rights were insulted and enraged by your remarks and performance." The actors could not resist concluding with the dig, "P.S. Since we are not rich, it took some time to collect the money for this."

Reaction was basically the same throughout Hollywood. Because so many record executives had been in attendance, it was said that Pryor's recording career was finished; most of the artists present indicated that they would never work with Pryor again. Universal Pictures was fearful that the negative publicity would hurt the impending release of *Which Way Is*

Up?, and timorous NBC was considering shelving the remaining Pryor shows.

However, none of the dire predictions came true. Money governs Hollywood, and as long as Pryor generated profits he would get away with anything. As *Which Way Is Up?* producer Steve Krantz pointed out, "The people in the rest of the country don't give a damn about his attitude toward gays."

Pryor had survived yet another battle, though, like his idol Muhammad Ali, each new bout was taking a heavier toll on him.

Pryor went to New York and *The Wiz* in style. He flew via chartered Lear jet from Hawaii, where he'd gone with Deboragh on a brief honeymoon. There, on the island of Maui, he fell in love with an isolated five-acre site, far from anything but trees and coastline. He bought it, though there was no time to do anything but say hello and good-bye to it before flying to New York.

Not surprisingly, Pryor was in no mood to act in a movie musical. Director Lumet was not surprised, blaming the TV experience for having left Pryor "just totally deballed. He was so tight and tense; and tension is the first thing that kills comedy."

Producer Rob Cohen concurred. Picking Pryor up at the Plaza Hotel en route to the St. George Hotel, where rehearsals were being held prior to shooting at the renovated Astoria Studios in Queens, he found him "in a very, very bad mood." Cohen describes Pryor as very sullen when he climbed into the car and talking bitterly as they made their way through midtown traffic about how he'd been betrayed by the industry people he'd trusted in California. He was certainly nothing like the eager, enthusiastic man with whom Cohen had worked on *The Bingo Long Traveling All-Stars and Motor Kings* less than two years before.

Cohen tried to defuse Pryor's bitterness by telling him that everyone in the cast, especially his old costar Diana Ross, was looking forward to working with him. Pryor dismissed the compliment, and Cohen began to worry that his depression would bring everyone else down.

Rather than throw him in with the other actors and director, Cohen decided to try to boost his spirits by taking him to the huge ballroom where the dancers were rehearsing. Wearing a tee-shirt and baseball cap, Pryor tagged behind Cohen as they entered the hall, where four hundred black dancers were in the middle of a frenzied Emerald City number. As the producer tells it, "All of a sudden, some of the dancers in the front row saw me and who was next to me, and stopped dancing. And it spread until the whole place stopped. They were just staring at him. Then they broke into spontaneous applause." Pryor was touched, holding back tears by breaking into his preacher character and saying, "We are gathered here today . . ." The dancers laughed uproariously, and Pryor was fine from that point on.

The Wiz was a $23 million epic that transposed the Oz tale from Kansas and Over the Rainbow to Manhattan. Caught in a snowstorm, Dorothy is hurled into an urban, very hip Oz where art deco and disco have merged with spectacular results. The winged monkeys have been turned into motorcycle-freak monstrosities; the witch is now Evillene, whose glittering wardrobe and great girth are almost a set unto themselves. The Emerald City is a chrome and light setting, with sequined, top-hatted dancers who look like refugees from an idealized Harlem nightclub. Everyone from the Tin Man to the human crows in the Scarecrow's field have incredible rhythm—everyone, that is, except the Wizard, who promises to send Dorothy back to New York if she can defeat Evillene.

As the great and powerful wizard, Pryor dwells within a twenty-foot-tall metallic bust of himself, complete with steel-wool mustache, smoke fuming from the nostrils, and spotlights shining from the eyes. However, as in L. Frank Baum's original tale, he has no mystical powers, and runs Oz through imposing special effects. Pryor describes the character as "a jive politician from New Jersey" who, when he's found out, meekly pokes his head through the empty eyesocket of the giant head, the portrait of vulnerability. The role may not have been a rounded one, but it is quintessential Pryor, the little boy behind the facade.

The Wiz was Pryor's first musical, and he says that he'd never have been able to pull it off had music supervisor Quincy Jones not "coached the hell out of me." Pryor was satisfied with the results of his work, though the film was a box-office disaster, returning under seven million dollars to Universal. It was a well-made and basically entertaining picture that just couldn't find an audience. It was too whitewashed for black moviegoers, too black for the whites, and too strident and gaudy for everyone. But it wasn't Pryor's failure, nor was it a total loss for him: *The Wiz* gave him what he needed—time to sort things out and regroup before facing the situation back at NBC.

Chapter Sixteen

In the fast-moving world of network television, where shows produce ratings or get the ax, Pryor was canceled after fulfilling his four-week commitment. NBC paid him off handsomely: he kept the two million dollars *not* to appear on any other network.

It was easy to turn his back on NBC, but less so on the fact that he had failed. He had said many times that he had done it for the money, but the facts don't bear that out, since he was drawing a salary of fifty thousand dollars a month and had assets in the millions of dollars. He could just about write his own ticket for any film he cared to make, at any fee. What had possessed him was the thought of conquering his old foe TV, the last stronghold of sterile entertainment. He may have come closer than anyone save for Archie Bunker in breaking new ground, but ultimately the system had been stronger. It was a bitter draft to swallow.

Possibly even worse, to Pryor, was having allied himself with people at the network who didn't care about art and didn't really care about him. It was the same sense of abandonment—in his words, "betrayal"—that he'd suffered when he walked out on Las Vegas. "I'm not out to be cruel," he has said of his irreverent approach to the media. But whether it was TV or the Hollywood Bowl, he was not about "to placate anyone either." Indeed, the only positive result of the NBC fiasco was that it reinforced his resolve never to do anything that wouldn't allow him just "to be Richard."

The professional setbacks and aggravations took their toll on more than Pryor's state of mind. Returning to Peoria in November for an early birthday celebration, he was outside the ranch-style house he'd bought on Mother's Day for his grandmother when he began to feel discomfort in his chest. As he later described the events of November 9 in a routine, "I was walkin' in the yard and somethin' say, 'Don't breathe no more.'" The pain worsened, and Marie made him go to the emergency room at the nearby Methodist Medical Center. Pryor was admitted, and though he instructed the hospital not to tell the media he was there, they managed to find out. The press gathered outside the hospital and waited for a verdict, Pryor informing them through a hospital spokesperson that it was nothing, he was simply exhausted. But when Marie was asked about her grandson's condition, she said, "He's doing as well as can be expected, considering he's had a heart attack."

Pryor quickly denied that he'd had a heart attack, though a year later would confess to an audience during the taping of his *Live in Concert* film that that was indeed what he had suffered. Like so many people, he said, he was embarrassed to admit it.

Years later, during his hospitalization after the fire, it was revealed that Pryor had a heart murmur, which may have been what was ailing him in Peoria. Pryor says that the condition has since "reversed itself"—Pryoresque hyperbole for the fact that it simply hasn't recurred.

Pryor left the hospital several days later and, instructed to relax for a few weeks, returned to the West Coast to consider career moves. Events helped make that easy for him. *The Wiz* opened at year's end and was shaping up as a film that would have its greatest impact—*only* impact, in fact—among a very limited black audience. Accordingly, as much as it may have galled him to do so, he fulfilled Paul Schrader's expectations by swinging to the white end of the spectrum and accepting a part in the film version of Neil Simon's *California Suite*. It was slated to go before the cameras in March 1978, giving him plenty of time to recuperate from the tribulations of the past year. However, Pryor couldn't let the new year begin without making the front pages.

Pryor's marriage to Deborah had its ups and downs, but for the most part he seemed happy; matured and apparently having found the right woman, he was becoming a family man. But that ended on New Year's day, when, having achieved a goal once more, he managed to shatter it in the most dramatic way possible.

He, Deborah, and two of her friends—thirty-seven-year-old Edna Solomon and twenty-five-year-old singer-dancer Beverly Clayborn—were sitting around the house just after dawn when Pryor got into an argument with the women. He became abusive with them, and they were abusive right back. Deborah recalls, "I thought the situation was hysterically funny at first. Just like a silly movie with everyone bad-mouthing everyone else. But," she adds, "things really got out of hand."

After two hours of arguing, Pryor ordered Beverly and Edna to leave. But Deborah didn't want them to go, and, aided by her friends, she tried to put her husband in his place. The results were predictable. As Deborah has said, under ordinary circumstances "Richard just can't argue. He waits until something gets under his skin so bad he blows up." But he'd been celebrating the New Year, and, full of spirits, he jumped to his feet. Snarling, "I'll give you bull-dykin' bitches five seconds to get out of my house!" he chased the three women out the front door. His anger far from spent, he climbed into his Mercedes and chased the women onto the lawn, ramming their Buick when they tried to get into it. Turning, they ran down the driveway and into the street, while Pryor backed up and rammed his car into theirs five more times just to make sure it didn't go anywhere.

Satisfied that the car was sufficiently wounded to stay put, Pryor climbed from the Mercedes, ran into the house, and returned with a .357 Magnum from his gun collection. Shouting, "No one's leaving in *this* motherfucker!" he leveled the gun at the car, blowing away the tires and windshield, putting a series of holes in the main frame, then blasting out the motor for good measure.

At that time the police pulled up in front of the house, having responded to a neighbor's call. Pryor stopped the assault and, telling himself, "Well, shit, it wasn't *that* bad. All I did was kill the car," he turned and calmly walked back into the house.

The police weren't impressed. Booked for assault with a deadly weapon, he was released on five thousand dollars' bail and instructed to appear at a pretrial hearing on February 16. In the meantime, Clayborn filed suit in Los Angeles Superior Court for $17 million. Wearing a neck brace, she said that Pryor had harmed her "physical and mental well-being." Commenting on the charge, Pryor was sufficiently overwhelmed to quip, "If she get the $17 million, I'll marry her."

Nonetheless, appearing in superior court in Van Nuys, Pryor opted to enter a no-contest plea. The assault charge was dropped, since there was no evidence that he had attacked or meant to harm the women, but the judge ordered him to make financial restitution to the women. He was also instructed to seek psychiatric care, was forbidden to own guns for the period of probation, and, in lieu of spending four months in the county jail, was told to donate 480 hours of his time to a good civic cause. Pryor was allowed to fulfill this obligation in the form of benefit shows. Late in 1979, having given five free concerts, his debt to society was deemed paid.

Just over a month after the shooting, Deborah Denise McGuire Pryor moved out of Northridge and into an apartment in Los Angeles. Registering for courses in psychology and real estate at a local junior college, she said that while she still loved Pryor very much, "a lot of things were said in anger that will be hard to smooth over." Shortly thereafter, she went to superior court in Santa Monica and filed for

169

divorce. Among her demands was that he pay her a modest $2,480 per month and that he be restrained from "annoying, threatening, or harassing" her.

In the aftermath of his latest public spectacle, Pryor took a hard look at himself. "I love my wife," he said sincerely. "I don't know how the situation got so out of hand . . . I don't know why I *do* self-destructive things like that. She's a fine person, a good human being, plus," he added impishly, "she's gonna be rich when we divorce." The reason actually went beyond the explanation he gave for his professional self-destructiveness. In this instance, he was driven by an unwillingness to be criticized. "I've been told that when a child hears often enough that he ain't worth shit, he begins to believe it, and that really messes him up later." Criticism cut Pryor to the quick, and while he couldn't control the press or the public, he refused to be censured in private. Unfortunately, so did the people around him.

Always one to look for the silver lining in every cloud, Pryor said after the shooting, "Well, in my working life I think I'm doing well."

And he was. When he was successful he was very successful, and even when he failed he proved that he could survive any artistic disaster Hollywood threw at him—witness *California Suite*. Not badly made in the same sense as *Adios Amigo, California Suite* is less bearable because of the spectacle of so much talent abasing itself.

Simon's play opened in New York in June 1976 and stands as one of his less successful works, both commercially and artistically. The play, like the film, told four different stories, unrelated, about couples in a hotel coming to grips with infidelity (Walter Matthau and Elaine May); divorce (Jane Fonda and Alan Alda); alternative lifestyles (straight Maggie Smith married to a gay played by Michael Caine); and how *not* to spend a vacation. The vacation segment starred Pryor as Dr. Chauncey Gump and Gloria Gifford as his wife, Lola, with Bill Cosby and Sheila Frazier as the couple with whom they are traveling.

Their trouble begins when only one hotel room is available, forcing the Gumps to sleep in a room that is undergoing repairs, flooding from pipes, sink, and toilet, and beset round-the-clock with repair people. Getting no sleep, they come to hate their well-rested traveling companions. Consequently, the couples, who could never disagree on anything before, now argue violently about everything. They finally end up in a fistfight that demolishes the once luxurious suite.

This segment, which was originally written for white actors, was changed to accommodate the black stars and came under attack from blacks for "tokenism." Simon dismisses the allegation as "crazy. I'm sure we'd have come under the same fire if we *hadn't* transplanted the roles." Regardless of who acts the parts, it's the same tale of dissension among the upper middle class. What's unfortunate is that the brickbats should, instead, have been directed at Simon, whose playlette in any form is badly written.

Cosby is right at home. However, even Simon agrees that Pryor was possibly miscast. He often puts on white, upper-class airs to spoof them in his act, but he just isn't smooth enough to play this kind of part straight. There's too much of the ghetto in him, and the contrived performance hurts him more than does the poor dialogue. "Richard is quite a good actor," says Simon, "and he tries to be a very good *legitimate* actor as well in some of his films. But he was constrained by the limitations of the script," which in Simon's view didn't allow the two Pryors to "merge together." He is at his best when he can do what he does best—his concerts."

Regardless of its failings, *California Suite* was a surprise hit, returning thirty million dollars to Columbia Pictures. Pryor hadn't, as he promised after his TV experience, just allowed himself "to be Richard" but, as Schrader had foreseen, had bent himself into a mold to advance his career. Fortunately, although this film certainly wasn't Pryor's best, it didn't hurt him.

Neil Simon described Richard Pryor as "the most brilliant comic in America. There's no one funnier or more perceptive." Sammy Davis, Jr., echoed that praise: "The freedom with which he works within his own sphere is unique and brilliant." However, Davis, who fought battles similar to Pryor's hastened to add, "I just hope they don't jerk him off into impotency."

That fear was obviously on Pryor's mind as he looked back over the past year and saw nothing of which he was particularly proud. Thus, in yet another radical move, he decided in April 1978 that what he needed was to do something extremely personal.

At first, Pryor holed up to write a new film script, only occasionally doing anything in public, such as a charity bout in Los Angeles with Muhammad Ali. Pryor came away with an even healthier respect for the fighter than he'd had before. "The nigger's so fast with his punches, you don't see 'em until they're comin' back. The man hit at my face eight times and just came within an inch of my nose, never touched me." However, Pryor does admit he became somewhat nervous when "my mind said, 'What happens if this motherfucker have a Joe Frazier flashback?' One of his jabs would give me brain damage for life."

But the script wasn't fulfilling him, and Pryor began to recognize that movies and fundraisers weren't what he needed either. He needed to get back some of the fire he'd lost, and sitting in a Beverly Hills restaurant late one spring night, drinking wine with some friends, he realized just how to go about it. He felt the urge to perform and did just that, standing up and improvising an act. "I just had to get up and work," he said, "that's all I know. Like the stuff, it just came out, man . . . I just emptied my head out."

Pryor stopped writing his script late in April and didn't start again until November. He literally put everything aside to work the local clubs again, and when he realized how good that made him feel, he arranged with Warner Records for a new series of concerts, which they would tape and release as a two-record set. The Warner people were delighted, Pryor was exhilarated, and the public lined up for tickets.

Like an athlete in training, Pryor honed his work for two months before going on the road to record it. His only stipulation was that he wouldn't do Las Vegas. "It takes too much out of me," he said, referring to both the nightly schedule and the need to launder his material. No doubt Las Vegas felt snubbed, but Pryor was on top now and was calling the shots—professionally, anyway. Women still had a way of sneaking up on him and whisking him off his feet.

Pryor appears to have felt that his personal life could be dramatically improved by avoiding another close relationship. "Being married is hard fucking work," he declared. "It's hard enough living by yourself, but living with somebody *all* the time—" He just shakes his head and shudders on the heels of a heartfelt "god*daaaamn*." However, shortly before marrying Deboragh he had met twenty-seven-year-old Jennifer Lee, of Gropseyville, New York, a white songwriter and actress who had appeared in *The Sunshine Boys,* among other films. After his divorce from Deboragh, he began to see Jennifer regularly. "She came to me when I was in need," he said, starry-eyed once more. And, as though wanting to talk himself into a marriage mentality, he was harsh in saying of his past excesses, "It's too easy to find reasons for messing up. It's my life and I'm responsible for it, and I'm going to do the best I can." He described Jennifer as the kind of supportive, loving woman with whom he would one day like to build a family.

Part of Pryor's effusion was *pro forma* for him where women were concerned, and another part of it was indebtedness to Jennifer, who was particularly helpful to him when Marie died. The death of the woman who had raised him, who was the reason he regularly returned to Peoria, hit him harder than anything he'd experienced before.

Pryor abandoned a concert tour and was with Marie when she died in the aftermath of a stroke. Says Aunt Maxine, "He just stood there shaking like a rag doll. He was just crying and talking, 'Mama! Mama!' He had a grip on her hand and they couldn't pry him loose without a struggle. They couldn't get him out of that room, and when they did, he broke and come right back in there." When Pryor was finally persuaded to go to the lounge, his aunt says, "That's when he really broke down. I tried to console him and he cried, 'Everything I've had and everything I've got is gone.

My mama's gone. I just loved her, I loved her.'" He wailed, "Mama, I did everything I could for you! I prayed, and I prayed—Mama, I prayed so hard. I didn't even *know* I could pray."

Yet, it was as much Pryor's own sense of relief as her death that upset him. "There's a moment," he told *Ebony,* weeping, "when you're ... well ... when you're glad she's dead. You feel that some kind of pressure has been lifted off you—then you feel sadness that such a great woman is gone."

The pressure he felt from Marie was different from the suffocation he experienced with his wives. Because Marie was such an imposing figure in his mind, he was still a kid when he was around her, still looking for her approval, seemingly unable to be his own man. As terrible as he felt at her passing, he affirmed, "I could finally take care of my own life now"—although it would be more than two years before he could mention his grandmother's name without breaking down.

Jennifer Lee wasn't Pryor's constant companion, but she was there whenever he was lonely or depressed. Fortunately, he didn't have time to dwell on his emotions. He was readying his show for the road, and he thrust himself into it fully. However, being Richard Pryor, he still managed to get into hot water now and then. One could say he'd made an art of it, managing to grab the spotlight even when he hadn't done anything wrong. In August 1978, police in Philadelphia raided the headquarters of a militaristic black group called MOVE. There, the officers found a diary that listed contributors; among the names was Richard Pryor. Pryor let his agent, Murray Swartz, field this politically sensitive issue. Swartz quelled potential backlash on the eve of the national tour by stressing to reporters that Pryor was not and had never been a MOVE supporter. Pryor had met with MOVE members back in 1974, when he was performing in the area, but it was they who had approached him to lend his talents to a fundraiser, and Pryor had turned them down—end of story.

The subject died with Swartz's disclosure. Whether he

liked it or not, Pryor was now too mainstream for even the sensation-hungry press to pin a revolutionary name tag on him.

Pryor hit the road in September 1978, costarred once again with singer Patti LaBelle. He opened the twenty-two city tour with a five-night, seven-concert gig at City Center in New York, where, as in subsequent stops over the next two months in Washington, D.C., Chicago, and other cities, he did from an hour to an hour and a half of the new material he had developed in Los Angeles. To no one's surprise, the shows were sellouts. He even broke Steve Martin's record at the Golden Hall in San Diego.

Many of the concerts were taped in their entirety, and the Warner album, called *Wanted, Richard Pryor Live in Concert,* was assembled from the best of those recordings. When it was released in 1979, the double album immediately went gold.

The record, like the concerts, represents the finest, most inspired, most balanced work of Pryor's career. He was as off-color as ever, but the shrill, hysterical edge was gone. Focused passion was the key element. Unlike the *Bicentennial Nigger* concert, Pryor was not playing to the audience per se, not hanging on their laughter. His Los Angeles tryouts had left him secure enough with the material to concentrate on the delivery, shaping his routines like a sculptor shaping a piece of marble.

Pryor's orientation was less overtly black than before, yet the concerts didn't lack ethnic flavor. He characterized all people more obliquely, his act more entertaining now because he didn't solicit outrage or compassion. He had "gone Hollywood" just enough to temper his bitterness without losing any of his insight. For example, he slipped audiences the prototype of the oppressed, confused, contemporary black in an unlikely manner, while discussing the population of China ("Who *counted* them 950 million motherfuckers? D'ya think they had some nigger goin', 'One, two, three—uh, didja get the one in the blue shirt?'"); zeroed in on the plight of the so-called black sexual giant ("I didn't have no time to

175

be kissin' on the toes. I wanted to get in the pussy in case it got away."); deflated the American middle class by turning their jogging pain into a very businesslike white-collar figure ("'I'll be fucking with you the next hour or so . . . moving from side to side, down your groin and up your ass.'"); and so on.

He also strayed further into anthropomorphism than ever before, and in talking about hunting or in taking the part of an animal, he was able, again, to talk indirectly about people and their foibles. His gem is a discourse on how different people urinate in the woods, graphically evoking the reluctant woman afraid of onlookers and bugs, and the man who flamboyantly writes his name in the snow. What Pryor creates in these bits are cartoons for adults, playing a stalked deer, a horny Great Dane, a lascivious squirrel monkey, a compassionate German shepherd, and a Jekyll-and-Hyde Doberman who good-naturedly lets a thief into the house and then, in Pryor's words, "when the burglar hits the door . . . turns into the Exorcist."

Pryor's genius has been alluded to by everyone who has ever seen or worked with him, and his concert tour bears them out. It ranks with the finest work of history's great artists. Naturally, a great deal of impact is lost on the record, for Pryor is a very visual, very expressive performer. Fortunately, Pryor agreed to do another concert—one that would be filmed, allowing him the satisfaction of "having my art etched in celluloid and shown 'round the world."

The Pryor movie concert was the brainchild of producer Bill Sargent, whom *Rolling Stone* magazine describes as "a fat, jolly, red-bearded Oklahoman who in twenty-five years has made, and lost, millions through his high-rolling ventures." Sargent caught Pryor's concert and saw dollar signs on the wall. Meeting with Pryor and Universal, he convinced the studio to put up the $700,000 necessary to film the concert, leaving it to his own Special Event Entertainment Theatre Network to handle the production. Pryor's fee would be a straight twelve percent of the take.

Because it had been an extremely draining tour—when

Pryor returned to Los Angeles in November, exhaustion forced him to cancel the last five days of a week-long stand at the Shubert—it was January 1979 before the concert could be staged. Pryor's choice of site was a curious one: an auditorium in the white stronghold of Long Beach, California. Pryor reveled in the ire and skittishness of local whites at having so many blacks descend on their community. He referred to it frequently during the concert, giving the film a slightly more militant feel than there had been during the tour.

Patti LaBelle was once again his warmup act—although she would not appear in the finished film—and Pryor went on for eighty minutes. The film was padded with scenes of Pryor arriving at the auditorium with Jennifer Lee in tow, very much in the background. *Richard Pryor, Live in Concert* was rushed through postproduction and opened on February 2, 1979. In an unusual break with tradition, Universal did not submit the picture to the Motion Picture Association of America, the industry's ratings tribunal. Instead, Sargent tacked a warning on all ads: "This picture contains harsh and very vulgar language and may be considered shocking and offensive. No explicit sex or violence is shown." Pryor was pleased with the disclaimer, noting, "I think that's a good idea. I have a vision of little old ladies coming into the theater by mistake and having coronaries." And, of course, in his view it was preferable to taking the risk of being saddled with an X rating, which would have cost them bookings and caused Universal to insist on edits. Sargent told it like it was when he said, "Who's kidding who? It helps sell tickets."

The concert movie quickly became the top-grossing film in the nation. Along with the rest of Hollywood, Sargent marveled, "One man, on a stage, all alone, with material he wrote—he's the scenery, he's the sense, he's the sound effects, he's everything—is outgrossing *Superman*." The producer smiled knowingly. "And why not? Talent and genius is talent and genius." As the *New York Times* accurately summed it up, "Prowling the stage impishly, slipping effortlessly from one hilarious impersonation to the next, he radiates an intensity that isn't often visible in even his very best feature-length acting performances."

177

Not surprisingly, *Richard Pryor, Live in Concert* remains Pryor's favorite film. He was more raucous then than he is today, and less compassionate; but those qualities gave him much of his fire—and were chased from him by a different fire. And while Pryor doesn't envy that sublime but doomed figure, he is proud of the work he did in that concert.

Chapter Seventeen

As soon as *Richard Pryor, Live in Concert* was in the can, Pryor decided to take some time off. But he got nervous almost immediately, which happens whenever he tries to relax. "I start thinking that I haven't worked in *years*," he says, and paces the house like a caged lion. As soon as he began to show his characteristic restlessness, Jennifer tried to get him to slow down. " 'Hey, man,' " Pryor recalls her having said, " 'you just came off the road. You been working for a fuckin' year.' And I say, 'Wha—? Okay.' You know, I get them anxieties. . . ."

Jennifer wasn't the only one who tried to make him take it easy. Shortly after his New Year's 1978 outburst, Pryor began seeing Dr. Alfred Cannon for therapy. He admits, "I had always been afraid of going to therapy because I had thought that it had some sort of stigma attached to it." But he went, and over the year Pryor and Dr. Cannon became close friends. Because of this personal bond, Cannon was able to make Pryor see what others had been saying to and about him for years—that whites were not his personal enemies, and that while his hostility might be great for comedy, it was eating him up. Pryor says that Cannon showed him how "for a long time I had the sense that I was inferior, which made me turn it into a feeling of false superiority . . . so I started dealing with myself. I cried a lot and I laughed a lot," and he says he also learned that, contrary to what he'd believed after earning so much in *Silver Streak,* "life ain't about money."

Cannon, a collector of African art, understood Pryor better than anyone, and Pryor realized this when Cannon "suggested one day that I go to Africa." Pryor suspected it wasn't just a matter of getting him to relax or to see in its native environment some of the art he'd admired in Cannon's collection. Thus, in March 1979, he and Jennifer flew to Nairobi, Kenya.

Pryor didn't go on a tour; he simply went, registered at the Nairobi Hilton, and rented a car. He stayed for just over three weeks, and, as Cannon had expected, it changed his life—after first humbling him. Pryor later griped, "Seven hundred million black people and not *one* of them motherfuckers knew me!"

Arriving at the airport, Pryor "felt something exciting in my bones and I *knew* that it was going to be different for me." It wasn't the airport itself, because he discovered that "people in Africa fuck over your luggage just like people in New York." But as he made his way into the countryside, Pryor describes the trip as being "spiritual." He felt the presence of his ancestors, of "all the bloodline from way back when," and it made him realize that black history, the good and the bad, did not begin in Peoria in 1940. When he visited a museum and saw a prehistoric skull, he says, "It was something to know that it was a black man who probably had the first thought . . . to know that . . . if we had just said 'fuck it' and turned it in, people would still be in trees." (Pryor hadn't changed so much that he couldn't poke fun at his ancestors, speculating that their first spoken words were probably, "Where in the fuck am I—and how do you get to Detroit?")

The sense of brotherhood Pryor felt in Africa was more wishful than fact. Pryor has always been selective in his vision and, as writer Richard Grenier pointed out in an essay on Africa, Pryor's idealized view was a false one. Grenier wrote, "As black American friends who have made the attempt to enter African society have always stressed to me, if you don't have a tribe in Africa, your skin color doesn't make

179

much difference. These tribes do not treat each other as 'brothers.' Indeed, they are rather given to massacring one another.''

Nonetheless, as ever, Pryor's perception of reality was all that mattered. And in that sense, the journey was an unqualified success. Seeing black heritage and black achievements filled Pryor with pride, which was one of the primary reasons Dr. Cannon had sent him. In fact, Pryor's elation was so great that at one point it made him feel dangerously invincible.

One afternoon when he and Jennifer were driving along a road, they spotted a half-dozen lions. Stopping the car, they watched the animals hunting and eating. Pryor has more than once portrayed himself as a coward and a nonintellectual, claiming that his kids are so much brighter than he that ''they usually get bored when I talk to them.'' But after driving through this land of proud, nonwhitened blacks (''blue-black,'' as he described them), he felt very wise and very brave. After watching the lions for several minutes, he opened the car door.

Jennifer asked, ''What are you doing?''

Pryor answered, ''I'm going over to those lions.''

''You're crazy!'' she shouted,

Without disagreeing, Pryor left the car and walked toward the lions. He advanced to within a yard of the nearest animal, a male, while a female nearby regarded him coolly and rolled over on her back.

''I just stood there,'' Pryor said, ''and the lion looked up at me real curious.'' He was locked to the animal, to the land. He felt as if he were a bridge between the beleaguered American black and the free native black, and he experienced the sensation of ''all the Pryors'' passing over him into what he calls ''the Motherland.'' There was a moment when he felt his bitterness subside and leave him, replaced by a sensation of pure exaltation. Only then did the twentieth-century man reemerge and realize that at his feet were the same animals that, a few minutes before, he had seen trap a cape buffalo and tear it apart.

Suddenly aware of his vulnerability, Pryor ''reached for

the door, but it was farther back than I thought . . . about ten feet away, and I said, 'Oh shit.' " Just then the lions started stretching in a way that Pryor says informed him, "You know your ass been out here too long," and he eased back to the car, Jennifer opening the door and promptly slapping him as he slid inside.

An equally important byproduct of his trip was that Pryor, who had made *nigger* synonymous with *friend;* vowed never to use the word again. He says that his resolution was a result of spending time in a society where everyone was black—the pilots, teachers, politicians, merchants, and even the drunks. Pryor describes seeing a man who looked like boxer Joe Frazier, only he wasn't a fighter, he was a bank president. The impact of being "home" was so great that on the last day of his stay, "I was sitting in the hotel lobby getting ready to leave and a voice inside me said, 'What do you see?' I said I see all kinds of people. The voice said, 'Do you see any niggers?' I said no, and I just started crying." Pryor was crying for having purged his soul of "a whole four hundred years of shit." He understood that "the reason black people used *nigger* as a term of endearment was because the more we said it, the less white people liked it." But, he saw now, "if saying the word *nigger* could change its meaning, it would be long gone by now." Using it simply reflected "a missing awareness of self," and that was something that no longer applied to him. At the same time, his realization purged him of his long-held feeling that it was impossible for whites and blacks to "sing in harmony." He was now of the opinion that "man is doomed if he doesn't make a multiracial society."

Although he said the concept of "nigger" was "nowhere in my psyche anymore," he refused to apologize for the number of times he'd used the word on his albums. "I'm not *there* now," he insisted, and he didn't think that people would hold it against him. If they did, all he could say to them was, "Allow me to grow. Just watch and see where my growth takes me. Maybe someday they'll say, 'Look at the motherfucker! He don't say all that shit he used to say, yet he's still saying some funny shit.' That'll be my growth."

For now, *motherfucker* was still okay. It would be several years before he pared his use of that word as well, realizing that since he wasn't using it very much in his private life, onstage or in film it was just a crutch, to get attention in case his material didn't.

Pryor was torn between going home and settling in Africa. He was terribly moved and wanted to cling to that emotional experience, declaring, "If peace of mind means keeping away from show business, then excuse me, showbiz, it's been a pleasure. Finito Bandito."

But Pryor couldn't turn his back on the money or the spotlight, and he plowed back into work. Helping to generate some enthusiasm was the fact that the story he had begun writing back in April was beginning to bear some fruit. The scenario, *Family Dreams*, had the kind of substance and pathos for which he was looking. He'd been unable to write the screenplay due to the tour, but, per his contract, he had given the synopsis to Universal. They liked it sufficiently to hire a writer to develop a screenplay while Pryor was away. Both he and Universal were happy with the results and, budgeted at $6 million, it went on the studio's fall schedule. There were still personnel and creative matters to iron out, but Pryor was glad to have it on the horizon, since there were slim pickings among the huge pile of scripts that had accumulated in his absence.

Pryor was understandably distanced from much of what he read, not only because of his experience overseas but because he was looking for something of substance and challenge, a movie along the lines of *Blue Collar*. Now that a few years had passed, and the pain of that project was less vivid, he realized, "I want to do something like that again...but everyone doesn't direct like that or write like that."

Pryor's words were sadly appropriate for the scripts and proposals stacked in his study. United Artists had come to him with the idea of doing a remake of *The Man Who Came to Dinner*, Pryor starring as an African president stranded in Georgia. He found the script lacking and the rewrites worse. Columbia Pictures put up one million dollars to reserve a few weeks of his time to costar with Marsha Mason in *Macho Man* by Neil Simon, based on a self-impressed character from one of Pryor's routines, but the script was never completed. Per the pay-or-play agreement, Pryor got to keep the money, though Columbia promised they'd be back with another property. In the meantime, a reworking of Neil Simon's *The Odd Couple* for Pryor and Bill Cosby never got past the talking stages, while Pryor collected another million-plus from producer Frank Yablans for one of his unrealized projects.

In the middle of all this activity sans productivity, Pryor took time in May to give Barbara Walters one of the most outrageous interviews of either of their careers. Pausing between outbursts of teasing and wrath, he gave her totally ridiculous statements, such as, "Whatever you feel about me when you see me right now is the truth," and, "Some of the things I say are true, some are not, but it all happened." Walters tried to get to the bottom of important racial and professional issues, but for the most part Pryor was more concerned with uncovering ways to crack up the crew members. He succeeded beyond expectation when he managed to coerce Walters into saying "nigger," thus setting her up for, "You say that very well. You've said it before, haven't you?"

While *Family Dreams* percolated at Universal, Pryor went to England to do a cameo as a balloon seller in *The Muppet Movie*—which, ironically, became the most successful film in his repertoire, outperforming even *Silver Streak*. He enjoyed *The Muppet Movie,* though very little else seemed to please him at that point. One development that particularly incensed him was the limited release in August of *Richard Pryor Is Back Live in Concert*. Bill Sargent's SEE organization had lifted the first twenty minutes of the seventy-eight-minute picture from the earlier concert film, while the rest featured virtually the same material as its predecessor—the difference being, according to a Sargent spokesperson, "It was photographed at a different concert—you can tell because Mr. Pryor is wearing a watch in the second part, and he isn't in the first part." Pryor detested the thought of the public flocking to theaters on the strength of his name, only to discover that they'd seen most of it before. He couldn't stop the film, though word of mouth buried it in short order, newspapers nationwide doing their part. As *The New York Times* reported, "If you cannot rest until you see Mr. Pryor wear a wristwatch, don't miss this recycled work." Otherwise, warned the critic, the prudent moviegoer would "stay home and remember the first movie fondly."

Family Dreams was finally ready to go before the cameras in October, though before its release it would undergo a title change to *Bustin' Loose*.

Pryor was simultaneously nervous and enthusiastic about the picture. Apart from the concert film, which was presold to his audience, he had never exercised so much control over a movie's material or casting. Indeed, he nearly came to blows with Universal over the choice of director. They wanted someone who was well established, while Pryor went to bat for Broadway director Oz Scott. After threatening to quit, Pryor got his man—along with the headache of knowing that if the picture failed, it was his responsibility entirely.

Scriptwise, Pryor felt that he had a lot going for him. The story gave him ample chance to act and to do a new character, Joe Braxton, a thief whose parole officer assigns him to escort teacher Vivian Perry and a busload of orphans from their residence in Philadelphia to a farm owned by Perry's parents in Washington State. In addition to playing Braxton himself, Pryor played Braxton impersonating a Texas conman, a blustering role that was thrown in for insurance laughs since he is really inconsistent with the sweetness of the rest of the story. Posing as the conman, Braxton swindles a bunch of gamblers in order to prevent the Perrys from losing their farm—and, in doing so, wins the teacher's love.

Given his background in broad comedy, Pryor courageously put most of his faith in the interaction between Braxton and the children, an oddball assortment that runs from a pyromaniac to a young Vietnamese hooker. He responds with brief, usually restrained outbursts as the kids dump on him, love him, annoy him, or otherwise incur his wrath.

Pryor took a personal hand in the casting, particularly in

the pivotal role of Vivian Perry. The first-draft script had been completed while Pryor was on the road, and as soon as he'd read it he asked Franklin to approach his client Cicely Tyson about playing Ms. Perry. Pryor and Tyson had never met, though in passing along the offer Franklin painted a portrait of Pryor as a coy, insecure man who didn't believe his poor little story had any chance of landing an actress of her caliber. Tyson laughed and replied that it depended on the script, which he left with her. Finding a lot of merit in it, she asked Franklin to arrange a meeting.

At the time, Pryor was performing in Atlanta, so Tyson flew there to catch his show and talk with him. She knew him mostly for his films, which she admired, and Franklin warned her to gird herself for his stage material. However, much to her surprise, it didn't bother her in the least. "I realized that he could say almost anything and not be offensive." Without being demeaning, she elaborated that that was because he projected the innocent wonder and bewilderment of "a little child up there onstage who had just learned a few bad words and almost didn't know the meaning of them." What struck her more was "the depth of his soul," revealed in the private conversation that followed, and she said that the chance to act opposite such a sensitive man was the factor that most influenced her to do the movie.

But there was a problem she hadn't anticipated. Pryor wasn't like her other leading men—well-trained and highly disciplined actors like Paul Winfield and James Earl Jones. Although Pryor had scrupulously adhered to the script in most of his previous films, he ad-libbed constantly throughout *Bustin' Loose*. It seemed he was trying to build a madcap presence within the basically gentle story, fulfilling his fans and at the same time letting loose some of his inherent irreverence. As Tyson points out, it was the first time he wasn't "screaming" in a movie, but quietly making points about love and commitment, breaking new ground internally and professionally.

Pryor's improvisations made Tyson uneasy at first. She would come to the set with her lines memorized, adhering to the actors' saw that the script is the solid structure on which one hangs his or her interpretations. But, she recalls, "I would say a line and he would come up with something new, something not in the script." That would cause her to fumble, which made Pryor very uneasy. "Listen," he'd tell her more than once, "I'm awfully sorry, but tomorrow I'm gonna learn my lines and I'm gonna do it right." However, each new day would be a rerun of the last, and before long the actress realized that the situation would not improve, that Pryor "is an actor who works creatively out of himself." Instead of trying to change him, she concentrated on putting him at ease, advising him to do whatever he felt was necessary and that she would "just roll with the punches."

Except for his insecurity, Tyson reports, "Pryor was very loose and funny... always kidding around. He had this very strong need to keep everyone up." But she knew that it was all a smokescreen. The actress says that all she had to do was "look at him and see the turmoil within him. He's very scrupulous about his work. And this makes him, as with any sensitive artist, frightened, wanting desperately to do the right thing."

Even though *Bustin' Loose* was all his, Pryor still wasn't happy. He was proud of making a nonexploitative, all-black film, but knowing that the eyes of the black world, the white world, and Hollywood were on him put him under inordinate pressure. He tried to keep it all inside, and the strain was enormous. His "legal" releases were few, such as sharing his pride in the project with Juliette Whittaker by flying her and some of her pupils to the Washington location and giving her kids cameo roles in the film. Otherwise, his only outlets were drinking and snorting as usual, which he did with such intensity that, in the words of his friend director Michael Schultz, this time it seemed as if he were "trying to really cash in the chips." Schultz, like everyone else, saw that Pryor was becoming "heavily overweight and puffed from excessive alcohol," but there was no one, not even David Franklin, who could help to ease his self-imposed burdens.

Bustin' Loose shot through the frigid northwestern winter, the studio sequences wrapping early in 1980, and the picture was slated for release in October of that year.

Relieved of the weighty undertaking, Pryor decided to involve himself with a few less-taxing works. The first was a cameo role, for a lot of money, in Universal's *In God We Trust*. This was star-director Marty Feldman's strained, misfired comedy about a monk who leaves his abbey in order to raise money and prevent foreclosure. Along the way he falls in with a wealthy evangelist, played by Andy Kaufman, who communes frequently with God, played by Pryor. Pryor's climactic appearance, decked out in long white hair, beard, and mustache, is embarrassing: his part is a caricature, not a character, and he hammed it up unmercifully.

Nonetheless, according to Kaufman, Pryor enjoyed the two days he spent on the set. It helped that the two men had known each other since 1972, when Pryor came over to compliment Kaufman after catching his act at the Improv in New York. Kaufman describes him as "very decent and great to work with," though he adds that "thanks to Marty and his wife there was a family feeling on this picture. We all felt like welcomed guests." Pryor responded to that, and was very loose with everyone—though the story would be considerably different on Pryor's next two films.

Columbia, as promised, returned with a starring vehicle for Pryor. He was still exhausted after *Bustin' Loose,* but the role offered three factors he couldn't resist. The first, and in this case the least important, was a fee in the neighborhood of two million dollars. That was a generous offer, but Pryor could have gotten close to that kind of money elsewhere. The second was a chance to be directed again by Sidney Poitier. *Uptown Saturday Night* had been less than satisfactory in that sense; what Pryor really wanted was the chance to work closely with the man. "Sidney's a great director," he had always maintained, "and I don't think there's a black actor or actress who doesn't want to work with him. That was one of my dreams ever since I saw *The Defiant Ones* and *Go, Man, Go,*" and the fact that it was coming true made him "happy." Yet, the third reason was no doubt the strongest in persuading him to accept Columbia's project. They were offering him the chance to act again with Gene Wilder.

Pryor had enjoyed working with Wilder before because

"we respect each other's work," but more important than that they respected "each other's person," which is rare in Hollywood. Understandably, Pryor was eager to get back in the saddle with his friend.

The picture in question was *Stir Crazy*, and it went into production on March 10, 1980. It's the unlikely chronicle of aspiring playwright Skip Donahue (Wilder) and his buddy, starving actor Harry Munroe (Pryor), who decide to leave New York and seek employment in Los Angeles. Along the way they are arrested for a crime they didn't commit.

Sentenced to prison for 125 years, the men try to act tough but fail miserably. Though Munroe struts into the cell booming, "Tha's right, tha's right, we bad—we don't want no shit," within moments his facade crumbles.

Fortunately for the new arrivals, their prison is one of two that is sending participants to a local rodeo and Skip, with a natural talent for staying in the saddle, agrees to ride if he's allowed to pick his own crew. He selects Harry and three other inmates—one of whom has a wife on the outside with a plan to smuggle the men from the stadium.

While Skip is riding, Harry slips under the grandstand and scurries into a large popcorn cart that the wife has planted there. She wheels him to a van, where he changes and dons a fake beard. The two enter the rodeo while the other inmates sneak off to the bathroom. There, Harry and the woman give them streetclothes and escort them out, while Skip lets his opponent win and convinces the dullard to toss the prize money into the grandstand, then sneaks under the grandstand in the ensuing hubbub. All of them go free.

Despite Pryor's rapport with Wilder, the two-month haul on *Stir Crazy* was plagued by almost as many problems as *Blue Collar*. Only this time, Pryor couldn't pin the blame on friction among the actors or with the director, all of whom were generally considerate and helpful, or on any moral conflicts with the script. Nor did he try. At the time of the shoot, Pryor states simply, he was "just about gone...destroying myself" by his inability to handle success, the thought of failure, or loneliness. He was preoccupied, still, with his grandmother's death, and longed to return to Kenya, yet found it impossible not to work, to take time off.

Perhaps worst was that people were constantly asking him for favors or money. These were not necessarily friends or family but people he knew peripherally or had known in the past, out-of-work black actors or technicians, acquaintances from Peoria—anyone who could get him on the telephone. "That was killing me, 'give me this' and 'buy me that' and 'do this for me.'" He says it "slowly ate me up" when these people would "come from nowhere, making their claims, feeding on what I've earned, feeding on me like they have a right to whatever I have." Because he's a self-described "soft touch," he gave when he felt the reason was justified, but he was no longer enjoying it as he had before. He became so resentful of people around him that he even broke up briefly with Jennifer, convinced that he needed more room to breathe.

Pryor's friend Burt Reynolds—who had built a home close to Pryor's lot on Maui—took a look at what had happened to Pryor and echoed what Franklin had said years before: "Richard is very capable of bringing genuine punishment upon himself. He seeks it out because like all of us he wonders if he deserves his success . . . he's frightened."

Analysis was no longer helping him, and he later admitted, "I kept going by using cocaine and alcohol." In the meantime, he appears to have taken it out on *Stir Crazy*.

Poitier minimizes the difficulties he had with Pryor, stating only that he "loved" working with him. However, in conversations with crew members, words like *depressed* and *erratic* surfaced frequently in connection with Pryor. He would make statements like, "I'm sick of the film business," and walk off the set; illnesses, too, were a frequent occurrence on location at the Arizona State Penitentiary in Florence. Pryor was often a half-day late coming to the set, blaming a bronchial condition aggravated by the crop dusting of fields surrounding the prison. The producers' insurance did not cover them for allergies, and while Pryor stayed in bed at the hotel the meter kept running on the film's budget.

When he did show up, there were allegedly frequent

confrontations between Pryor and the crew members, who didn't want to be in Arizona and resented the fact that it was Pryor who was keeping them there. This tension came to a head when a cameraman was said to have approached Pryor one day late in April and, holding out a piece of watermelon, let it fall at the star's feet. Pryor remained calm but walked off the picture, staying away for several days while Columbia quashed rumors that another actor was being called in to redo the part, that a double had been hired for behind-the-head shots, and that the script was being rewritten to eliminate the rest of Pryor's scenes. "The film has only three more weeks of production," noted an exasperated spokesperson. "If we replaced every actor on every picture who had flareups or emotional problems . . ."

Stir Crazy lurched to completion in May, Pryor's behavior tempered by Wilder's presence and the fact that his own reputation was on the line. However, Pryor was on a roll and went right from that battleground to a worse one.

Pryor had agreed to do a cameo for Columbia in their comedy *Wholly Moses,* playing the pharaoh opposite Dudley Moore's prophet Herschel, who, overhearing God's commands to Moses, thinks they're for him. While *Stir Crazy* was being held for Christmas release, Columbia wanted *Wholly Moses* out in July to cash in on the lucrative summer trade. Time was tight, and within a matter of days Pryor had gone from a prison grays and iron bars to the regal white robes and alabaster scepter of an Egyptian monarch.

During what was scheduled to have been a week-long gig, Pryor was said to have oppressed everyone in sight, not only arguing with cast and crew over artistic matters but shooting down anyone who complained about his showing up a half-day late—usually detained because he was freebasing and didn't feel like leaving the house. At one point Pryor became so disgusted that he walked off the set for a week. Since his part was small, there was talk about recasting the part; but Columbia wanted his name on the marquee and director Gary Weis hung in there, finally managing to squeeze out all the scenes he required from Pryor.

At the beginning of June, to coin a phrase, Pryor didn't seem to know which way was up. He wasn't happy despite all his wealth and stature, and while Dr. Cannon had shown him that riches weren't a solution to what ailed him, Pryor didn't know what was. He decided that until he sorted it all out, what he really needed was to have some fun. To this end, he tentatively committed to costar in the forty-five-minute Roman-era episode of Mel Brooks's new film, *A History of the World, Part One*. What had passed between him and Brooks on *Blazing Saddles* took a backseat to Pryor's need for a few laughs. However, instead of making the film, Pryor would end up fighting for his life.

Chapter Eighteen

"I spent a lot of time being a hustler...struggling, stepping, pulling, clawing. Then you get to a point where you don't have to do that—so what do you do with your hands?"

Pryor's question is less rhetorical than it sounds, for, without knowing it, he turned them on himself. Everything that had happened on *Stir Crazy,* on *Wholly Moses,* in his personal life—all the fighting and turmoil—was only a preliminary bout to the main attraction. "I had all this stuff seething inside of me," Pryor divulges, "and not being able to express that—" He pauses, and says of the fire, "Everything was settled that night...the slate was clean."

There remain many mysteries about what actually happened on the night of June 9, 1980, not the least of which is exactly how Pryor managed to set himself on fire. What is known are the psychological events that preceded the blaze. As Pryor has said, "My bitch left me and I went crazy freebasing for eight months straight," virtually since the end of his tour. He admits "doin' so much I embarrassed cocaine dealers," and resisted the efforts of friends like

Jim Brown to help him quit. Indeed, when anyone tried to "rule" his life he redoubled his efforts to be independent.

Pryor's carefully rebuilt reputation for reliability was demolished, along with his health and mental stability. He didn't care. He felt that his pipe was all he needed, and in his routine he personified the bong, talking about how it promised to take care of him, how it smooth-talked him into staying home and not bothering with anything or anyone.

On the night of the fire, Pryor had been up for five days straight, acknowledging that on the first three of those days he'd been freebasing. Freebasing originated in Colombia in the 1930s and takes its name from the freeing of cocaine (i.e., "base") from impurities, thus producing a more intense high. Freebase is made using a solvent and ether. Ether and Pryor's favorite solvent, a 151-proof Jamaican rum called Overproof, which is more than three-quarters pure alcohol, are extremely flammable substances and if carelessly handled can explode.

Freebasing cocaine is the most exhilarating use of the drug because it goes directly to the brain. But the effect lasts for no more than two minutes and produces what one user told *People* magazine was "the urge to have more . . . the more you smoke." Pryor fell into that trap, thus bringing on side-effects that ranged from severe depression to paranoia.

Pryor has offered two different stories to "prove" that he wasn't freebasing the night of the fire. His most frequent claim is that he had simply decided not to do it anymore. In light of the drug's psychologically addictive nature and Pryor's weakened resistance, this is questionable. More than likely, as Pryor has also said, his connection simply didn't come through. He didn't have the cocaine and thus "elected" to quit.

Pryor's version of what happened the night of the fire first came to light in a press conference held by David Franklin on June 11. The attorney simply announced that contrary to the rumors of freebase having been the cause, Pryor had had a glass of rum in his hand and it ignited.

Pryor later elaborated, saying that he was in his bedroom

with a friend and "since we didn't have no coke, we were drinking the rum. My partner and I were sitting there drinking and talking . . . all I needed was a little boost." The bottle was on a TV table beside Pryor, who was sitting on the floor, and when he reached for a cigarette lighter on the table he spilled the liquor. Pryor went and got a towel to mop it up, then tried to light his cigarette. The lighter was empty. Since he was going to refill it, he decided to gather up all the other lighters in the house and refill them at the same time.

While Pryor was sitting on the floor, testing one of the lighters, it lit. Still seated on the floor, he brought the flame to the cigarette dangling from his mouth. The bottle of rum was still on the table, at the same level, some of its contents coating the neck and sides of the bottle. As he brought the lighter near, the rum ignited.

"I heard a noise like 'Pow!'" Pryor says, "and suddenly I was engulfed in flames." Screaming for help, he groped for something to smother the flames, but "everywhere I touched there was fire. My buddy ran and I jumped on the bed and grabbed the blanket and tried to put out the fire."

Pryor's Aunt Dee, who was staying with him at the time, came running at the friend's behest. She scooped up the blanket with which her nephew had been fumbling, hurriedly wrapped it around his torso, and snuffed the flames. Pryor slid to the floor while she slapped out the few flames that had caught on surrounding articles.

Pryor told *Ebony*, "I was sitting on the floor waiting for the ambulance, and I said, 'I'm going to die.' I didn't want a lot of photographers coming in my house and taking pictures of me laying there dead . . . burned up. I could just see the cameras . . . click . . . click . . . me laying there dead . . . pictures in the papers." This unusual vanity prompted Pryor to jump to his feet and run from the house. He would later say, "I ran out of my house so fast that I must have some Olympic records coming to me." He sped into the driveway, the only thing on his mind "to make a four-hundred-yard dash to *somewhere*."

The police tell a slightly different story. They claim that Pryor was probably freebasing, and the only reason they didn't press drug charges was that they found no evidence in his house. Immediately after Pryor was lifted into the ambulance, the police cordoned off the street in front of his home and firemen tried to get inside. One of Pryor's business managers informed the staff to admit no one, so it was fifteen hours before the arson squad, armed with a verbal search warrant, threw ladders against the driveway gate and entered the grounds.

One investigator subsequently confided to a reporter that they wouldn't have been surprised to find "a factory up there"; accordingly, they approached armed with a shotgun. When the door was answered, the officers insisted that they be admitted to search the premises for "unsafe materials." Not surprisingly, they found nothing incriminating. They found only rum and broken glass. Captain Dan Hostetter of the Los Angeles County Fire Department arson unit told reporters that neither drugs nor flammable liquids were found in the bedroom, adding, however, that the maids had moved things around. But Pryor had admitted to Zielinski and Helm that he was freebasing and had been overheard by passersby. He was also said to have confessed to doctors Richard and Jack Grossman, the codirectors of the burn center. However, it is possible that Pryor was speaking from anguish, feeling he was being punished for having freebased before, not for having done it that night.

Larry Murphy is the vocational nurse and respiratory specialist who took care of Pryor for the duration of his hospital stay. Talking to him, one gets the impression that he knows the truth. However, he says only, "Even if I knew, I couldn't and wouldn't divulge it." He feels that "Richard has told America and his fans whatever he wanted them to know about that particular situation," and refers interested parties to the album *Richard Pryor Live on the Sunset Strip*, recorded at a concert after the accident. "Richard tells us what he wants on that album. Go back to it and listen."

What Pryor *seems* to say is that he wasn't freebasing. "Have you ever heard of a motherfucker burning up freebasing— other than me?" That's not an admission of catching fire while freebasing, merely asking if the audience has ever heard of anyone doing that. Then he cries with exasperation, "I burned up because I *quit* freebasing!" Yet, that may not be the "confession" to which Murphy refers. For Pryor also asks rhetorically, "If nobody else burns up freebasing, why do you think it happened to *me*?" The answer, which the audience well knows since it cheers at that point, is that whether it's catching fire or shooting up cars or staring down lions, such things don't happen to everyone but they *do* happen to Richard Pryor.

If the rum story is a lie, what could Pryor's reason have been for concocting it? Surprisingly, it would not have been fear of prosecution. For the most part, police are not interested in apprehending the users of drugs like cocaine; they're after the sellers. And although the authorities could have turned Pryor's home inside out searching for evidence, mere possession of paraphernalia isn't a crime. Even Pryor's statements to Zielinski and Helm wouldn't have been admissible in court, since he could hardly have been aware, at the time, of the ramifications of what he was saying—a key aspect to any confession. And there were no witnesses who were willing to talk. The worst that might have happened is that the police would have kept Pryor under surveillance.

It isn't likely that he was protecting the reputation of whoever was in the room, since that person's identity has never been revealed in any case. Equally unlikely is that he was concerned about the presence of a morals clause in any of his contracts; he was too valuable a commodity for that.

The most rational explanation is Pryor's concern for public and peer reaction, which was a threefold consideration. First, the public tends not to be sympathetic to celebrities who harm or kill themselves with drugs. They'll ignore its "limited" use by eccentric talents but won't tolerate mishandling of any kind. Second, a drug accident implies, in the words of an L.A. attorney who advises his clients to keep quiet about such things, that "you're so blown away you can't handle anything, which makes it impossible to get a job if you survive." Lastly, there is a certain romance in *denying* it. If not consciously then subconsciously, not telling the truth would have appealed to Pryor's sense of creating an aura of mystery about himself. It would not have been the first time that Pryor lied to that end.

Apart from the medical personnel at the burn center, the only people who know for certain what happened are Pryor's aunt and whoever Pryor was with that night. Speculation about his partner's identity has ranged from Jim Brown to the concert promoter who called Franklin in Atlanta with the news. Brown is actually the least likely candidate, for Pryor's friend of fifteen years was known to disapprove of cocaine, and his presence wouldn't have coincided with Pryor's comment that he was drinking rum because they were out of cocaine. A girlfriend is also unlikely, since Pryor would hardly have referred to a woman as his "buddy." Besides, he and Jennifer Lee had reconciled and he had been with her earlier in the day, though she had gone back to her Los Angeles apartment late that afternoon.

The fact that no one has spoken up lends weight to the freebase story. It suggests someone looking to avoid even minimal legal hassles, and besides, a voice in support of the rum story would have helped Pryor's cause, not hurt it.

As with the police, the consensus among the press is that Pryor was freebasing. According to *Rolling Stone* magazine, which was present at the Franklin press conference, "No one bought the rum line for a minute," a sentiment echoed by *Newsweek* and other publications. Of course, opinion, not evidence, is all that supports that suspicion, and Pryor complains, "It upsets me to hear that people think I was freebasing. Why can't they hear my side of it?"

But it is difficult to dismiss the freebase story, particularly in light of the final paradox that comes from Pryor himself. He reports that in his autobiography *Up From the Ashes*— which he also insists will most likely never be published— he's going to be telling the real story of the fire. If the "real" story has yet to be told, then just what has he been telling people?

Across the street from the Sherman Oaks Community Hospital on Van Nuys Boulevard is the institution's burn center, one of the most modern in the nation. Located minutes from Pryor's home, it was here he was rushed after the accident.

Larry Murphy was on duty when Pryor arrived. "I just happened to be in the emergency room when he came in, and

I just couldn't believe it. He was pretty cooked but he was sittin' up. I said to a coworker, 'Wow—that looks like brother Richard Pryor,' and my first reaction was that I really hurt for him. My second reaction was more comforting—the fact that he was here, in the best place.''

A quick examination determined that Pryor had suffered third-degree burns over much of his body above the waist and below the ears. This meant that if he survived, the wounds would require grafting. As Pryor joked in his Sunset Strip concert, he was so badly burned that the doctor said, ''Why don't we just get some cole slaw and serve this up?''

Pryor was dazed by it all, though he says, ''I knew I did *something* 'cause there was too many white folks paying attention to me.''

Murphy recalls, ''He came in hurting, but not really knowing what it was going to be like, what was in store. He was almost comical once the medication took effect, certainly having more fun with us than we were with him.'' Murphy knew what Pryor did not—that if he survived, the real pain was three days down the road. ''It takes that long before the burns really let you know what they're gonna be. Once we get the dead tissue off and the raw skin is exposed, you're hurtin' a hell of a lot more.''

Pryor was rushed into surgery to clear away the largest chunks of charred tissue, after which he was placed on a bed of ''egg crates,'' a mattress made of small cones. Doctor kept constant tabs on his blood pressure and heartbeat, his kidneys likewise monitored to ensure that they didn't shut down from the waste overload. He was fed intravenously, since the healing process requires a minimum of one thousand calories per day and burns deaden the appetite.

There were concerns that Pryor would suffer a heart attack or lose his eyesight from the proximity of the flames, but there was virtually nothing else that could be done for him. As the initial report from the hospital explained, ''He's about as sick as you can get and be alive. He's stable, but in these cases things can turn around in thirty seconds.'' Pryor was given a slim chance of survival, his doctors pointing out that seventy-five percent of the patients his age and in his condition didn't pull through. The prognosis was even worse for Pryor because his constitution was weakened due to what Richard Grossman described as "all the junk he's put in his body."

When Pryor woke up on the morning after the fire, his first thought was that he was glad to be alive, and he intended to stay alive. "I got a strong will and I'm a strong man and I wanted to live," Pryor says. His second thought, he recalls, is that he knew he'd "fucked up because my dick didn't want to move."

Pryor also took strength from the people around him, all of whom showed extraordinary concern for his well-being. On the night after Pryor's arrival, officer Zielinski phoned the hospital to enquire about Pryor's condition. Zielinski was quoted as saying that he was angry with reporters who were constantly calling and asking if Pryor had been stoned, said he didn't care himself what Pryor had been doing—only that this man, of whom he was not even a fan, become well as soon as possible. Pryor was especially helped by the presence of thirty-year-old Larry Murphy, who stayed with him for the first eighteen hours of his ordeal, and would end up putting in 172 hours over the first two weeks of Pryor's stay.

Others quickly rallied to Pryor's side. Pryor's actor-friend Stan Shaw (costar of *Roots* and *Bingo Long*) all but pitched a tent at the burn center, and ex-wives Deboragh and Maxine were frequent visitors, along with Dee, Pryor's children Richard, Elizabeth, and Rain—and of course Jennifer Lee. So many of Pryor's women were present that, after the first skin-graft operation, when Richard Grossman went to the waiting room to report on the surgery, he innocently called out, "Mrs. Pryor?" All the women in the room shot to their feet.

An innocent, plaintive figure keeping constant vigil, Jennifer Lee was never permitted to see her lover. On the first few days the restriction was purely medical. "The doctors say I cannot visit with him until he is completely out of danger," Jennifer told a reporter. "So I'm just going to hang in here now, and keep reminding him of how much I love him." Yet, even after Pryor was able to have visitors, he didn't want her at his side, didn't want her to see him scarred. Eventually, however, ex-wife

Maxine convinced him to let her in. The rest of the time, Jennifer kept in touch with him by passing him notes on his meal trays. "I'm just trying to give him positive energy, good thoughts, strength, and expressions of my love in the notes," she explained. "I want Richard to know I am close to him." A hospital spokesperson told reporters that she had succeeded, the messages helping to put "the sparkle back in his eye."

However, of all the people who stayed with or visited Pryor, no one was more helpful to Pryor—or more formidable—than Jim Brown.

Brown was the first person Pryor asked to see, fueling speculation that he'd been present at the time of the fire. More likely is that Pryor was looking for moral support, and Jim Brown gave him that and more. He arrived at nine every morning, at which time many other people would already be waiting, from friends to professional associates to journalists and religious fanatics. Brown would take the list of their names to Pryor's room, returning with messages for those who waited or admitting the privileged few. The rest of the time, Brown was at Pryor's side, encouraging him through the many harsh medical procedures he had to endure.

Pryor's daily routine at the hospital was long and filled with what Murphy calls "scheduled pain." Virtually from the bginning of his stay, he was awakened every morning at six-thirty or seven o'clock, made to eat a light breakfast, then walked to a whirlpool for the first of his two hourly treatments.

These sessions were absolute torment, for it was here that the dead skin was scrubbed away. Though debriding increases a patient's fluid loss at a time when they can least afford it, the wounds must be cleaned to prevent infection and to prepare for eventual grafting. According to Murphy, the whirlpool is literally a battleground to which "some of the biggest men come in bragging and go out humble." He reports that while Pryor may not have been the bravest man in the world, he had a positive mental attitude, "the ability to cope." Murphy says that the cut on the Sunset Strip album that recounts the first time Pryor went into the chemically treated water of the tank "is very accurate."

In this routine, Pryor says that Murphy sat him in the tub, talking to him as though he were a child. Feeling good—the dead skin was insulating his wounds, minimizing the pain—and tiring of Murphy's slow build, Pryor lost all patience when the specialist started to make a big deal about a sponge.

" 'Here, feel that?'

"I said, 'What is it?'

" 'It's a sponge.'

" 'Yeah, motherfucker, now *wash* my ass!' And the motherfucker went *whoooooosh*. I screamed, 'Ahhhhhhhh! Dooooon't.'

" 'But I gotta—'

" 'No, ya *don't*!'

" 'But just lemme get—'

" 'Fuck you! I don't care if I *do* die, but you ain't gonna touch me with that motherfuckin' sponge *no more....*' "

Pryor elaborated in an interview, "The first time he hit me across the ass with that scrubbing brush, I let out a scream they probably heard all over that hospital. [But] Brother Murphy said, 'I have to hurt you to get you better.' He talked to me like a baby. He just kept telling me, 'Richard, I've got to get this dead skin off you or the skin grafts won't take, man.' And I could tell from the way he handled me, from the look in his eyes, that he wanted to help me, that he loved me."

Murphy recalls that Pryor immediately stalked from the tub but that he quickly "regrouped," and thereafter they "had no problem cleaning him."

Following his morning whirlpool bath, Pryor went for the first of two daily visits to the hyperbaric tank, an iron-lunglike unit that speeds the healing process by subjecting the user to oxygen-enriched air at two to three times the normal atmospheric pressure. The higher oxygen content of the blood stabilizes the functioning of vital organs, improves metabolism, and decreases swelling. After that two-hour session, Pryor's burns were dressed in gauze saturated with the powerful antibiotic silver sulfadiazene. Pryor would then rest briefly, eat, and repeat the routine. Rarely was he allowed to sit around, for, as Jim Brown told a reporter, "They are keeping him busy to keep him alive."

Brown wasn't just composing headlines. In these early days, activity, focusing his will and attention, was Pryor's only hope. The rest of him was falling apart, and quickly—so much so that the doctors were not sure he would pull through.

As if his condition were not severe enough, within days of his arrival Pryor contracted pneumonia. This is not uncommon for burn patients, due to a condition called atalectasis. Their injury becomes what Jack Grossman compared to "a leather girdle," restricting breathing and causing coughing. The pneumonia came and stayed, and Pryor underwent frequent treatment to force air into his lungs. At the height of its hold, from June 17 through the 20th, a lung specialist paid regular visits, along with a kidney expert who was called in to watch what a spokesperson described as "an abnormality that existed before he was burned." Jack Grossman said he had no reason to believe that abuse of drugs or drink had caused the damage to Pryor's kidneys, but that an unspecified problem had been heightened by Pryor's debilitation.

Pryor was on the critical list for the first two weeks of his stay. Psychologically, there was also an incredible strain. According to Murphy, Pryor suffered less from feelings of futility and depression than disorientation and a sense of being ashamed, both of which are natural for burn patients. "You're talking about someone who is taken out of their environment, is in pain, whose loved ones are in pain. Then someone starts telling them when to eat, when to go to the bathroom, and on top of this causes them nearly continuous pain. But he bit his lip and took it, and as soon as he could he did the work himself."

Pryor's alertness was at once an asset and a bane. It helped him work up a fighting spirit but left him constantly aware of the gravity of his condition, of his tenuous hold on life. "I didn't know what was going to happen to me," he says in retrospect, "but I didn't think about dying at all. I was concentrating on getting well. I walked the second day I was in the hospital and did everything I could possibly do to help myself.'' Though vanity prevented him from ''looking in a mirror for six weeks,'' he was otherwise as tough as he could be. He refused medication except when the pain was unbearable. As he told Murphy, ''This is real and I'm gonna deal with it and we will fix it.''

He also wanted to impress Jim Brown. Brown had warned him about the kind of life he was leading, but Pryor hadn't listened, and now he wanted to pull himself back by the bootstraps. Brown was only too willing to help him. ''I got strength off of Jim,'' Pryor says fondly. ''For three hard weeks he was there. When I went to sleep, he was there. When I woke up, he was there. And I kept saying to myself, 'I can't give in to the pain . . . not in front of Jim Brown.' '' That, Murphy observes, ''helped him deal with the stress and the pain outstandingly well. In any given situation, the doctors can only do so much. You have to have the help and the confidence of the patient, or else we have a very difficult time.''

As soon as Pryor was able, he began walking around the ward, giving encouragement to fellow patients as well as seeking it. He saw accident victims like himself, stood weeping over a child who'd been burned in a scalding tub, watched in awe ''this Mexican man burned head to toe. They would bathe him and scrape him and he never blinked.''

Despite the other patients and the staff's tender loving care, and Jim Brown and all of Pryor's other friends, Murphy isn't sure that Pryor would have survived without his sense of humor. ''He *did* work superhard, and so did everyone around him, but it was his comedy that took the upper hand when it was needed, when he was suffering and refused medication, or was in pain that no medication could handle. The jokes gave him the strength to deal with his ordeal.''

Pryor's capacity to make light of personal misfortune took on new dimension after the fire. ''I gotta tell you how I burned up,'' he would tell a concert audience a year after the accident. ''Before I go to bed, I have a little milk and cookies. And one night I had that low-fat milk and that pasteurized shit. And I dipped my cookie in and the shit blew up. . . ." It was a feat that impressed even ex-wife Deboragh, who had doubted he could do it because the pain had simply been "too real." But, as Larry Murphy recognized, "That's something I don't think a lot of people understand about him: his comedy and his humor carry him higher than anything. More than money."

Chapter Nineteen

Pryor was in surprisingly good spirits, and Jim Brown's presence was one of the reasons. Larry Murphy says that having Brown around didn't hurt hospital morale either, since "the ladies on the staff went a little apeshit over him," while Jack Grossman lauded the way "he stepped in and took over completely everything that had to do with Mr. Pryor's affairs and his family."

Unfortunately, certain members of that family didn't appreciate Brown. Neither Brown nor Pryor has ever said who the dissenters were, but apart from his children and ex-wives, his only surviving relatives were his uncle Dickey, aunts Dee and Maxine—Leroy's sister from Bloomington, Illinois—and various cousins. Whoever the antagonists were, they had frequent run-ins with Brown. The biggest row was over the control of Pryor's nonmedical affairs. Brown made decisions when Pryor could not, and was apparently suspected by some of maneuvering so that he would ultimately be able to involve himself much more in his friend's finances, projects, real-estate holdings, and so on. That was neither Brown's objective nor his style, and after a few weeks he began to resent the confrontations. He pulled back, grumbling, "I'm a straight-walking, black, bad, tall, straight-talking fool. I either run it or I don't [and] can't override what I call a lack of knowledge."

Brown started coming in earlier in the morning and

departing shortly thereafter, staying out of Pryor's personal matters entirely—which, unknown to either man, left him a target for vultures. While Pryor was hospitalized, members of his family began dividing up his possessions. With the known exception of his children, he discovered that "when I was in the hospital fighting for my life, there were people close to me, people I trusted, members of my family . . . in my house deciding what they were going to have. My watches are missing. My money is missing. Some of my jewelry is gone." Pryor breaks into sobs, even today, when he talks about the theft of an old one-hundred-dollar bill his grandmother had given him for good luck. "I'd always believed in my family, but . . . people I trusted were making deals with other people about my shit, thinking I was going to die."

Pryor would recover many of his belongings, though never his faith in the good intentions of so many of the people in his life.

With or without Brown, there were plenty of people working to keep up Pryor's hopes. Though the doctors didn't permit him to have a phone, calls flooded in, from fans to enemies to actors to politicians. Of these, the only call Pryor took was from Ted Kennedy. The nurse who brought him the phone explained, "This was special [to Pryor] and he wanted to talk to Teddy. They had a real nice talk. It just really perked him up." (Placed a few days before the Democratic National Convention, the call won Kennedy a good deal of press but didn't help him get the nomination. The good wishes from third-party candidate John Anderson were merely conveyed to Pryor.)

Despite the ban on phone calls, Pryor didn't want for visitors, though only his friends were allowed to see him. Elliott Gould, Sidney Poitier, Rosalind Cash, and Marlon Brando were among the many who came to the burn center and were allowed in. ("White people never came to see me till I burned up," Pryor later quipped.) Brando even arranged for a private TV hookup in Pryor's room so he could watch the Roberto Duran–Sugar Ray Leonard welterweight bout on June 21. Sammy Davis, Jr., made a point of stopping in to see the other patients, as did Redd Foxx, who had earlier sent flowers and a telegram that read, "I knew you were looking for me, but I didn't expect you to send up smoke signals." Pryor received so many flowers that he cracked, "I can always open a flower shop if the doctors don't let me go back to work right away."

Murphy notes that while everybody "got a little silly" over the flood of celebrities, their presence kept everyone on their toes. "We had to stand in the way to keep Richard out of stress, which kept us busy. But it was good in that it reinforced the fact that we were in the public eye. Not only did we have to do a good job, we had to do it under unusual pressure. I think we handled it very well."

Many other people dropped by but were not admitted, and even the privileged few didn't stay long. As Brown noted, "There's very little time for visitors; they get in the way of the nurses. Burn patients don't just lie there in bed, they're kept moving around." Nor did Pryor particularly want to entertain guests when he was allowed to sit still, preferring to watch television. "He was really interested in the news," Murphy reports, "especially the news about him." More than once Pryor heard that he had died or wasn't expected to live through the night, which Murphy says caused him to "laugh or get pissed off," depending on his mood.

Pryor was grateful for all the attention, but, as usual, it was the common folk who really won his heart. Books, gifts, telegrams, and thousands of letters arrived daily, and were immediately turned over to eighteen-year-old Richard, Jr. The recent graduate of Peoria Heights High School was there every morning, and when he wasn't assisting Jim Brown he was sorting the letters, weeding out the smattering of hate mail and passing along the rest. The young man said, "My father has been encouraged by it all and it gives him renewed confidence," and Pryor himself later acknowledged that the letters meant more than he could ever say. There would be twenty-five thousand pieces of mail in all, and Pryor vowed, "If it takes me twenty years, I'm going to answer every one. I got letters from people saying, 'We don't necessarily like what you do in your comedy act, your language, but we think you're a nice man.' It embarrassed me. I saw how stupid I was . . . never knew that people liked me that much. When you've lost your sense of self-worth you say to yourself, 'Wow! All those people out there are praying for me. All their energy is flowing into my hospital room.' All you can do is lay there and say, 'thank you' . . . and really mean it.''

Everyone who came to see Pryor was impressed with how much the outpouring of love bolstered his spirits. ''There's something happening to him,'' Rosalind Cash said of the impact of the mail and visitors. ''That survival thing; you can see it in his eyes and it's a beautiful thing to see.'' Psychologically, he was indeed ready to take any steps that would lead to his recovery. ''On a scale of one to ten, I give this man a ten,'' Murphy said with conviction. ''Though I didn't give him any better care than I provide for any other burn patient, he gave us a free hand and put the drive out.'' Pryor shrugs off Murphy's praise, saying that all he did was ''ask everybody what I had to do to get well, and I did what they told me.''

Building up strength was crucial to the healing process, and to this end Pryor kept on his feet as much as possible. He used a walker to move around the room or go to the bathroom, proceeding in what one nurse described as ''a painful shuffle.'' Stan Shaw remembers, ''The first day Richard got up, he pushed his IV pole in front of him and walked by himself. He was so childlike and helpless. He tried to make a joke but he was hurting. He could hardly talk.'' But Brown says what was important was that Pryor did it himself, at the same time ''putting the nurses on to make things easier and lighter around him.''

But Pryor yearned for a few big steps, and it was his decision to undertake the first of the graft operations. The doctors had hoped to begin on June 18, but his wounds, according to Jack Grossman, ''were not ready to receive any grafts.'' Five days later, despite the pneumonia that required regular draining of his lungs, plus low resistance and kidneys that were barely functioning, the doctors felt they could leave the debrided skin open no longer. The risk of infection was

simply too great. Besides, it would take a week for the skin used in grafting to regenerate, and the medical team was already looking ahead to second and third operations.

After being apprised of the dangers, Pryor considered for a moment, then nodded and told Jack Grossman simply, "Okay—let's go." On June 23, in the first of the grafts, skin was peeled from Pryor's calves and thighs and stretched over portions of his chest, shoulders, back, arms and ears. The operation lasted ninety minutes, and in the days that followed it became clear that a remarkable sixty-five percent of the grafts had taken. At the same time, Pryor's kidney functions climbed to one-third the normal rate and the pneumonia began fading fast. Pryor was upgraded from the critical list to merely "serious."

During the first two weeks of his stay, Pryor's chances of survival had crept from one-in-three to fifty-fifty, and after the first graft there was little concern that he would die. Three-quarters of his upper torso received skin transplants in the following weeks, the second graft done on July 2, the third a week later. Plastic surgery was performed on his chin and ears, the lobes of which had been burned away. Pryor jokingly wished they could have done more, quipping, "I'm still as ugly as I ever was."

Because Pryor was running up large bills, and it was not yet clear how high they would go—the hospital alone cost fifteen hundred dollars per day, excluding the doctors—Redd Foxx announced on July 5 that he would mount a telethon to raise at least a half-million dollars for Pryor's medical expenses. At a time when no one had any idea when or even if Pryor would be able to go back to work, Foxx said simply, "We don't want Richard to go into debt." He felt confident that "with the pleasure he has brought to millions, they will want to contribute to his welfare." Foxx himself started the ball rolling by "tossing a thousand in the pot," adding that "Frank Sinatra is doing the same."

The "Skin for a Friend" show was aired July 18 and 19 on Channel 30 in Los Angeles. It was, in a word, a fiasco. Instead of running for twenty-four hours, as announced, it

was cut off after fourteen and one-half hours—though no one involved was particularly surprised.

From the start, everything had gone wrong. While one-hundred-odd stars had pledged to donate their time and influence for the show, few actually came through. As airtime neared, the telethon was becoming a comedy—or, more accurately, a tragedy—of no-shows. Muhammad Ali and Alex Haley declined to come, and even Sammy Davis, Jr., couldn't make it, appearing instead on tape. The only celebrities of note who found time to make it were Stevie Wonder, Donny Most of "Happy Days," and Robert Guillaume of "Benson." Bill Cosby found it inconvenient to appear but donated a tub.

The second setback was Foxx's inability to get airtime on a major network. NBC, ABC, and CBS were unwilling to preempt a full day of programming, thus leaving the telethon without a national audience. This was no doubt one reason many would-be guest stars dropped out.

A third, though less significant, blow came when organizer Foxx himself withdrew as host, claiming, Sanford-like, that a back ailment had acted up. Industry scuttlebutt had it that when the telethon began to show all the earmarks of disaster, he wanted to distance himself from it. Altovise Davis, wife of Sammy, was summoned to replace him, along with actor Leon Isaac Kennedy, husband of sportscaster Jayne.

The telethon raised a meager $141,000, and Foxx was ripping mad. Asked to comment on falling so far short of his goal, he snapped, "If anyone fell short . . . it was the major networks for not taking the telethon. We could have raised a lot more if it had been televised nationally." Fortunately, a week after the telethon, it was announced that a one-million-dollar insurance policy, plus coverage due him from the Screen Actors' Guild, would take care of Pryor's bill. When he realized he wouldn't need the money from the telethon, Pryor asked that it be turned over to the hospital under the auspices of the Richard Pryor Burn Foundation. Officials were grateful, though no less so than the patients who would benefit from the endowment.

After Jim Brown's departure, Pryor was comforted by his children's devotion. Not only did Richard, Jr., step in and manfully try to fill Jim Brown's shoes, but fourteen-year-old Elizabeth prepared her father's favorite dishes, particularly moo goo gai pan. The kids' goodness and generosity helped him gain perspective on his own misadventures. "Lying in bed in the hospital," he reflects, "I had to think about *why* I was hurt, trying to find the truth."

Pryor didn't believe that he was being punished for his many sins. (He insists, "If God wanted to punish my ass, he would have burnt my *dick*.") But Pryor did feel that he'd courted disaster by leading "a life of pretense." Not on the stage; there, he was utterly honest about his private life, often to the point of embarrassing those who were involved in it. To this day Pryor isn't sure why he's able to tell the truth to two thousand people yet lie or fall silent on a one-to-one basis—though it's obvious that a crowd can't talk back, can't turn around and use the information to hurt, seduce, or betray.

Resting in his bed one day, Pryor says, "I started to cry," and let out a lot of anger at the way he'd been "a manipulator . . . a real deceiver and a schmuck." He told himself, " 'You're forty years old and you're a punk. Nobody knows you're full of shit but you, and that's enough.' " What he meant was that he'd invented a false self-image, "a much-loved, very happy . . . hip motherfucker who knows everything about life and people and getting high." Having been foolish enough to set himself on fire, he admitted—and with self-reproach so severe that the rum story becomes even more farfetched—"I didn't know shit about a damn thing."

Thus, Richard Pryor, now expected to survive, was hardened, and swinging more toward self-esteem than ever before. "The fire just made me aware of here and now. I'm too old to be hip. I just would like to be Richard now for a while and find out about that person and enjoy him." He'd said that before, of course, but as Stan Shaw pointed out, the blaze had made him "much stronger and wiser," while Murphy remarked that the fire had taught him "a lot about courage and life."

The only voice of dissension was that of Jim Brown,

who, like the others, saw these changes—but wasn't ready to regard them any more seriously than reformations Pryor had made in the past. "The accident is gonna show Richard that he has a lot of fans who are truly interested in him. He's gonna find out he has some friends. But when he gets back outside, I don't think it's gonna make one bit of difference unless this whole process is fortified by key people in his life, unless those of us who care about him . . . take some time out and assert ourselves in dealing with him." Brown was simply being practical. This wasn't the first time he had seen Pryor swear off marriage, drugs, Hollywood, Las Vegas, stand-up comedy, and white people, only to do an about-face. "Richard has a tremendous ability to reject bullshit, but along with [that] are the individual weaknesses of all of us. If we drop away and leave him out there alone, I don't think this [the fire] will make up for all the things that have gone before."

Others who knew Pryor or followed his career were openly skeptical. New York's *Amsterdam News* wrote, "Close associates doubt the accident will change him from a man of confusion. He'll . . . keep on doing what he's always done in life—getting involved in unpleasant incidents that only do harm to himself." *Daily News* reporter Lorenzo Carcaterra echoed these fears when he predicted, "He'll probably try to find danger again. But the smart money says that when he does, he won't come back."

Pryor was aware of what people were saying, but he was remarkably unfazed. Dismissing his previous promises and confrontations as trivial, he says, "Every man or woman eventually goes through a test. [The fire] turned out to be a damn good experience." He insisted that he'd "committed suicide" the night of the fire, that "the other person's dead. He was a horrible man."

Pryor was now instinctively developing a new devotion to God. Murphy indicates, "You find many burn patients saying prayers, though in Richard's case he wasn't praying for strength. He had confidence in himself. He was praying because he wanted to thank God for his life."

Pryor says that his bond with God began the instant he was set ablaze. "When all of a sudden there you are,

burning up . . . you don't call on the Bank of America to help you. You don't call on nobody but God. Dear Jesus! Lord! My Master! You know, all those people, those names you'd forgotten." That reflexive reaction set him on a more cognitive search. Resting in his bed at night, he saw that worse than the agony of the fire was that of having been lonely most of his life. The letters from fans, the visitors, the phone calls—all made him feel good, but it was like applause from an audience. The only time he didn't feel alone was when he prayed, so he formed his own "family" with God. It would help him through the disappointment of learning about his family's thievery behind his back, gave him a companion who would never abandon him, never condone or allow self-destruction, never lie to him. Everyone was busy saying that what Pryor had to do was toughen himself up to deal with temptation, but he felt that all he needed was self-love, which he said "God has . . . given me. It took me all this time to find out it was okay to be me. If anybody was born again, I was."

Against all odds and expectations, Richard Pryor was released from the hospital on July 23, 1980, a few days before the announced date so that thousands of fans would not gather to see him. It had been less than seven weeks since he'd been admitted, and considerably less than the minimum of three months he'd been expected to stay.

"We started seeing tremendous improvement in the past three weeks," Jack Grossman said. "The tissue healed remarkably well and his attitude was fantastic." Grossman said that Pryor would need "a couple of touch-up operations for the scars . . . but he looks marvelous. He's up and around, driving his car." Grossman informed reporters that Pryor had even gone to the movies. But his regimen wasn't over. "Burn patients are patients for life," Grossman advised. A nurse was sent home to give Pryor physical therapy three times a day—stretching, swimming, and other exercises that were painful, given the tightness of the skin, but vital to ensure that the scar tissue didn't constrict his movement. He was also placed on a high-protein diet and told to return to Grossman's office once a week for a checkup.

Proud of his healthy, disciplined new self, Pryor sat down for a taped TV interview with Barbara Walters on the day he was released. She had wanted to conduct a phone interview to tag onto the scheduled August 5 rebroadcast of their previous interview. However, Pryor told her not to show the old tape; he wanted to do a new one. Walters dropped everything, leaving the Republican National Convention to fly out and do the interview in Northridge.

His hair cropped close, his skin obviously scarred and discolored, Pryor was nonetheless alert and in good spirits. He went through a litany of resolutions, telling her that he was a much-matured man whose hates and ambitions and self-indulgences had all been vanquished by his newfound joy in life.

Pryor spoke to *Ebony* and other magazines, repeating over and over again that his Mr. Hyde days were over. Drugs? Absolutely stricken from his life. Liquor? "I don't think I'll even drink. Maybe some beer, but not wine or anything. This," he said of his healing body, "wants to live."

David Franklin, who had been listening to the promises of change since Pryor had entered the hospital, summed up all of Pryor's pledges and confessions by whispering quietly, "I hope so."

Chapter Twenty

Alone now, Pryor was starting from scratch in many ways. He felt good to know that he was "equipped with a lot of stuff that I hadn't been using; good stuff that I'd been denying myself. It's something when all those things you avoid all your life come, 'Uh, Richard, can I speak to you now? You're not doin' anything, you're not too busy,

are you?' You face the demons and get them out of your life.''

Pryor did not return to his house in Northridge. "I was supposed to continue therapy,'' he allows, ''but as soon as I could stand up, I just said, 'Let me out of here,' '' and headed for the house he'd built on Maui. There, in his all-wood home overlooking the Pacific, he spent the rest of the summer and fall convalescing in what one houseguest described as ''paradise . . . sun-dazzled, with days that drip like molasses . . . and thousands of miles of ocean.'' In addition to Burt Reynolds, his neighbors included Kris Kristofferson, Carol Burnett, and former Beatle George Harrison—an eclectic group, and one he was sure he'd enjoy. And enjoy them he did. Pryor fell in love with everything about Hawaii. "When I first saw this place again, I cried. I thanked God for letting me live to see it. There's no wickedness, the people are pure and innocent. You might *mildew* to death here,'' he told a reporter from *People*, ''but nothin' else is going to happen to you.''

Very few people visited Pryor there, which was just how he wanted it. "It's hard for people just to drop in. I have . . . my privacy. And I'm going to keep it that way. I feel at peace here.'' He had a housekeeper, and his children were regular guests, but other visitors were rare. One of the people who came for a stay was a photographer friend, who commented that Pryor was taking it easy and was ''so happy he doesn't know which way to go with it.''

Pryor took it easy for a while. As he told an interviewer from *Playgirl*, ''After what I went through, it takes time before you can laugh again.'' He no longer needed jokes to survive and rarely thought of them.

Personally, Pryor was in a state of flux. For a long time after his release, it appeared that Jennifer Lee was out and Deborah McGuire back in. Though Deborah claimed she wasn't as close to Richard as some of his male friends were, he saw her regularly for the rest of the year before they parted again, amicably. ''I do know that I *love* Deborah,'' Pryor stated at the time, ''but I don't *know* her. And she doesn't

know me. But I think we could be friends." Of Jennifer, whom he was not seeing at the time, he said, "I thought we were friends, but that's what *I* thought. Obviously I should have stopped and asked her what *she* thought." He has never elaborated, though there are allusions to the fact that she wanted to get married and he did not.

Things weren't any more settled in other areas. Restless, Pryor discovered very quickly that the kind of lifestyle he was trying to accommodate just wasn't him. "People tell me, 'You ought to just lie on the beach and close your eyes.' I can't do that." A pause, then, "I gotta keep one eye open outta fear that somebody is gonna sneak up and hit me with a board."

What Pryor was saying once again, is, that he simply didn't know how to relax. There was unfinished business, and he was itchy to address it.

Wholly Moses had been rushed into release on June 20, somewhat ghoulishly trying to capitalize on his misfortune. If it had been a better picture, perhaps it would have. But *Bustin' Loose*, which was to have been released in October, had been held back. The filmmakers felt that it needed some additional work, the bulk of it involving the location work in Ellensburg, Washington. Although Universal was eager to get the film into the marketplace, they would have to wait for Pryor.

He wasn't yet ready to go before the cameras, but that didn't make him any less restless. Utopia quickly became tiresome. He would wake up each morning with a glass of fresh fruit, protein powder—the body burns up protein rather than fat after a physical trauma—eggs, and yogurt. Then he would go fishing from a nearby pier, wearing a straw hat to protect his skin from the sun, or he'd jog, or drive slowly around the island on a Moped or Jeep. He even bought a single-engine Grumman and learned to fly so that he could pick up occasional guests at Honolulu and shuttle them the sixty miles to Maui.

Instead of thinking about a movie, he began to work on a new act. He had once said, "You need pain to be funny," and rather than shy from the extreme pain of the fire, he decided

to embrace it more fully. Deboragh hadn't been alone in thinking the accident had been "too real" to serve as the basis for a new routine. She didn't mean that the pain had been too real, for it had been physical pain, which by Pryor's own declaration was easier than emotional pain. What was "too real" about the fire was that, in Pryor's own words, he'd really "fucked up." That was the millstone. He'd tried to blunt that with the rum story, but his mortification remained acute. The only way to exorcise that was to seal it in vinyl. Along the way, he would go public with a lot of other things that had been building up inside of him: his discoveries about the word *nigger,* the eye-opening trip to Africa, his failed relationships, and the inhumanity he saw in prison. It would be the Gospel According to Richard Pryor, his way of letting the world know that that unstable, raucous man was indeed dead.

While Pryor was mending in Hawaii, word around Hollywood was that his unreleased *Stir Crazy* could be another *Silver Streak.* Pryor was one of the few who didn't believe that. After screening the film, he said, "When I saw *Stir Crazy* I said, 'My career is over . . . this is it. I'll never work again." However, Pryor admitted, "I don't like watching myself," and seldom does so. "I think I'm awful, I think people will think so—it takes me a long time to be able to get a movie and look at it." Consequently, he removed himself from the critical jury where *Stir Crazy* was concerned, and was receptive when Columbia asked if he would help promote the film. Quality notwithstanding, a successful movie would only enhance his career.

Returning to Northridge, Pryor visited Jack Grossman and was pronounced fit enough for a limited amount of publicity work. He also caught some flak for neglecting his scheduled visits, but in Pryor's mind, returning to a therapy-free life meant the accident was forever behind him. He needed that psychological boost more than he needed physical rehabilitation.

When it became clear that Pryor was back and intended

to take care of business, Universal contacted him about wrapping up the *Bustin' Loose* location scenes. Pryor felt that by March, three months hence, he'd be healed enough and confident enough to face a camera again. Meanwhile, Pryor devoted himself to the movie promotion—something he hadn't done since *Greased Lightning*. Most of his duties were in Los Angeles and New York, where he would get the maximum exposure with a minimum of travel. In both cities he did interviews and participated in media events, the most lavish of which was a combination *Stir Crazy* and birthday party in Hollywood, attended by Warren Beatty, Mary Tyler Moore, and others. Its New York counterpart was a similar gathering at Tavern on the Green in Central Park.

While he was in New York, Pryor received a call from the director of the Fortune Society, a drug rehabilitation center. He was asked to visit the Kennedy-sponsored center and discuss with ex-offenders what he had learned about drug abuse. Pryor was uneasy about making soapbox pitches of this type, but he also knew that his recent experiences would undoubtedly benefit the youths. Perched on an old sofa in a lounge at the Park Avenue facility, Pryor gathered the kids around him. "I used to smoke base," he said somewhat self-consciously, "but that stuff will kill you." Pryor proceeded to tell them about his new highs—life and achievement. He concluded, "What is good is getting high on energy. I get high on myself now and I really like Richard. Pryor was enthusiastically received, and after his chat he patiently answered questions and posed for pictures with each of the teen-agers.

Pryor's trip to New York had humanistic as well as materialistic benefits. Though *Stir Crazy* opened to scathing reviews—among the worst a Pryor film had ever received—seven months later the picture was still in release. Audiences made it one of the top ten grossing films of all time. Pryor chalked it up to the fact that "the public wanted to laugh, and me and Gene seemed to have some kind of chemistry together that, aside from how rotten something we're doing is, *we* are interesting in it. The combination is something you couldn't have predicted, a white guy and a black guy comedy team—

you couldn't have made it up." He added that he and Wilder "have a thing together that just hits on the screen when we work . . . a nice little magic combination. And that's hard to find with people, but we 'just be us,' and it works real good. I think that's all it is, because *Stir Crazy* didn't have much to it."

Poitier agreed that the duo had an unbeatable chemistry. "Pryor's obviously a genius, and when he works he is usually very funny. But for some reason when you pair him with Gene Wilder . . . they are probably the funniest pair that's ever been onscreen."

Though fans of Laurel and Hardy or Burns and Allen might disagree wth Poitier, there's no question that Pryor, the frightened kid putting up a tough-guy facade, and Wilder, the shrieking loon hiding behind a veneer of continental sophistication, had a seesaw effect on each other. One served as ballast while the other was in the air.

The public thanked Pryor and Wilder by spending one hundred million dollars at the box office—more than the combined grosses of Pryor's previous films.

Columbia wasted no time commissioning author Bruce Jay Friedman to write a sequel, titled *Deep Trouble*. The studio was pushing for a start during the summer of 1981, but, though the script was completed, there was never any time in Pryor's schedule and the project eventually fizzled out. More than once he and Wilder talked about reteaming, either to remake some of Laurel and Hardy's classics or for Wilder to direct Pryor in a film. It took years for anything to come of these plans. Wilder's efforts to spark similar madness in *Hanky Panky*, with Gilda Radner in the "Pryor role" and Poitier directing, proved a commercial disaster.

For months after the fire, Richard Pryor seemed the calmest man on earth. There were no more headlines, no confrontations; people around him said that he had found peace. But if Pryor had changed, the world had not. Returning to the mainstream, he was reminded that treachery and

temptation were still out there in force. And in the spring of 1981, the old dog proved that he still had some fight in him.

The *National Enquirer* reported that Pryor was using cocaine again, but he ignored the front-page story until thousands of letters arrived from angry fans. As much to show that the story was a lie as to lash out against the newspaper, Pryor hit them with a ten-million-dollar libel suit in May 1981. At the same time, he made the grandstand gesture of agreeing to discuss his personal experiences before the United States House of Representatives Select Narcotics Committee's hearings on drug abuse, to be held in Hollywood that spring. He would end up backing out of the appearance due to a "scheduling conflict." Whether that's a euphemism for an attorney's advice not to put his illegal affairs "on the street," as he referred to confessions about his private habits, is not known. Regardless, he made up for it that August by giving Peoria fifty thousand dollars to combat drugs and help any "deserving people . . . regardless of race, color, or creed." Whatever he felt about drugs in his own life, he wanted to warn others away from using them.

How did Pryor feel about cocaine nearly a year after his accident? He was not as much of a convert as one might suspect. Perhaps the *Enquirer* overstated its case by insisting that Pryor had used the drug in the hospital (an angry Stan Shaw retaliated, "This man was struggling to *breathe*!"), but when asked by a reporter whether he'd "cleansed himself completely of drugs," Pryor responded, "I don't want to be a hypocrite so I won't answer that." On another occasion he elaborated, saying that while he stayed away from his pipe, "I hear him saying, 'That's okay, Rich, I'll take care of you.' I'll hear him every day of my life." But he knew that cocaine "ends up sucking you," and that returning to it would "kill" him. It was for that reason that he decided to make Maui his permanent residence. Hollywood, he said, offers "too many temptations for people like me who fly." He would end up flying again—but not just yet.

Pryor's move against the *Enquirer* wasn't as big a surprise as his unexpected legal assault against David McCoy

Franklin. Pryor had heard things about Franklin that he didn't appreciate, among them that during his hospitalization Franklin reportedly claimed, in private, that Pryor had indeed been freebasing, not drinking rum. Pryor contemplated a slander suit, but rejected that when his financial advisers uncovered a more serious problem: the possibility that for some time Franklin had been mismanaging Pryor's funds. The cornerstone of their suspicions was a pair of apartment complexes that the men had bought with equal investments of $200,000 each in 1978 and sold in January for a large profit. In March, Pryor filed a suit at the Fulton County (Atlanta) Superior Court, claiming that Franklin had not accounted for some of this money and in addition had mingled hundreds of thousands of dollars of his money with that of others, in transactions made with little or no bookkeeping. "Literally hundreds of checks have been drawn . . . to various persons," read the heart of the claim, "many of which do not state the purpose for which they were drawn."

To no one's surprise, a wounded Franklin disputed the charges. "I don't know why he filed the suit," he told the press, adding that it was more sensationalism than substance. However, he refused to elaborate. As an aide to the lawyer expressed, "Mr. Franklin feels that when someone is suing you for a million dollars, it's wise to make no comment."

The case eventually became the property of the California labor commissioner, who, on August 12 of the following year, found against Franklin. By that time the accusations had expanded far beyond their original, comparatively modest parameters and Franklin was ordered to pay Pryor the sobering sum of $3,110,918. *Variety,* in reporting on the judgment, declared it "probably the toughest action of its kind on record," the court's thirty-five-page list of infractions including such charges as "blatant self-dealing," "egregious abuses," and "unconscionable and continuing wrongful acts of conduct . . . including numerous acts of embezzlement, fraud, and defalcation while acting in a fiduciary capacity."

Pryor's attorneys at Lavely and Singer in Los Angeles

219

described Pryor as "very pleased" with the verdict, even though the ruling was "yet another painful reminder that a person whom Mr. Pryor had trusted and relied on for five years grossly abused that trust." The case is presently in superior court, where, on September 7, 1982, Franklin appealed for a new trial.

Despite the court battles, Pryor showed no signs of the contentiousness that had marked his public and private dealings in the past. Howard Koch, who would produce Pryor's next film, suspected that previous problems were gone forever when he heard someone on the set ask Pryor where he was born and heard the star reply, "The Sherman Oaks Burn Center."

Koch was not alone in this impression. Pryor returned to active duty on *Bustin' Loose,* and those who'd worked with him before the fire found that he'd become a different man during the ten month layoff. "Before the accident he was very loose and funny," Cicely Tyson said, but afterward "he was the other way. He would come out and shoot his scenes, and then he would go back into his dressing room." She held that "it took a lot out of him to come back to work that soon," but his reserve was due to more than just fatigue. Director Michael Schultz was present when Pryor did the "looping"—adding voice to scenes that had been shot without sound. He hit it on the head when he said, "Up on the screen was a Richard Pryor that was heavily overweight and puffed from excessive alcohol. Richard looked at himself . . . and tears came to his eyes. The accident really brought him around to seeing the beauty of things, instead of trying to destroy it."

During the shoot, the *Bustin' Loose* set was closed to visitors to minimize Pryor's exposure to disease. Though he wore costumes padded so that his 130 pounds would photograph the same as when he was twenty pounds heavier, Pryor's face fluctuates from beefy to thin in the final scenes. Less noticeable is the way a kerchief he'd worn loose in the prefire shots was now tucked neatly around his throat to conceal scars. Other sequences in which he'd

performed with an open-front shirt had to be reshot from beginning to end to accommodate turtlenecks.

Bustin' Loose opened that summer and was another hit for Pryor. While it didn't reach the astronomical levels of *Stir Crazy*, Universal wasn't disappointed. The picture wasn't a madcap comedy, yet it still grossed nearly forty million dollars. The box office was reassuring to Pryor not only because he had created *Bustin' Loose* from top to bottom but because it meant that large numbers of people would turn out to see him in a seriocomic role. That was important because, as he subsequently announced, his goal in undertaking any new project would be "to make people think" through pathos and laughter.

As a somewhat grotesque postscript, *Bustin' Loose* was cited in a handful of reviews for its coincidental references to Pryor's character burning up. Apart from the numerous blazes set by the young pyromaniac in the film, there were scenes in which Pryor said to Tyson, "You set me on fire," or she warned him, "Don't set yourself on fire." Viewers who thought that Pryor was punning his accident could not be convinced otherwise.

Chapter Twenty-one

Pryor's changed outlook prompted Stan Shaw to predict, "You'll see more of this new Richard Pryor in his work." There was no question that Pryor would have had difficulty doing a film like *Stir Crazy*, which, perhaps more than any other reason, is why the completed script for the sequel has been collecting dust on a shelf at Columbia. He was looking for relatively restrained motion pictures that were closer to the emotions he was feeling.

In this respect, *Some Kind of Hero* was the ideal vehicle for him. A blend of the old and new Pryors, it contained a lot

of anger and bitterness blunted by a gentle determination of spirit.

Some Kind of Hero was developed by Howard Koch for Paramount, based on the 1975 novel by James Kirkwood. Kirkwood, coauthor of Broadway's *A Chorus Line* and *P.S., Your Cat Is Dead!*, cowrote the screenplay and remained faithful to his book, with the exception of expanding the role of Toni (Fritzi in the novel), a Beverly Hills callgirl played by Margot Kidder.

In the film, Corporal Eddie Keller (Pryor), a prisoner of war in Vietnam, is forced to confess in writing to war crimes in order to get medical attention for his good friend Vinnie (Ray Sharkey). Finally released after six years he receives a hero's homecoming but learns that the document he signed prevents him from collecting his back pay.

Alone and broke, Keller goes to a bar, where he meets Toni, a prostitute, who brings him back to her apartment, at no charge. After a delightful evening she tells him not to return, that all she wanted was a one-night stand.

But Keller continues to see her, and it isn't long before they fall in love. Unable to get a job or parlay his "hero's welcome" into a bank loan, he decides to rob the place. He loses his nerve, but Keller follows two men, robs them and discovers he has stolen hundreds of thousands of dollars in negotiable securities.

Keller contacts some mobsters who offer him cash for the bonds and notes. Realizing that they don't intend to let him live, Keller phones Toni to come and get him. Once the transaction is made, he subdues the two men who have come to his room. Phoning the police, he waits until the officers arrive, then slips out. He drives into the night with Toni and newfound fortune.

Pryor enjoyed *Some Kind of Hero,* and it shows. It gave him "the opportunity to do some work that doesn't depend on my being zany. I'm a character and not a caricature." This was important to him since, as Robin Williams has also discovered, "the serious roles mean longevity." While Pryor gives a lot of credit to director Michael Pressman, who "stopped and helped me the many times I thought I

couldn't . . . go inside and find new places," everyone else singles out Pryor's efforts. Pressman dubbed him "the best actor I've ever worked with—free, open to suggestions, conceptual, and incredibly talented. He embraced this film and his role with total dedication." Koch agrees. He cites one scene in which Pryor, in his prison cell in Vietnam, improvised by singing "Queen of the Nile," adding an entirely appropriate sense of "whistling past a graveyard" to the scene. Koch marvels, "That's his ability—to come on with something in the middle of nothing and, all of a sudden, turn it into a tremendous thing." He adds, "I'd heard about his explosive unpredictability. So I was waiting for that. But it never showed. He couldn't have been nicer, more cooperative . . . he was a doll and I'm not bullshitting. *Everybody* was crazy about him."

Pryor was particularly devoted to one of the actors who, according to inside sources, had a drug problem. Pryor spent time trying to get him to conquer his addiction and, in Koch's words, was "devastated" when, despite his efforts, the performer's problem got worse.

However, of all his relationships on *Some Kind of Hero*, Pryor's closest was with Margot Kidder. She describes it as "wonderful working with this extraordinarily serious and dramatic actor," but was even more impressed with him on a personal level. She found him cooperative, courteous, and "the most real human being in the world. He is just all-knowing about the human condition . . . he has that reality, that truth, that life force that is inextinguishable. He's full of power and wisdom and I was devastated when filming was over."

Some suspect that because Kidder and Pryor share some steamy love scenes onscreen, they were carrying on away from cameras as well. Kidder, who has always been open about her sexual liaisons, dealt with those rumors bluntly: "I adore Richard. He's a warm and special person [and] I love him very much. But we weren't having an affair." Pryor was no less smitten with his costar and her wisdom. They were totally honest with each other—she described him as the kind of man around whom she could "pick her toes" without

feeling self-conscious—and it came as no surprise to observers when Pryor straightened out some of the filmmakers for what he perceived as "the disrespectful way they were treating Margot on the set." He described their macho backlash as "fear" of her confidence and outspokenness, traits that many of the men couldn't handle. It was the first time since the infamous days on *Wholly Moses* that he'd thrown his weight around on a film, though to utterly different ends than before.

Some Kind of Hero shot at a hectic pace through May and June 1981, in an effort to complete it before the industry could be hobbled by a proposed directors' strike. The pace made it easier for the performers to stay in character and on their toes; but Kidder, while shooting the climactic scene in which Toni drives up to the hotel to carry Keller away, discovered that everyone must *always* be on their toes in a Pryor film. Instead of emerging in his army threads, Pryor jumped from the hotel lobby wearing a padded Superman costume, cracking Kidder up by poking fun at the film that made her a celebrity.

Some Kind of Hero didn't open until spring of the following year, and the reviews were mixed. Most critics complained that the film was really two unrelated pictures, the often brutal forty-five-minute sequence in Vietnam, where the humor is a pressure valve for the audience (as when Keller taunts his captors by signing an early confession "Mr. Meoff" and, when questioned about the name, pulls at his crotch and taunts "Jack Meoff"); and the often Keystone Cops–like scenes in Los Angeles, i.e. the failed bank robbery and the "feet don't fail me now" flavor of the bathroom holdup. However, Pryor's reviews were almost uniformly excellent and the picture brought in some thirty million dollars—less than *Bustin' Loose,* but fine for a basically downbeat two-character comedy-drama.

Pryor spent the summer after his hectic shoot shuttling between Northridge and Maui, molding his concert material. His accident-spawned insecurities about the public shunning him had been shored up by the reception of *Bustin' Loose* and

his own good work on *Some Kind of Hero,* but normalcy was quick to return in other ways as well. No sooner was he working again than the lepers congregated to be cured—the out-of-work actors and technicians looking for work, the writers with scripts, the aspiring directors. Pryor was as giving as ever, though his generosity was less guilt-ridden than part of a more benevolent attitude. He no longer seemed to perceive himself as a devil who bought redemption through charity but as a guardian angel. Learning that Larry Murphy, who was a Vietnam veteran, hoped to be a chest surgeon, Pryor insisted on putting him through school. Two years after beginning his Pryor-sponsored studies, Murphy declared, "I'm totally indebted to him. I can't thank the guy enough. He has a big heart, and I don't think his fans or even the people who love him know how tender and loving this man is."

Jackie Wilson knew. After the singer collapsed, Pryor directed his agent to send every penny of royalties from his own most recent album to Wilson's children. That, in Pryor's mind, was obviously the way for the industry to aid one of its own, something Wilson would appreciate more than an outright gift of money. Local institutions also profited from his metamorphosis. Pryor performed for free at a local club to help its ailing finances, and in the fall he did a stint at the Comedy Store to raise money for cancer research—money that, fittingly, would go to the John Wayne Clinic at UCLA. In October of that year he also allowed himself to be "jailed" by Ed McMahon on the charge of "impersonating a black person," to be bailed out in an auction benefitting the Christian Children's Fund in Los Angeles.

Unquestionably, Pryor's most unusual public service was performed early in the summer, when he was approached by directors of the Sheenway School, a private cultural center in Watts, to help cool simmering hostilities between thirty gangs in Watts, Compton, Inglewood, and other areas in South Central Los Angeles. Joined by actress Mabel King—Evillene in *The Wiz*—Pryor met with twenty-one teen-agers on the junior board of the center. Chairing the meeting, Pryor tried to convince them that violence wasn't a solution to local problems. When challenged to suggest an alternative, he prom-

ised that if the kids would help defuse the tension and keep crime down, he would donate two hundred thousand dollars to the school. As a show of faith, he gave them fifty thousand dollars on the spot, earmarked for thirty-five scholarships and equipment for a new recreation center. The kids were pessimistic but they did as he asked. To the surprise of everyone but Pryor, the street responded and he honored his pledge. Dee Blunt, the center's director, singled out Pryor's efforts as having kept the peace during that hot Los Angeles summer.

All this compassion left Pryor short in other areas, especially in his dealings with women. "He attracts women like flies," Howard Koch noticed. "If we'd opened the doors of the studio we would have had thousands of them there." But Pryor apparently felt that he was overdosing on basically anonymous relationships, and in August, in a private ceremony in Hawaii, he married Jennifer Lee. Friends and family were surprised, not only at the fact that Pryor was tying the knot yet again but because he had insisted several years before that "I would never marry another white woman. It's too hard." But Pryor saw no point in denying, as he said after the wedding, that "I loved her and she loved me and we got to love each other. For real, not just the word part." Still governed by his heart, he acted impulsively, though he had become a realist in one way: this time he drew up a prenuptial agreement to secure his assets.

The marriage was fine at the start, as Jennifer adjusted to her husband on a full-time basis. "Marriage is a lot of responsibility," she discovered, alluding to Pryor's eccentricities but readily defending them. "He's a genius. We don't exactly have a marriage with white-picket-fence values." Her words were more prophetic than she knew. Within three months Pryor was in Hawaii Circuit Court suing for divorce. He subsequently withdrew his hasty complaint, though the marriage was off to a sputtering start.

Pryor wanted to bring his new routines to the public, but he was wary of going back to the stage. On movie sets he had directors and fellow actors for support; in concert, there was

only the thousand-headed monster to be fed. Not only had he been away for years, but a lot of what he had done back then had now been burned out of him. But he wanted to exorcise his remaining demons in public. To give himself added impetus to do so, he struck a deal with Columbia pictures to film the concerts. He agreed to do two performances at a local auditorium, the movie consisting of the best of each show. The site was selected and four million dollars allotted to produce *Richard Pryor Live at the Hollywood Palladium*— of which three million was handed over directly to Pryor. Pryor, in turn, earmarked the first fifty thousand dollars of the box office from the concert itself for Jesse Jackson's PUSH— People United to Serve Humanity—campaign to raise money for underprivileged black children.

Late in the summer, having labored for over a year, Pryor pronounced the material fit for a trial run in Los Angeles. With close friends like John Belushi encouraging him, and others like Robin Williams actually joining him nightly for professional and emotional support, Pryor went through the crucible of the Comedy Store and other Los Angeles clubs, honing and refining the material. Pryor played to enthusiastic crowds, earning a standing ovation each night after closing with the story of how he caught fire due to that queer blend of milks.

The small houses left Pryor feeling relatively secure with the material, troubled only in that it was more introspective than his fans were used to. He told himself that they'd have to chalk it up to growth, reminding himself that "nobody can stay the same unless he's Plastic Man." But on the night of the first concert he was a shambles inside, wanting to get over this hump but emotionally winded by what he perceived as the awesome size of it.

He pulled himself together, heartened by the presence of friends Robin Williams, Lily Tomlin, Stevie Wonder, and boxer Sugar Ray Leonard. Dressed in a fire-red suit and black shirt, Pryor looked remarkably fit as he strode down the aisle and mounted the stage. The thousands of fans gave him a tumultuous reception, leaping to their feet and clapping, cheering, stomping, supporting him in every way they could.

Pryor went to the microphone and acknowledged the welcome with a gracious smile. He basked in their love and, when he felt ready, prepared to start the show—and panicked.

"I was so nervous," he said later, "I went blank. It was the pressure." Instead of sticking to the program that he'd painstakingly worked on, he was seized by the fear that he wouldn't be funny, so he opened with the surefire burn routine. "It went great," he sighed, "but then the show was over. There was nowhere to go." That wasn't quite true: after scoring heavily with what was supposed to have been the comic and dramatic highlight of the show, Pryor had nowhere to go but down.

At first, he tried to regroup. Completing the routine, he attempted to go back and do the show from the beginning. But the material wasn't playing with him or with the audience. He paused frequently, lost his train of thought, forgot the material. He apologized, saying he was anxious about being there. The audience seem to understand, particularly when he told them that he was beginning to think "I ain't funny anymore . . . it's hard to get up here again." They encouraged him with their calls and applause. He heard one person near the stage cry out, "We love you, Richard!" He smiled, said, "Thank you, I needed that," and struggled to continue. But inside he was telling himself, "We knew you were gonna fuck up. We were waitin' for you."

Giving in to his fears, Pryor stopped again, only this time he turned his back on the audience and walked off the stage. A *Newsweek* reporter later wrote that he left behind "a shocked audience that was rooting for him in his comeback show." The audience wasn't so surprised at his anxiety; they understood what he was going through. These were his people, who had followed his career and prayed for his physical and professional recovery. They just couldn't believe he held their support in such low regard that he'd cave in at the first sign of trouble.

"I should be grateful I have a job," he said after the disaster, "but I don't understand some stuff . . . I'm trying to find out what I want to be and I don't know." He searched for words that would more accurately pinpoint his feelings, but

228

they eluded him, and he finally dismissed his failure and insecurities in one line: "I want to stop."

But the worst was yet to come. Pryor's associates told him what he already knew—that he couldn't turn his back on the concerts. It wasn't just the money or a matter of saving face, though both were pressures he was feeling at the time. Giving in now would allow him to regard failure as a viable option. After twenty-one years in the business, having achieved success unparalleled in the history of entertainment, Pryor knew he couldn't accept that. The show had to go on the following night.

It was not a dubious audience that showed up for the second concert, but a hopeful one. Most didn't care that they may have wasted their time coming; they cared about Richard Pryor, and their hearts went out to him. And when he came out as he had the evening before, the reception was even louder, and applause longer. Looking slightly uncomfortable and described by one acquaintance as "demoralized," Pryor climbed to the stage and gazed past the multicamera setups filming the concert. His heart was drumming in his throat as he pulled the microphone from its stand and, sweating more from anxiety than from the hot stagelights, said solemnly, "Let's talk about something serious—fucking."

The audience broke up, and Pryor was rolling.

The motion picture that would emerge from the concerts underwent a title change to *Richard Pryor Live on the Sunset Strip* and consisted, obviously, of the bulk of the second show, with only a few clips from the first night. The film was released in March 1982, at which time *Newsweek* said, "*Sunset Strip* doesn't match the devastating perfection of *Live in Concert*, but as a historical document of a superb artist in transition it's unforgettable." That it is, and more.

Actor Ned Beatty, who would costar with Pryor two years later in *The Toy*, said that one night he and Pryor were talking about how honest they allow themselves to get in their work, and Pryor admitted that while he tries to be as truthful as possible, he "was really pushing into difficult areas" with the concert. Richard Donner, who would direct *The Toy*, wasn't surprised to hear that, having always regarded the film

as "a lot more emotional comedy and . . . a whole different vein in Richard's life, a much richer vein."

After the concert, Pryor acknowledged that on the second night, more than ever before, he and his audience were "right on that edge of crying and laughing, it's so real." Hitherto, society had always been his target, but now the focus had changed. He had created a comic Inquisition in which he was judge and defendant both.

Self-deprecating is too mild a description of the public flogging to which Pryor subjected himself. Typical is his stint as Mudbone, who says of Richard Pryor, "He fucked up. That fire got on his ass and fried up what little brains he had. 'Cause *I* remember—*he* could make a motherfucker laugh at a funeral on Sunday, Christmas day. But he got some money and went all the way crazy."

Needless to say, the fire recurs like ghosts in Shakespeare. He lights a match, holds it in front of him, and asks, "What's that?" Answer: "Richard Pryor running down the street." He talks about the changes a fire will make in one's life: "You stay away from fireplaces, will *not* go on the Fourth of July picnic, and refuse to use gas in your car." Asking someone in the audience for a light, he extends his cigarette and recoils slightly, cooing, "Careful!" He discusses the sole benefit of burning up, namely that you can do "the one-hundred-yard dash in about 4.6." About the only stone left unturned was the scorcher about Pryor's favorite charity, the Ignited Negro College Fund, which everyone in Hollywood openly disdained, while passing it along to anyone within earshot.

Pryor gives equal time to his freebase pipe, a silky-voiced confidant who promises Pryor his undivided attention, claims to understand him, and offers to take care of him. Pryor paints himself as a helpless fool for listening. It's a vignette that encapsulates Pryor's years of decay into several riveting, tragicomic minutes, a routine that inspired Donner to dub *Richard Pryor Live on the Sunset Strip* "the greatest antidrug film ever made. It should be a compulsory film for kids to see."

Most of the reviews of the concert and subsequent film

and record album commented that Pryor had mellowed, that he wasn't as brutal and therefore as funny as before. To some extent this is true. There were, as he had vowed, no "niggers" in his act, and he was no longer at odds with the world. He was his sole target, someone who, when he wasn't getting high or burning up, was beset by other kinds of disaster. A sexual Lilliputian, he claims to have had no chance to develop due to the "great pussy drought of the fifties" and thus found himself unable to match "electrical equipment" in bed, could only arouse a Playboy Bunny he dated by doing small-boy impressions, and managed to get caught cheating by his wife. ("No, I was *not* in the pussy," he tried to tell her. "I had my dick *out* but I wasn't fuckin' nothin'.")

Pryor revealed that he was ineffectual in other ways as well. The Mafia laughed at his attempt to rob them in a club they owned in Youngstown, in a dramatization of the time he tried to collect his paycheck, and he was easily intimidated by prisoners on the set of *Stir Crazy* ("Why'd you kill everybody in the house?" he asked one inmate, who shrugged and said, "They wuz home."). Even his concert characters are prone to failure, as, when recounting his trip to Africa, Pryor takes the part of a smug cheetah on whom a terrified antelope puts a move, leaving him to face the herd with egg on his face.

Rob Cohen said that the difference between Pryor before and after the fire was not that he was less funny, but that his anger had been redirected. The audience was no longer laughing at itself but at the quasipathetic figure on the stage. Before, says Cohen, Pryor was governed "by a lot of anger...at the white establishment, love and compassion for black people, and pity for their supposed helplessness." Cohen believes that Pryor changed when he saw the way all people "rallied around him and gave him a new perspective on life." That's when he got down on himself not only for the accident but for having been so angry at so many people for all those years.

Pryor concurred. "There is a realization that I can't make life perfect. Before, when I'd gotten disappointed, there would be depression. Now I can deal with the mistakes...walk

amongst the good and the bad. We're here just a short time, and it has to be used for the good.''

Cleansed now, inside as well as out, Pryor looked toward the future. Unfortunately, despite its many revelations, his shakedown at the Palladium left him with little emotional or intellectual fuel to make the journey.

Chapter Twenty-two

With *Richard Pryor Live on the Sunset Strip* and *Some Kind of Hero* awaiting release, Pryor and Jennifer ushered out 1981 by taking a vacation in the Caribbean. At the onset of that trip, Jennifer happened to overhear ''palimony'' attorney Marvin Mitchelson in the phone booth next to hers at the Los Angeles airport. Leaning over, she quipped, ''I'm Jennifer Pryor. If I ever need to get in touch with you, where can I find you?''

By the time Jennifer reached the Caribbean, newspapers nationwide were carrying the story of a presumed breakup. Returning to Southern California ahead of Richard to oversee work being done on the house, she vehemently denied the rumors, calling it all a misunderstanding. ''I hope I'll stay married to Richard forever,'' she said. ''He is my knight in shining armor and I'm going to be with this man as long as I live.''

That was February. In March, surprising Pryor and the public alike, Jennifer sued for divorce. This time it was for real, Jennifer working around their marriage contract and asking for ''spousal support, property rights, and attorney's fees.'' She cited nothing more than the *pro forma* ''irreconcilable differences'' in her claim, leaving Pryor genuinely puzzled and distraught. ''I guess I don't know how to do it,'' he said of marriage. ''I thought this time I was never going to get divorced. I was in love a bunch. I must have made her

real mad.'' Neither Pryor nor his ex-wife has said much else about the reasons for their parting, although it is obviously to Jennifer that Pryor was referring in the Palladium concert when he talked about his own infidelity. The fact that Jennifer was devoted to him emotionally, and is the kind of woman who would have taken marriage vows very seriously, leads one to the logical conclusion.

Jennifer's departure was just one of two blows that struck Pryor that month. The second was the drug-induced death of his good friend John Belushi. ''He didn't seem like a man who would do that,'' Pryor grieved. ''I never imagined John Belushi with a needle. He just seemed like a guy in a samurai suit.'' Pryor was acutely aware of the fact that Belushi had friends, like himself, who would have helped if he'd asked. But his own experiences had taught him that people in that frame of mind neither solicit nor heed the advice of others. All he could do in the wake of the shock was utter disconsolately, ''I'm sorry he didn't know that we loved him.''

If, as Pryor has stated, his work was a balm for personal setbacks, he had much to console him in the spring of 1982. *Richard Pryor Live on the Sunset Strip* earned an astounding eight million dollars in its first three days in the marketplace, far exceeding all the competition. It ended up making nearly thirty million dollars, adding another five million during a reissue in the fall of 1982. A week later *Some Kind of Hero* opened to lesser but still very healthy numbers, giving Pryor an unprecedented one-two punch at the box office.

Pryor admits having been a nervous wreck before the two films came out, and their success gave him a needed boost. However, with it came the feeling of self-importance. Ever since he could afford it, Pryor has kept himself insulated from others behind a somber-looking staff. But now the public was his servant as well, telling him that everything he did was golden. On one level, he seemed to take that as a mandate to dish up whatever he felt had merit. ''I'm getting a lot deeper about stuff . . . a lot more sensitive about things,'' he said. ''I want to do a lot of stuff, but I want to do it right.

I'm going to take charge of my own destiny, do my own films.''

But Pryor is a man on a pendulum, swinging from one extreme to another, although he says he was ready to do his own movies, there was a clear edge of wariness. Everyone always praised him for being better than his movies, for rising above the material. Yet, if he wrote the material and it was awful, would the public be as generous? Pryor thought of Woody Allen, Mel Brooks, Gene Wilder, and Marty Feldman, whose good acting failed to rescue their efforts behind the typewriter and camera.

Pryor, the writer and potential director, was like Pryor the interviewee. He could go inside and wrench up all kinds of emotions in front of a crowd, onstage, or on a movie set. But alone, with a journalist or a typewriter, it was a different matter. Encouraged by the staggering fees he could collect simply for his performances, Pryor did not follow his heart and ''take charge'' of his artistic destiny. Indicative of his turmoil is the fate of *The Charlie Parker Story,* a picture he'd wanted to make for some time.

After *Some Kind of Hero,* Pryor tentatively accepted Universal's offer to play a newscaster in *Color Man,* scheduled for a June 1982 start. However, deciding he wasn't entirely satisfied with that project, Pryor opted for a two-picture deal with Columbia and Rastar Productions. One of the two films was supposed to be *The Charlie Parker Story.*

Charles Christopher Parker was a jazz saxophonist and composer, born in 1920 and dead at the age of thirty-four, the result of drink, drugs, and debilitating confinement in a California mental institution. It was Pryor's desire to stretch himself dramatically with that film, just as Diana Ross had done a decade before playing Billie Holiday. A script was completed late in the fall of 1981, and shooting was supposed to have begun in May 1982. However, Rastar was a bit more keen about the other project on their two-picture slate, a comedy, and pushed it to the fore. Pryor could have thrown around his weight and made *The Charlie Parker Story* happen, but there were various reasons not to: he had just appeared in the relatively somber *Some Kind of Hero* and it

would be wise to rally the *Stir Crazy* buffs back to his camp; he was forty-one years old, still young enough to be credible as an aspiring young what-have-you as he was in *Stir Crazy,* a persona with which the public identified; a hit comedy would create a larger audience for whatever he did next, presumably the jazz film; and the longer he waited to play Charlie Parker, the more ''life'' he'd have under his belt, the more depth and texture he could bring to the role.

There was one other reason. Pryor's costar would be Jackie Gleason. Pryor had grown up on ''The Honeymooners'' and was in awe of the man; and he was convinced that acting with him would be an exciting and memorable experience. He wasn't disappointed. ''Gleason's a great man who knows it frontwards and backwards,'' Pryor said afterward, ''who is a professional *on the dime.* I learned a lot from him.''

Thus, in May 1982, for a salary of approximately two million dollars, Pryor went ahead with a remake of the 1979 French film *Le Jouet,* which had been directed by Francis Verber, helmer of the enormously successful *La Cage aux Folles;* in the translation, Rastar's new film became *The Toy.*

Pryor starred as Jack Brown, an out-of-work journalist who, to prevent foreclosure on his mortgage, takes a job as a ''cleaning woman'' in a department store. Young Eric Bates (Scott Schwartz), son of U.S. Bates (Jackie Gleason), one of the wealthiest—and cruelest—men in Louisiana. When Eric meets Jack, a Bates' employee, he offers him several thousand dollars to be his playmate for the week he's home from military school. Since the money would allow Jack to keep his home, he reluctantly accepts.

Jack moves into the Bates's mansion, where Master Bates humiliates him at every turn—just as his father degrades all of his employees. Offended by the viciousness of U.S. Bates, Jack persuades Eric to publish a newspaper about his father. The journal is an exposé of Bates's questionable business and moral ethics, and a copy is distributed to every Bates employee. The tycoon, mortified, confronts his son and Jack in a hostile meeting. After everyone's anger is vented U.S. realizes that his son was driven solely by his need for a father's love, which the enlightened U.S. vows to provide.

The Toy was filmed on location in Baton Rouge, and, according to director Richard Donner—who has directed such actors as Gregory Peck in *The Omen* and Marlon Brando and Gene Hackman in *Superman*—no one matches Pryor for the talent and imagination he brings to a role. "Working with him was one of the most thrilling experiences of my life," exclaims Donner. "A lot of times, when an actor is established, he has usually established himself with a set characterization and, although they keep saying, 'I want to break that mold,' there is a desperation to *keep* the mold for fear that if they do change it, they're going to lose the love of the public. That's not the case with Pryor; it never even came up. Working with him is like playing four-wall handball blindfolded—it's working with genius. You have to be on your toes every second because you just never know where he's coming from next."

Comedy requires spontaneity, and Donner reports that when Pryor and Gleason got going, there was a great deal of improvisation. There was so much, in fact, that young Scott Schwartz moaned, "They were constantly changing the script and the action." But Donner was in heaven. "They came up with schtick that just *destroys* you," he marvels.

Nine times out of ten it was Pryor who got the improvisation rolling. Wilfred Hyde-White, the distinguished British actor who plays the Bates butler, observed, "They are very different in their manner and they're different in their approach to their work." Gleason, like Cicely Tyson, preferred to stick to the script. "You discipline yourself," he said, doing the scene the same every time once it's set. But Pryor would have none of that and elaborated, "Gleason don't waste no moves. When they say action, he knows exactly where he's gonna turn his head. [But] I don't like being tied down to stone. I feel different at different times; I like to go with what I feel rather than what I'm saying." The only consistency he ever promised Donner or Gleason was, "You'll like it, what I'll do; don't worry."

Gleason went along with him. "You figure how he's going to perform and you adjust," he explained, adding that he didn't mind because of the high esteem in which he holds

236

his costar. "Pryor is an uninhibited, absolutely all-out comedian. And he is a very, very good actor. And those two
propositions, when they're put together, are quite invincible."
Hyde-White agrees. "Richard is very, very bright, very quick
indeed; no good trying to get ahead of him." Fortunately for
the film, Donner says that Gleason discovered exactly how to
play off Pryor. "Richard pours forth this wonderful, insane
comedy, but Jackie tops it with total sanity."

Typically, not everyone had kind things to say about
Pryor, and those who held him in contempt, and resented his
power, spread rumors as usual. Irate crew members, acerbic
journalists, jealous rivals; it's difficult to pinpoint exactly
where rumors get their start. Typical of the tales circulating
through Hollywood during the making of the film is that, one
of the actors, in the course of berating Jack, ad libbed and
referred to him as a cockroach. Without missing a beat, Pryor
allegedly walked off the set and returned to his hotel room.
Neither the crew nor the actor could understand why Pryor
took offense. When the producer's representatives tried to
speak with Pryor, he refused to admit them into his room or
take their phone calls. The next morning, he showed up on
the set, as if nothing had happened, and just went on
working.

Donner gets upset at the mention of such stories. "Shit,
never," he growls, "it *never* happened. If it did, it happened
when I wasn't there—and I was there all the time. It's a
figment of somebody's imagination. Maybe he's just an easy,
visible target, but it's bullshit, and you have to wonder where
they think these things up." He reflects for a moment, then
divulges what was apparently a confidence: "These things
hurt him, not just in his career but inside. They hurt him."

However, it's a matter of public record that *The Toy* was
not trouble-free. Whether the problems were due to Richard
Pryor depends on whom one chooses to believe. Late in the
shoot, Pryor admitted himself to Our Lady of the Lake
hospital with what a Columbia Pictures spokesman described
as "a mild respiratory condition." The publicist took it upon
himself to define it as "a cold, I guess." Pryor was in and out
in one day, though he returned later in the week for a longer

stay. Stories immediately surfaced that he was having a "sick-in" reminiscent of *Stir Crazy*, or that he was back on cocaine and had become very ill. Donner fumes, "*These* stories I heard, and they really got me angered." He reveals that Pryor entered the hospital at the behest of producer Phil Feldman, because the shooting schedule had left Pryor dangerously rundown. This seems likely, since he was in virtually every scene and refused to give his still-weakened system the rest it needed. Drugs? "Absolutely not," Donner insists. "I never even saw Richard take a joint. He had a couple of glasses of brandy one night after dinner [even though he had "sworn off" alcohol except for beer] but that's the only thing I ever saw him take. And I spent a lot of time with him." A sick-in? He had no reason, says Donner, because there was never a moment of trouble. "Pryor became a great love and friend of mine and, obviously, that couldn't have happened if there were any kind of ill feeling on the set."

Visitors to the set tend to substantiate Donner's story. They saw Pryor joking with everyone, technicians as well as his fellow performers, and saw no hint of dissension. Scott Schwartz comments that the only time Pryor wasn't clowning around was when he was in character and the cameras were rolling. "I'm here to have fun," Pryor declared, and, underlining that philosophy, went so far as to do most of his own stunts in a climactic slugfest/pie-fight that erupts at a lawn party when guests of Bates are revealed to be members of the Ku Klux Klan.

Fun was the byword behind the cameras on *The Toy*, and Donner was amazed at how many times he had to stop the proceedings because the cast or crew was laughing. Though these delays cost him time, it was an atmosphere he worked hard to maintain, commenting, "You need that kind of energy when you're doing comedy. Everyone's got to be sharp." Gleason agrees that an unusual amount of energy is necessary a comedy because "an actor has two hours to make a point a a play or a picture, but a comic has to get those laughs immediately."

All of the good feelings are geniune, and there's no doubt that everyone had a grand time. Ned Beatty, who plays

U. S. Bates's aide in the film, told a reporter that the teaming of Pryor and Gleason "was one of those things, if you're a comedy fan, you hope and pray that it would happen someday." Unfortunately, as often happens between the bowl and the lip, this spoonful of froth slipped and sullied everyone involved.

Pryor endured a critical drubbing after the film's Christmas 1982 debut, because for the first time he plays a character is utterly unbelievable. Before Eric "buys" him, Brown dresses up in a maid's costume, complete with breasts, to honor Bates's edict that only ladies wait on his table; the ploy fails to generate *Tootsie*-like charm because he doesn't bother to shave his mustache, making the scene silly rather than humorous. Also unbelievable is this would-be writer, this serious thinker, driving a kiddie car through Bates's outdoor party and pelting guests with pies; Eric should have been the one flinging meringue, with Pryor anchoring the slapstick with adult reactions. The Spiderman pajamas are never explained, Brown runs *across* a pond to escape piranhas (at superspeed), and then there's the ancient "walk this way" joke, with Pryor sashaying behind a maid.

However, equally damaging is that when Donner wasn't doing broad comedy he was trying to make *Kramer vs. Kramer*, emphasizing the tender relationship that grows between Brown and Eric. Donner envisioned Brown as "sort of a wonderful everyman," yet due to the flimsy nature of the script not even Pryor could bridge the gap from one extreme to the other. That he'd been able to accomplish this in *Some Kind of Hero* is a virtue of Kirkwood's ability as a scenarist. *The Toy* just didn't have any weight.

And, to some extent, it may not have had all of Richard Pryor either. Just before the picture went into production, he said that if it weren't for *The Toy* he'd be in Zimbabwe, helping beleaguered blacks and trying to get a better understanding of what he himself was all about; to "shut down" all systems, was how he put it. Watching his uninspired performance, it's obvious that Pryor had started early.

Even at his worst, as in *The Toy*, Richard Pryor still draws his fans, can still be counted on to generate millions of

dollars in profit. To a large extent *The Toy* fulfilled the prophecy of Sammy Davis, Jr., that Hollywood would neuter Pryor. But the mellowed-out comedian didn't quite see it that way. "A little laughter, some tears—that's good," he said, then clarified, "that's *box office*."

Had Pryor sold out? He continued to insist in public that he was taking roles if they paid him enough money. Watching him on the set of *The Toy* and on his next film, enjoying himself but not searching too deeply for that internal spark that kindled his genius in other projects, one might take Pryor at face value. But avarice is too easy a rationale for going through the motions. Insisting that he's greedy is Pryor's way of distancing himself from the picture and the anticipated criticism. It's his way of saying, *Don't be too hard on Richard Pryor, 'cause he's just treading water. This ain't the artist at work, it's the commodity.*

Pryor says as much when, pressed on the matter of his career as he viewed it late in 1982, he agonized, "I don't know what I want to *do* anymore. I don't think about movies very much. I don't have that performing urge anymore . . . a 'have to work' kinda thing." Greed greased the path, he acknowledges, and kicked him into gear. But it had reached the point where the fees were so astronomical that he wasn't sure it would continue. "I don't want to work myself to death," he stressed. "I want to take some time for Richard and just enjoy myself a little bit."

Veteran director Billy Wilder commented that around Hollywood, the cry of every producer in a bind was the same: "Get Richard Pryor." One producer made up his mind to do exactly that, only he didn't just grease the road with money: he tore up the cobblestones and replaced them with gold.

In 1977, producer Alexander Salkind and his son Ilya made motion-picture history by paying Marlon Brando more than three million dollars for less than two weeks' work on *Superman*. It was the highest salary ever paid to any performer. Gene Hackman, who labored for several months as the villain of the thirty-five-million-dollar picture and its equally costly sequel—the films were shot simultaneously since the cast was

onhand and the sets were built—pocketed an impressive two million dollars. By comparison, screen newcomer Christopher Reeve received a paltry quarter-million dollars for his heroic efforts as the Man of Steel.

Superman and *Superman II* were massive box-office hits, and when it came time to put *Superman III* into production, the Salkinds had a problem: what to do for an encore? They were set to pour nearly forty million dollars into the new picture, but spectacle alone wasn't a guaranteed box-office draw. To ensure that the Man of Steel had what *Newsweek* referred to as "legs of steel," the producers went after Richard Pryor.

The Salkinds approached him just before *The Toy* was set to roll, and as much as Pryor wanted to take some time off, there was no way he could refuse their four million dollars. He didn't even bother to read the script.

There were other factors, of course: he was looking forward to working again with Margot Kidder, who, although her part was small, filled him with her vitality, which lingered long after her departure. And he genuinely loved the character of Superman. "Richard is a Superman fanatic," Christopher Reeve discovered. Pryor able to cite chapter and verse of the Superman mythos from both the TV series and the comic book. "He gave you the impression that he'd have done the film for free," says Marc McClure, the film's Jimmy Olsen. "I couldn't believe how excited he'd get talking about Superman."

Superman III is the saga of computer genius Gus Gorman (Pryor), a loser whose programs can embezzle funds, spy on others, or control the weather. Looking to boost his fortunes, he joins forces with international villain Ross Webster (Robert Vaughn), who plans to control the world by manipulating oil supplies and sees, in Gorman's computer, a way to get rid of the one obstacle in his path—Superman.

Just before the film went before the cameras in June 1982, at the Pinewood Studios in England, Christopher Reeve said of Pryor, "He's a terribly gifted man, and it's going to be a gas working with him." He wasn't disappointed. Everyone describes him as very loose, always clowning around. He was even a

model subject for the press. When the company moved to Calgary, Canada, to spend August and part of September filming the Metropolis exteriors, he gave generously of his time to local reporters, praising the city and its people whenever possible. According to Marc McClure, Pryor had such a good time that members of the cast speculated in private that Pryor had done the picture simply as an excuse to be a kid again.

Pryor was indeed at ease, even more so than he'd been on *The Toy*. However, that had little to do with the film and its personnel. His cooperation with the Canadian press can be attributed to a resurgence of the "*Ebony* syndrome," Pryor's willingness to help out the little guy. But his high spirits boiled down to one clear cause, which had nothing to do with the cast or the nature of the film: *Superman III*, he says, "was fun to do because it was my last movie and I knew it." Pryor meant what he said. He cohosted both the 1982 Oscars and the Motown twenty-fifth anniversary celebration, and appeared on the "Tonight Show" with Bette Davis—who reports that he was "terribly nervous because of the show *and* meeting me"—but he stayed away from anything heavyweight. Charlie Parker notwithstanding, once *Superman III* was in the can, he refused to look at another script.

Epilogue

Richard Pryor is forty-three years old.

Everyone who has known him, written about him, or watched him in concert or on the screen has said that he can go wherever he wants. Pryor's problem is that he doesn't know what he wants. He wanted creative freedom: he has it. He wanted wealth: he has that too. More elusive has been his search to find that woman to "treat like a queen."

When *Superman III* wrapped, he announced, "I'm taking off for a year, just to understand the territory." He began by going on his long-delayed trip to Zimbabwe. "I've been through enough pain. I've been hurt enough. I want to go someplace where they like me, where they'll be nice to me." He seemed to feel that the combination of the motherland along with his postfire sensibilities would help him *"to understand the territory,"* to come to grips with the fact that he had the power, money, and freedom to do anything he wanted in life. Anything.

Pryor's second trip to Africa was no less rewarding than the first. Though he didn't manage to involve himself in any revolutions, Pryor went into the mountains and spent time by himself. "Hardly anyone knows me there, and that was great," he says, "to sit in a park and be alone, [be] private, like I really have a personal life now." He cherished the anonymity, telling a reporter from NBC on his return that "if you knew you were going to have to give that up when you come in show business, I think a lot of us would change what we do." That was Pryor the extremist talking again, though

the leisure and quiet of Zimbabwe was a balm to his troubled spirit.

Richard Pryor had done more than mellow; he'd come to an emotional halt. Ned Beatty, after spending time with Pryor on *The Toy*, said that all actors are "manic depressive . . . up when you're working and if you're not working find yourself in a hole somewhere," and that Pryor was just slightly more extreme, "on the edge . . . sending us signals from somewhere slightly where we're not."

Pryor laughs at that. "Yeah, I have a friend who used to say, 'Earth to Richard,' to help me come out of it. 'Cause sometimes," he says of his soul-searching art, "it can take you out there."

In the past, that was very true. However, it wasn't what ailed him in this case. Larry Murphy comes closer to the mark when he says that the accident opened Pryor up in ways he'd never suspected, not the least of which was teaching him that "he's not just a comedian, that he bleeds like everybody else, has needs like everybody else." Pryor agrees that the accident showed him "a lot of stuff about feelings," but the problem now was that Pryor found himself unfulfilled every way he turned. "I'm grateful," he is quick to say of his career, "I really am. I could be in Peoria parking cars, hoping to get a tip. This is what I enjoy doing, so that's why I chose it—and I did it well." But it no longer satisfied the new and improved Richard Pryor. Indeed, he was as restless as when he'd walked away from the Aladdin, admitting that despite his calm manner since the fire, he remained as "fucking aggressive" as ever, although he didn't know which way to go with it. Sometimes he'd feel an overwhelming need to be "a loving soulmate" to a little baby; at other times, all he wanted was to throw himself headlong into a project like *The Charlie Parker Story* and throttle it with every ounce of talent at his command. Individually, however, one could not be had immediately and the other could not sustain him.

As Pryor pondered his future, mundane realities were never far behind. He was still grist for the rumor mill, and libelous articles in some of the more sensational tabloids had

him back on cocaine or getting into brawls at nightclubs. Then, in November 1982, he was on the receiving end of a lawsuit brought by another attorney. Whether this was tangled up in Franklin's dealings or was a separate matter has never been made public.

If Pryor was upset by the suit, he said nothing, though it serves to illustrate the joys and the danger of being Richard Pryor. "If you've never been an eighth-grader, you have to depend on others," he once said. So he depends on others, and if they disappoint him he wanders off, grumbling about them under his breath. Sometimes he grumbles too loud and gets in trouble; sometimes he talks himself into doing more and gets *them* in trouble. In either case, what it proves is that for all his money and his awards, for his degree in Black Street History from San Jose State College, Richard Pryor is still the kid from Peoria, street-wise but frightened. He's afraid of not being liked, yet he's afraid that if he *is* liked, he'll be hopelessly disoriented. He's also afraid of failing, and, perhaps worst of all, fearful of not using his power wisely.

Richard Pryor has overcome every obstacle he and life have heaped in his path. He came through each confrontation black and blue but stronger than before, and has freely passed on much of what he's learned to other black comics, in particular friend Eddie Murphy. "I've had some fabulous things said about me, I've had some bad things said about me," he says. His response to it all—and the facts certainly bear him out—is to "just do what I do." His current dilemma is figuring out what to "just do".

What Pryor is doing now is working hard. Neither *The Toy* nor *Superman III* were box-office successes; worse, both were soundly beaten by *48 Hrs*. and *Trading Places*, the Eddie Murphy films in release at the same time. In both cases, awful scripts and bad direction were the problem; Pryor couldn't help but suffer from the critical fallout. Thus, he has propelled himself back into filmmaking with a fury.

In the middle of 1983, Pryor signed a lucrative five-year, forty million dollar pact with Columbia. The money went to the creation of the Pryor Company, which will make four pictures in the five to six million dollar range, with Pryor

producing but not necessarily starring. He has complete creative control over those projects as long as they remain within budget. To make sure that they do, Pryor appointed Jim Brown as president of his new firm, which is located in Burbank.

In addition to the production package, Pryor has agreed as part of the deal to star in at least three films for Columbia during the lifetime of the contract. His fee will be in the neighborhood of five million dollars per film, along with a healthy share of the profits.

The first of the Columbia films will be the long-delayed *Charlie Parker Story,* scheduled for release in mid-1984. The production of that important film put the Pryor/Richard Dreyfuss vehicle *Ain't No Hero* for Warner Brothers on the back burner, probably for good. After making the jazz film, Pryor will fulfill that longstanding ambition of remaking Laurel and Hardy classics by doing *The Music Box* with pal Burt Reynolds, followed by *Double Whoopee* with Gene Wilder, and then the long-planned redo of H.G. Wells' *The Man Who Could Work Miracles*.

Apart from the challenge of once more making the name Pryor synonymous with quality filmmaking, he took the deal because it would allow, in his words, "people who heretofore haven't had the chance to do films" to work in the industry, specifically blacks and members of other minorities.

But while he was busy doing things for others, Pryor also expressed a desire to do something for *himself.* Movies weren't personal enough, so he announced a final concert tour. That, more than anything, is indicative of the spark he apparently feels he's lost. He started breaking in new routines at Los Angeles' *Comedy Store,* audiences greeting Pryor with standing ovations each night ("I get nervous when people go 'Yee-*haaa*!' ", he informed them one night, " 'cause I know what comes after that: 'let's get a couple of black boys and hang 'em up!' ") and being treated to Pryor's up-to-the-minute feelings about herpes ("Uh . . . I forgot," he tells a girl who has the disease, "I, uh, gotta have an operation tonight."), pets ("A ball will go into the street my dog'll run up to the gate and screech, 'I'm not going out there, Rich.

It's tough out there. If you want your ball, go get it your motherfucking self.' '') and drugs ("I haven't had drugs in five months and," he stutters, his torso twisting and quaking, "the stuff is starting to wear off." Worse, he says, since giving up cocaine there's nothing to do when he goes home " 'cept go to sleep.' '').

Pryor says it took him longer to get in comedic shape than he expected, and he refused to take his act on the road—or put it on film and vinyl—until it was perfect.

Though he opened to acclaim at Radio City Music Hall in New York in August of that year, the material, like Pryor's *Sunset Strip* work, isn't as angry as his previous routines. Pryor doesn't deny that. "People call me up and say, 'You're not like you used to be,' and I say to them, 'That's right, but do you *know* what I was really like then? Do you know what kind of insanity I was into?" He says he wants to entertain *and* be nice to himself. For him, this concert represents that balance.

The sharp pre-fire Pryor, that guy who aspired to be an incubus but found himself welcome anyway, is gone for good. If his new movies reflect that emptiness, and if his audience dwindles as a result, Pryor may well do what he did the *last* time he felt frustrated: scrap it all and push off in another direction entirely. *He* says it won't happen. He maintains, "I don't have the same desire to succeed. I don't have that push, push, push I had until I burned up." But Eddie Murphy's outgrossing him, and Pryor has enough pride left to want to be number one. If the young, energetic Murphy already has the crown in theatrical dollars, Pryor may well throw down the gauntlet in another field.

The autobiography? Three years after announcing *Up from the Ashes*, it remains uncompleted. Some associates claim it has yet to be begun. Pryor himself says that even if he writes it, he doubts anyone will read it. "It's nice to watch someone *else*'s life story," he says, "it's entertainment. [But] if it's *your* life, you go, 'Hold it! Wait! No!'"

What else is there for him? Broadway? A novel? A jazz album?

Possibly all of the above. He has the ability.

247

Politics? There was a movement afoot to run a black candidate for President in 1984; since nothing causes Pryor's passion to rise as the plight of the poor, the nation's minorities, and world unrest, he just might seek the office—and win. And do a hell of a job to boot.

Consider, at worst, Pryor in a Presidential debate. . . .

ABOUT THE AUTHOR

JEFF ROVIN, age thirty-one, is the author of over thirty books. Among them are historical novels, science fiction, and books on film and TV including *The Great Television Series*, *Of Mice and Mickey*, *Always, Lana* (with Taylor Pero), and *The Films of Charlton Heston*, written with the actor's cooperation. Rovin has also written about celebrities for *The Ladies' Home Journal*, *Omni*, *Moviegoer*, and *U.S.A. Today*, and publishes the topselling monthly magazine *Videogaming Illustrated*.

THE PRIVATE LIVES
BEHIND PUBLIC FACES

These biographies and autobiographies tell the
personal stories of well-known figures,
recounting the triumphs and tragedies of their
public and private lives.

☐	23809	**BLACK AND BLUE** Richard Pryor	$3.50
☐	05035	**OUT ON A LIMB** Shirley MacLaine (Hardcover)	$15.95
☐	23662	**"DON'T FALL OFF THE MOUNTAIN"** Shirley MacLaine	$3.50
☐	05020	**LIFE WITH JACKIE** Mansfield & Block (Hardcover)	$14.95
☐	23816	**THROUGH THE NARROW GATE** Karen Armstrong	$3.50
☐	05044	**GIANT STEPS** Kareem Abdul Jabbar & Peter Knobler (Hardcover)	$14.95
☐	20805	**ALWAYS, LANA** Pero and Rovin	$3.50
☐	20704	**BURIED ALIVE: The Biography of Janis Joplin** Myra Friedman	$3.95
☐	23886	**HAYWIRE** Brooke Hayward	$3.95
☐	23133	**'SCUSE ME WHILE I KISS THE SKY** David Henderson	$3.95
☐	20756	**MONTGOMERY CLIFT: A Biography** Patricia Bosworth	$3.95
☐	20857	**AN UNFINISHED WOMAN** Lillian Hellman	$3.50
☐	23005	**A SHINING SEASON** William Buchanan	$2.75

Prices and availability subject to change without notice.

Buy them at your local bookstore or use this handy coupon for ordering: